IMAGES
of America

COLORADO SPRINGS

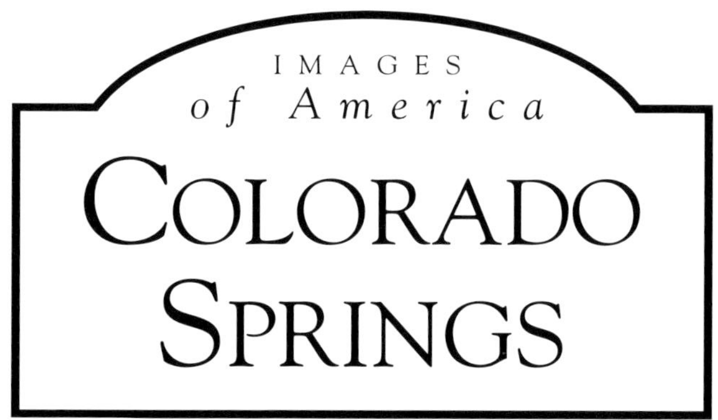

Elizabeth Wallace

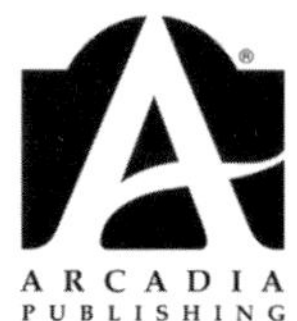

ISBN 978-0-7385-2091-9

Published by Arcadia Publishing
Charleston, South Carolina

Printed in the United States of America

Library of Congress Catalog Card Number: 2002117611

For all general information contact Arcadia Publishing at:
Telephone 843-853-2070
Fax 843-853-0044
E-mail sales@arcadiapublishing.com
For customer service and orders:
Toll-Free 1-888-313-2665

Visit us on the Internet at www.arcadiapublishing.com

Contents

Acknowledgments

I extend sincere thanks and appreciation to the Colorado Springs Pioneer Museum, Special Collections of Colorado College, Pikes Peak Library District, the Denver Public Library, the Colorado Historical Society, the Cheyenne Mountain Heritage Center, Dr. Lester L. Williams Museum, the Palmer Lake Historical Society, and the Lucretia Vaile Museum, as well as Dick Over, Bill Luke, Adna Wilde, and Eve and Robert Gladstone. With special thanks to Susan and Rogers Davis, curators of Palmer Lake Museum, for their help and guidance and also to Dr. Robert Larson for his suggestions and comments regarding the contents of *Colorado Springs, Colorado*.

Finally, special thanks to my dear husband and family, whose interest and encouragement helped keep me on track and focused.

Introduction

Through a careful selection of photographs, Elizabeth Wallace has captured the remarkable transition of Colorado Springs from a frontier town, founded in 1871 by Civil War general and railroad builder William Jackson Palmer, to those years just prior to the city's explosive growth, which started during World War II. Although only a few people call it Little London today, during these years Colorado Springs drew a substantial number of English "lungers" seeking the warm, dry climate considered essential for the cure of tuberculosis. The charm of this burgeoning new town was enhanced by a number of natural attractions, such as Pikes Peak, the Garden of the Gods, Seven Falls, and the Cave of the Winds. But it also boasted some extraordinary man-made attractions, including the world-class Broadmoor Hotel, and the many mansions built by those who struck it rich during the gold rush of the 1890s at nearby Cripple Creek. This bonanza brought to Colorado Springs such prominent citizens as Spencer Penrose and Winfield Scott Stratton, who both contributed significantly to the city's economic and cultural climate.

The photos chosen by Elizabeth Wallace are enhanced by informative captions, which not only describe their significance but also provide a fascinating narrative of the popular resort city during its first 75 years of growth. The beautiful region around this community, comprised of hundreds of square miles of mountain and prairie, is also represented by some of these photographs. Thus, communities such as Manitou Springs and Cripple Creek, which are still closely identified with the city, are included. The overall result of Wallace's effort is an excellent book, which will be of interest not only to Coloradans and other Americans but also to the many enthusiastic travelers from abroad.

Professor Emeritus Robert W. Larson, University of Northern Colorado, and author of several books on the American West, including Red Cloud: Warrior-Statesman of the Lakota Sioux.

One

The Founder, General Palmer, Family, and Friends

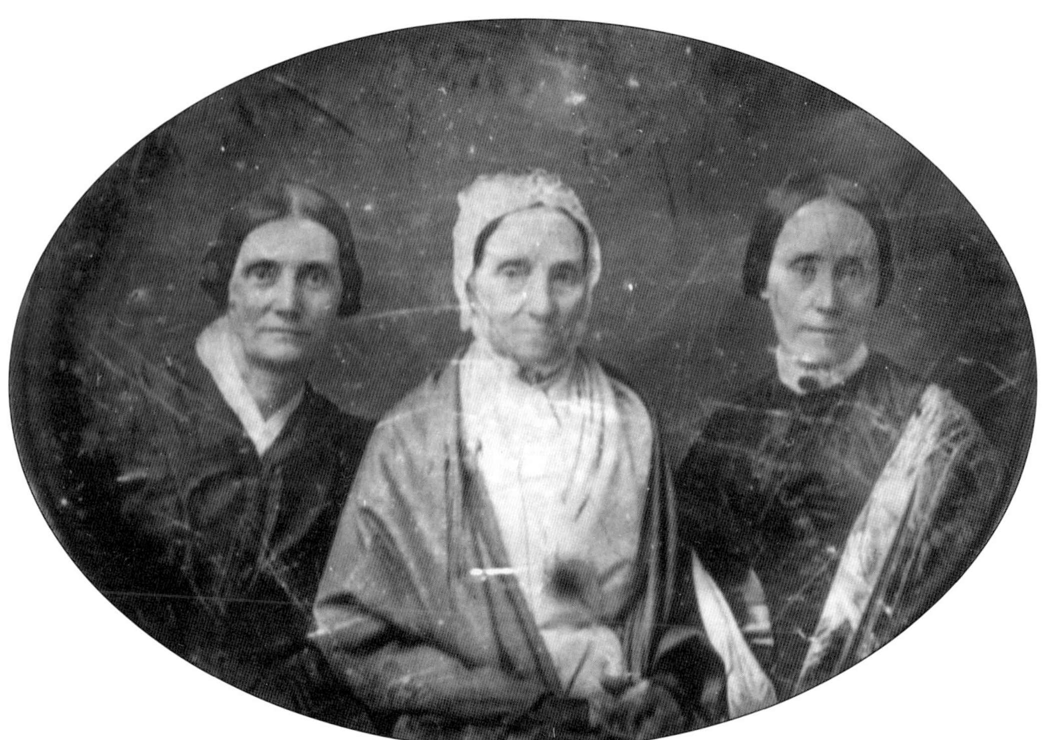

Matilda Palmer, The General's Mother. (*c.* 1850) Believed to be a daguerreotype, the image above pictures, from left to right, Matilda Jackson (mother of William Jackson Palmer), Sarah Hancock (mother of Matilda and Jeanetta Jackson), and Jeanetta Jackson. The Quaker family moved from Delaware to Philadelphia where, after some schooling, William Palmer joined the military. He was a determined and charismatic man who rose quickly through the ranks and gained a following of men who would later share his plans in Colorado. (Courtesy Colorado Springs Pioneer Museum.)

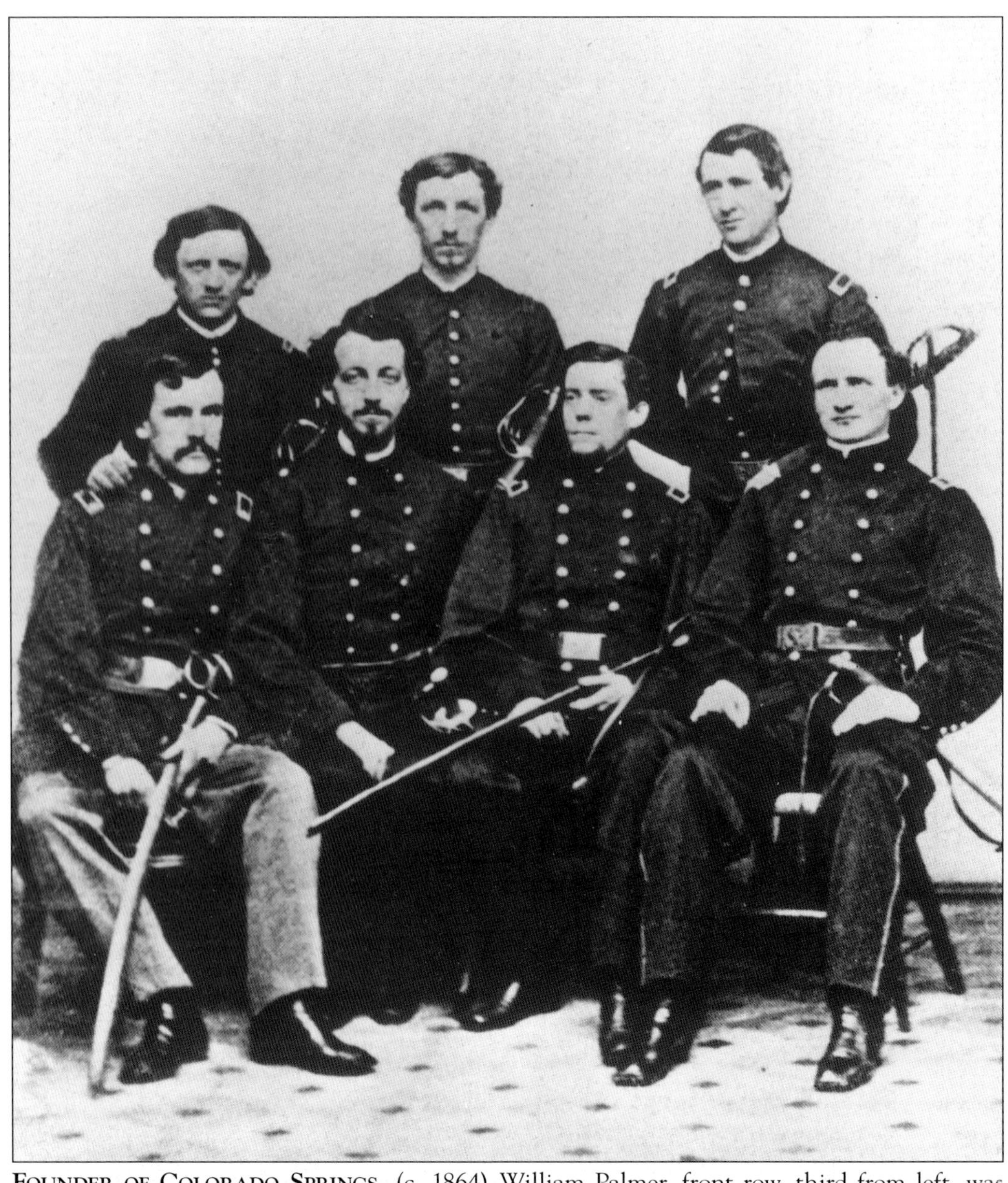

FOUNDER OF COLORADO SPRINGS. (c. 1864) William Palmer, front row, third from left, was born in 1836, on a farm in Delaware. His Quaker family moved to Philadelphia where William attended a few years of high school before joining the 15th Pennsylvania Volunteer Cavalry, where he soon attained the rank of General. After visiting an uncle in Europe, his attention turned to railroads and he surveyed the Pikes Peak region for the Kansas Pacific Railroad. During this time, he met and fell in love with a young girl called Queen Mellen whom he hoped would share his dreams of a successful railroad of his own, a fashionable new town, and a family. Some of his visions were realized, but in 1906 a horse-riding accident paralyzed him and changed his life forever. He was now unable to attend the annual reunion of his beloved cavalry regiment in Philadelphia. Since he was a wealthy man, he invited the whole regiment to Colorado Springs; they stayed at the Antlers Hotel and paraded through the town led by their General, who was seated in his White Steamer car. (Courtesy Colorado Springs Pioneer Museum.)

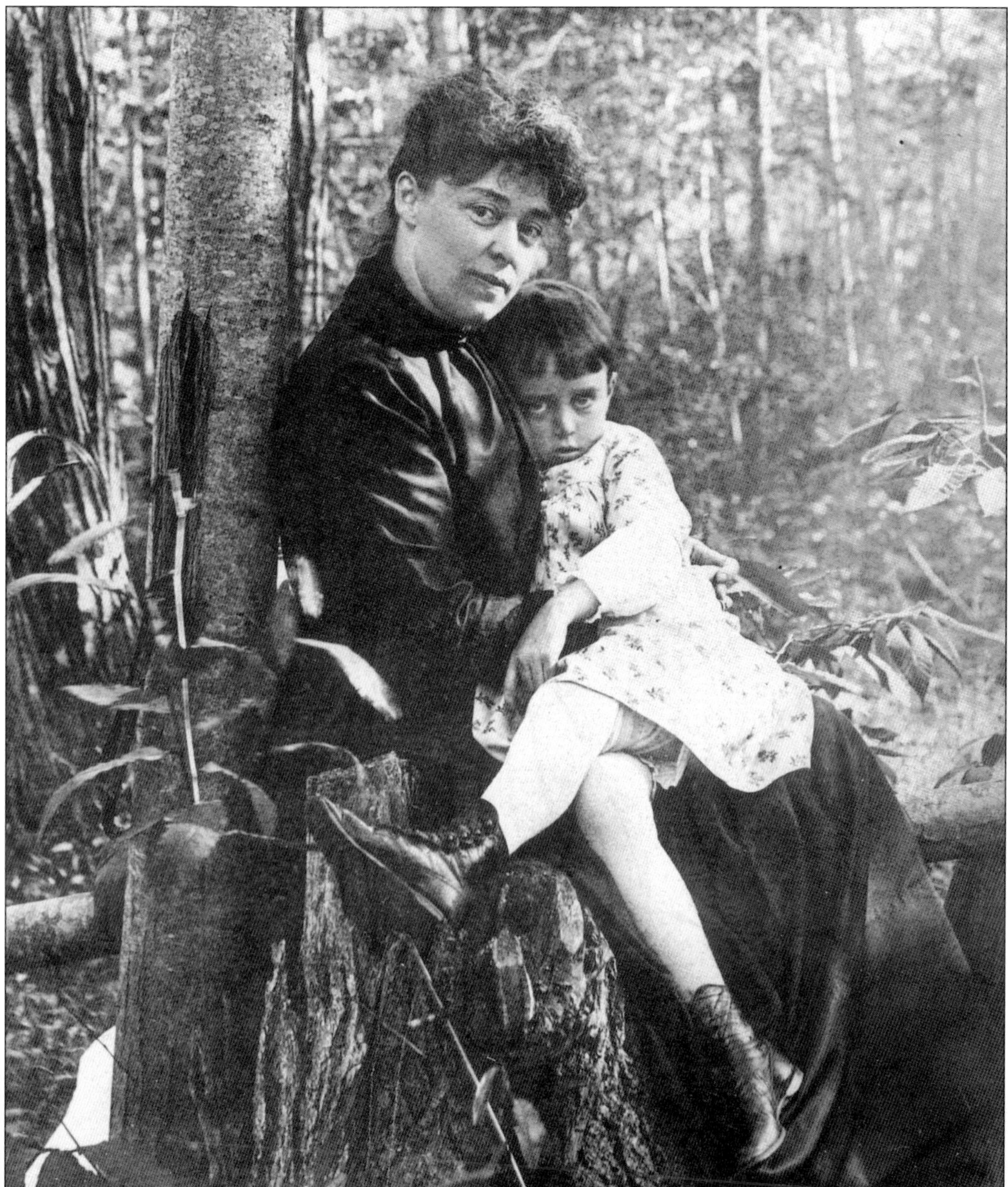

QUEEN PALMER AND DAUGHTER. (c. 1886) Queen Palmer sits holding Dorothy, her second daughter, who is about six years old at the time. Elsie, the first daughter, was born in New York, while Dorothy was born in Colorado and Marjory was born in England. The Palmer family lived for a while at Loseley Park, a stately home nestled in the heart of the Surrey, England. It was built in 1562 by Sir William More and is a magnificent home complete with a walled garden containing five individual gardens, each with its own character and style. Queen and the girls also lived at Ightham Mote, a medieval manor house in Tonbridge, England, which is full of ancient tales and where important members of society hid their loved ones over the centuries. General Palmer spent much of his time in Colorado Springs, but visited his family in England about twice a year. He sometimes stayed in his offices in West London before visiting his family in the countryside. (Courtesy Colorado Springs Pioneer Museum.)

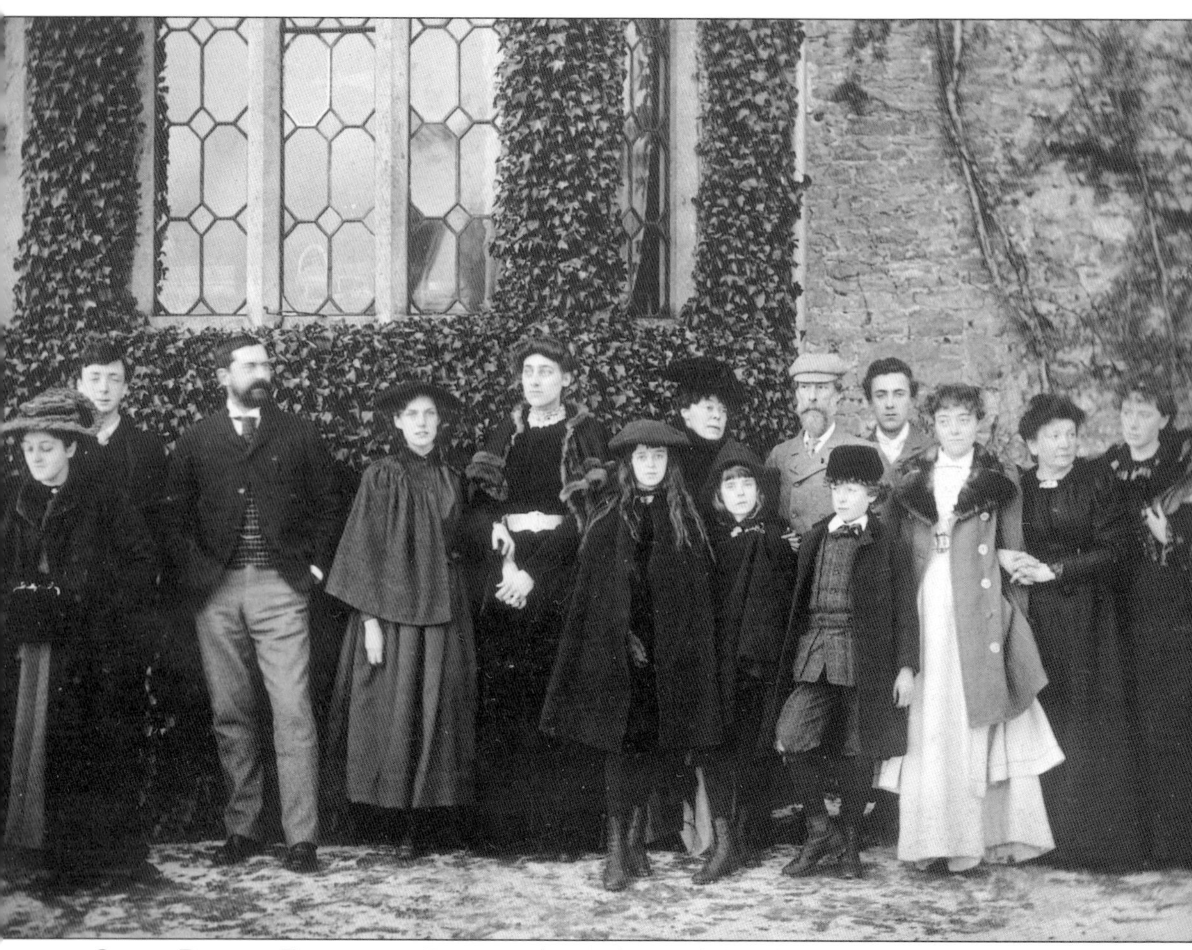

Queen Palmer, Family and Friends. (c. 1893) From left to right are Elsa, Paul, John Singer Sargent, Dorothy Comyns Carr, Vetti, Dorothy Palmer, Queen Palmer, Marjory Palmer, Fred Jameson, Arthur, Phil, Elsie Palmer, Madame Haas, and Marie Meredith. While living at Ightham Mote in England, Queen Palmer was known to have entertained many literary and artistic friends. Henry James, the famous novelist, visited Queen from his home in Rye on the coast of England, where some said he nursed a bruised ego after a bad review. He leased Lamb House in 1895, and wrote *The Spoils of Poynton*, *The Awkward Age* and *The Wings of the Dove*. John Singer Sargent was a frequent visitor to the Mote and painted two paintings of Elsie Palmer, one called *The Lady in White* and the other *A Game of Bowls*. On December 27, 1894, just a year after this photograph was taken, Elsie cabled her father telling him her mother was seriously ill and not expected to live. Palmer left Colorado immediately but was not with his wife at her death. Queen Mellen Palmer died on December 27, 1894, at 44 years of age. (Courtesy Colorado Springs Pioneer Museum.)

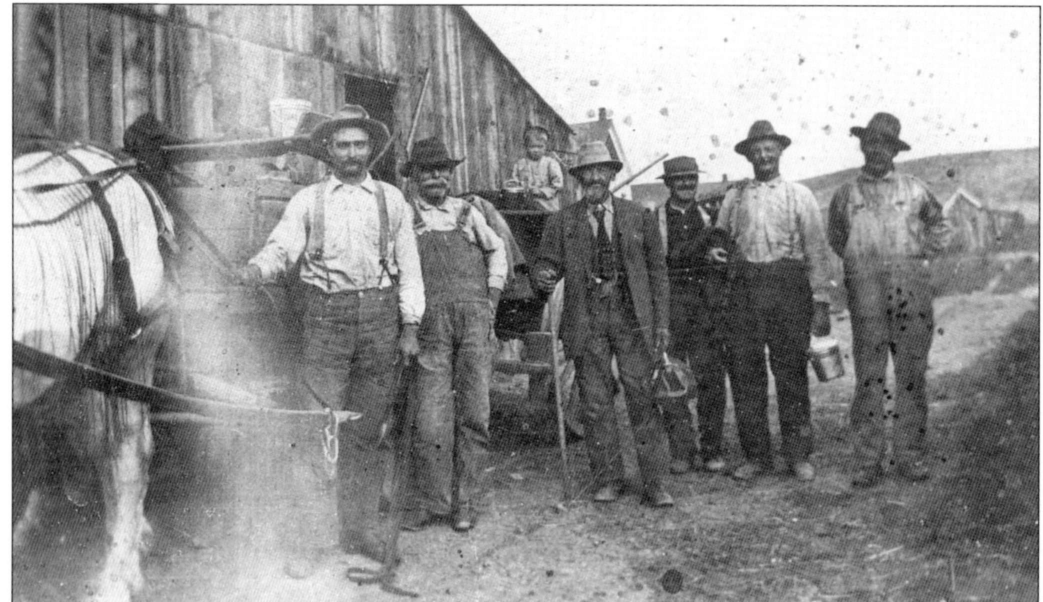

Workmen of Glen Eyrie. (*c.* 1890) Six unknown workmen pose for this photograph at Glen Eyrie. One man holds a lunch pail and another wears a three-piece suit and tie. A young child sits in the wagon. The house at Glen Eyrie, although a beautiful home on completion in 1872, was later updated and improved with state-of-the-art appliances. (Courtesy Colorado Springs Pioneer Museum.)

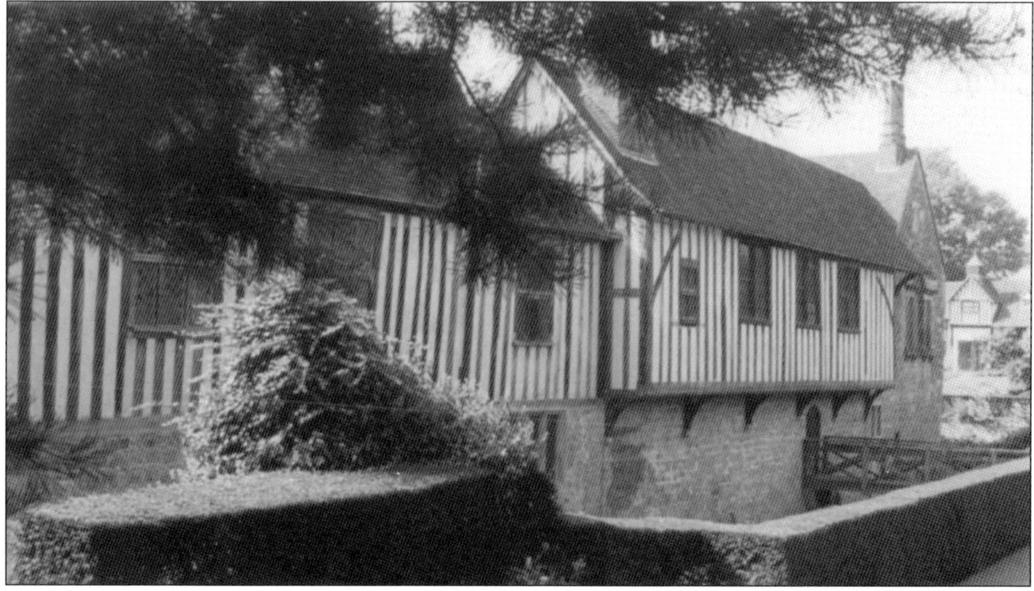

An American Purchased the Mote. (*c.* 2001) The Mote has long been a refuge for many, including the Lord Mayor of London, who hid his Catholic wife from Queen Elizabeth's vengeance. In 1890, General Palmer leased the property, but another American would eventually own it. Charles Robinson from New England purchased the Mote and tried to restore it to its former glory but the cost was too great for his coffers and he willed the property to the National Trust on his death. (Courtesy Eve and Robert Gladstone.)

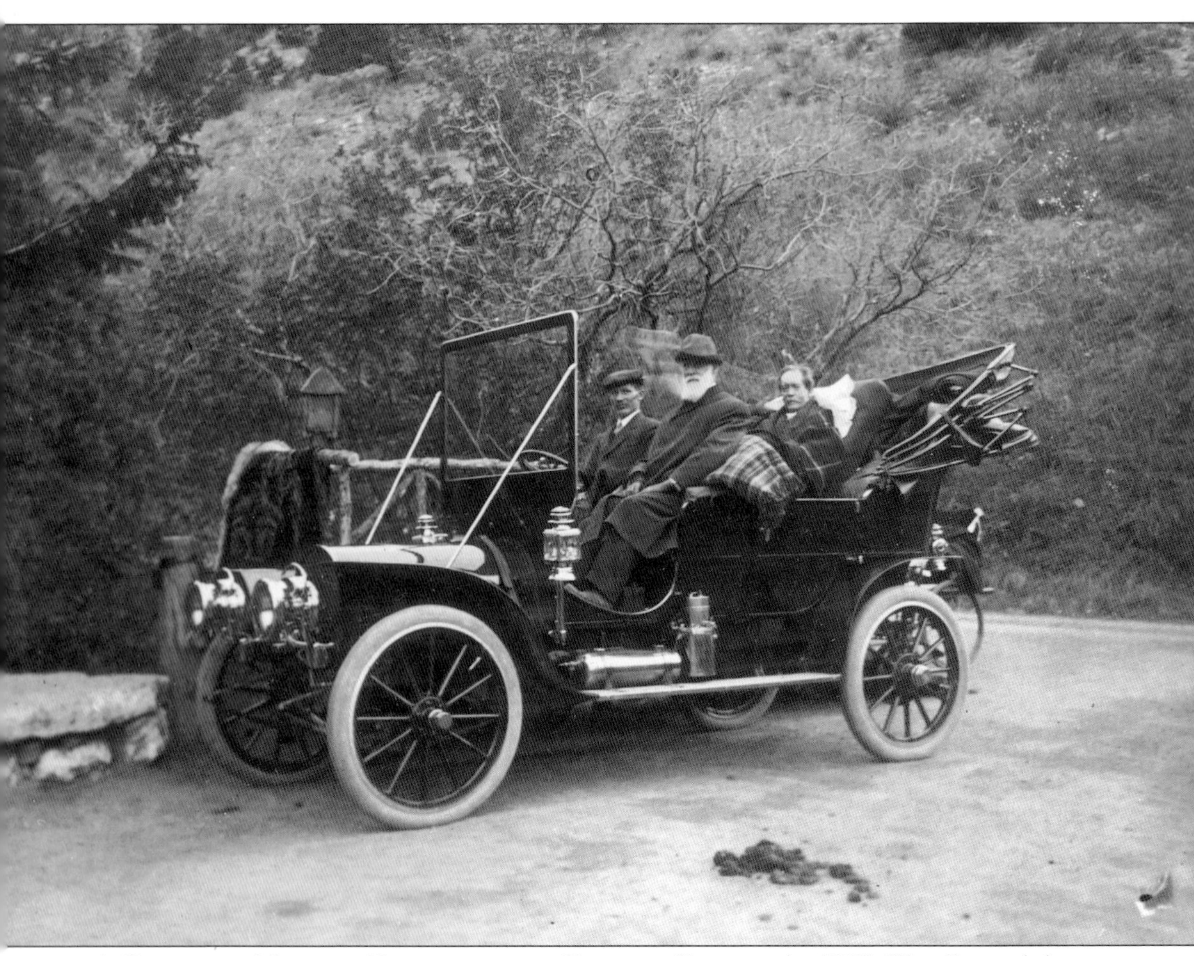

A DIFFERENT MODE OF TRANSPORT FOR GENERAL PALMER. (*c.* 1907) The General, known for his love of horses and in particular his Arabian horse The Moor, was riding School Boy, an unfamiliar saddle horse, on an outing with his daughters and a friend on October 27, 1906, when he was thrown from the horse. It's believed the accident happened near the Gateway Rocks in the Garden of the Gods; it was Dorothy who rode hard to Glen Eyrie for help. In the meantime, a passing motorist, W.A. Otis, picked the General up and placed him in his car. The accident left Palmer paralyzed and he could no longer ride his beloved horses. Despite the obvious pain, Palmer still wanted to travel, so he purchased a car and had the back seat padded with pillows in an attempt to provide some comfort. His determination to live gave him two more years to see his daughters grow to womanhood, but on March 10, 1909, the General fell into a coma and died three days later with his daughters at his side. (Courtesy Colorado Springs Pioneer Museum.)

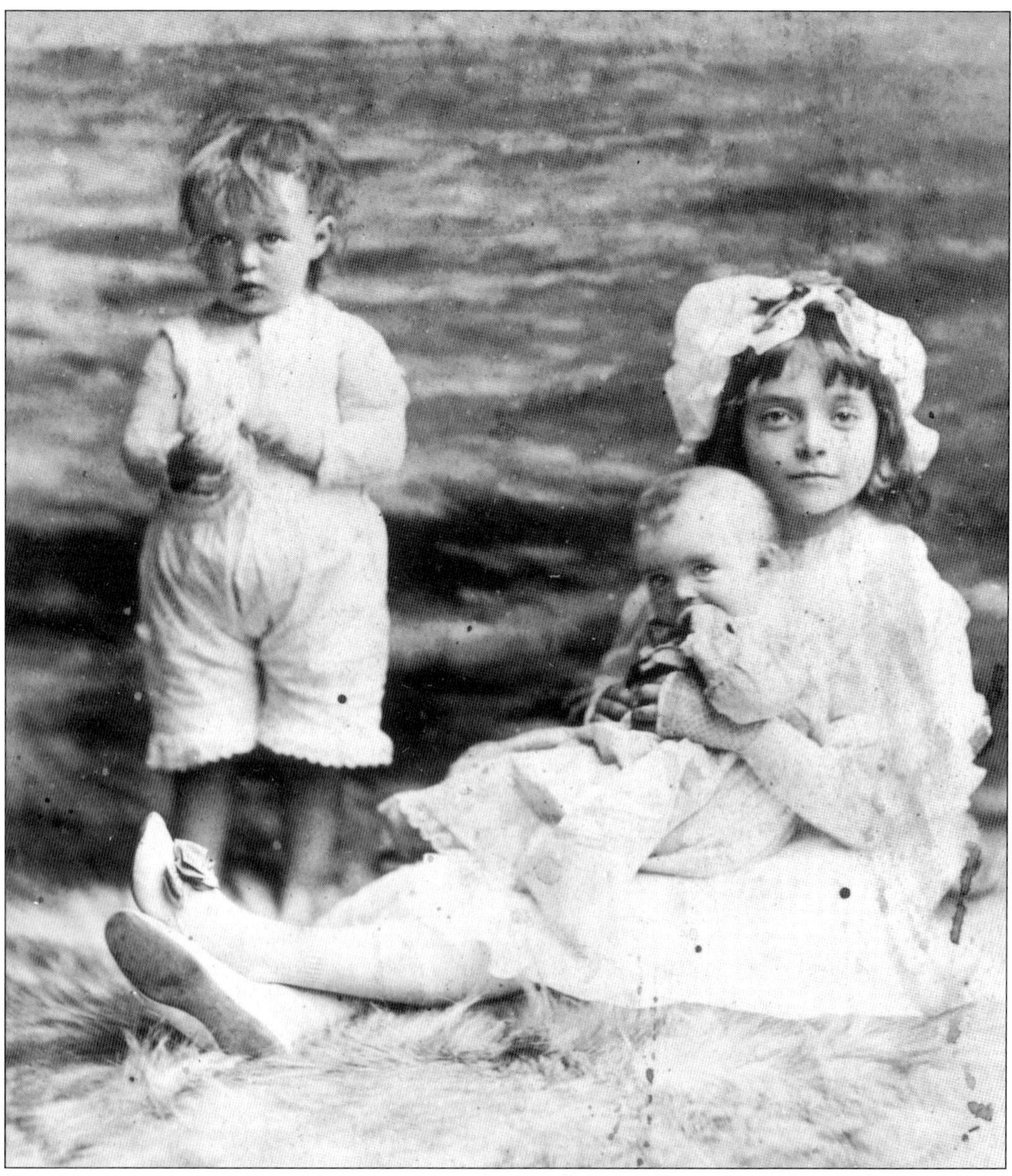

THE YOUNG PALMER GIRLS. (*c.* May 12, 1882) From left to right are Dorothy, aged one and one half years, wearing bloomers and standing next to her sisters; while Elsie, aged nine and one half years, holds little Marjory, who is six months old. All three girls were born in different locations. Elsie was born in New York, Dorothy in Colorado, and Marjory in England. There is some speculation that Queen Mellen Palmer spent years living apart from General Palmer because she was unhappy living in Colorado Springs. However, letters Queen wrote from England to Palmer suggest she was following doctor's orders by living at sea level because of her weak heart, and there was no marital rift. When Queen died in 1894, Palmer quickly made his way to England to finalize his wife's business plans and organize the return of his daughters to Colorado Springs. Queen was buried in England, but 18 months after William died in 1909, Queen's grave was disinterred and her remains were brought to Colorado Springs where she and Palmer rest in the Evergreen Cemetery, Colorado Springs. (Courtesy Colorado Springs Pioneer Museum.)

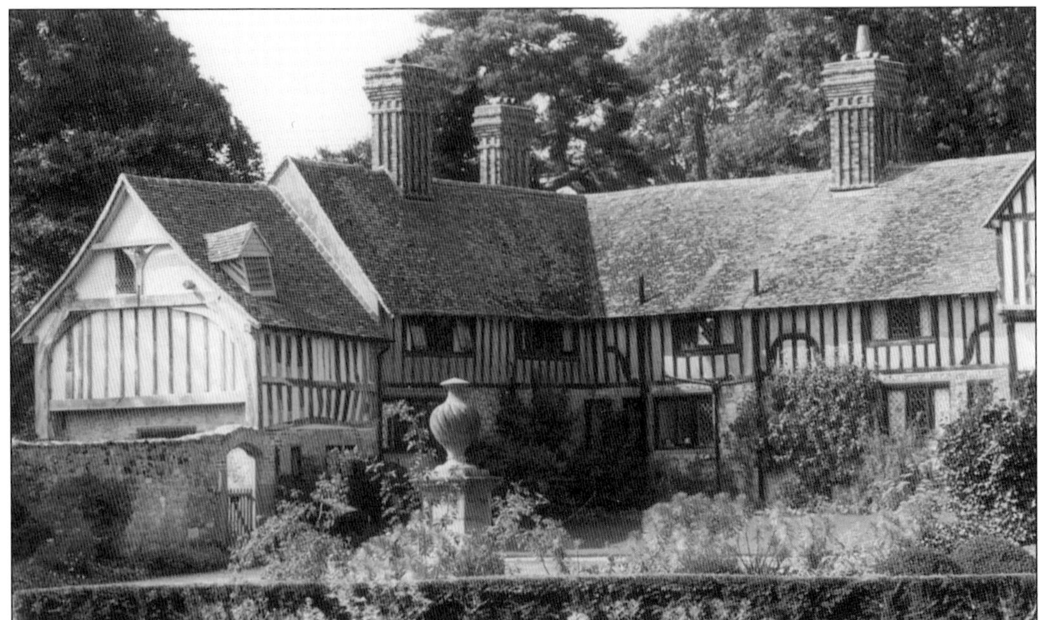

IGHTHAM MOTE—A MEDIEVAL RETREAT FOR THE PALMERS. (*c.* 2001) The Palmers leased the manor house in 1890 and commissioned John Singer Sargent to paint a portrait of Elsie Palmer, aged 19 years, in a beautiful white dress seated in front of some special carved paneling for which the Mote is known. The painting is called *The Lady in White* and now hangs in the Fine Arts Museum in Colorado Springs. (Courtesy Eve and Robert Gladstone.)

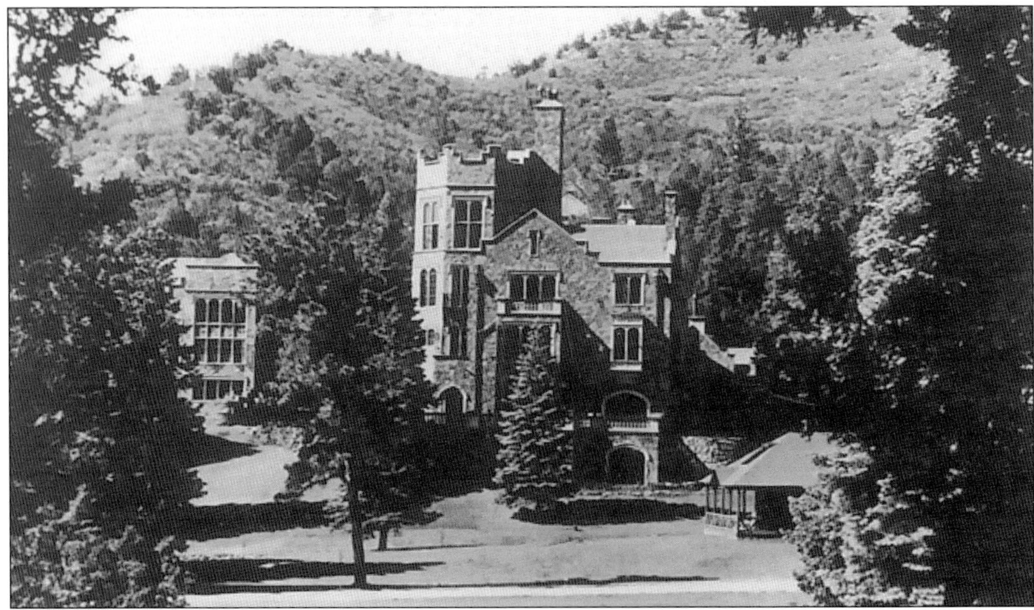

A CASTLE IS BORN. (date unknown) A facelift for Glen Eyrie consisted of a sophisticated telephone system, a custom built four-story elevator, washing machines, and a refrigeration system. Ancient tiles from England and local blocks of stone from Pikes Peak kept masons, carpenters, and other workman busy for years. Most of the work was completed during 1903-4 while Palmer and his girls were vacationing in Europe. (Courtesy Special Collections, Colorado College.)

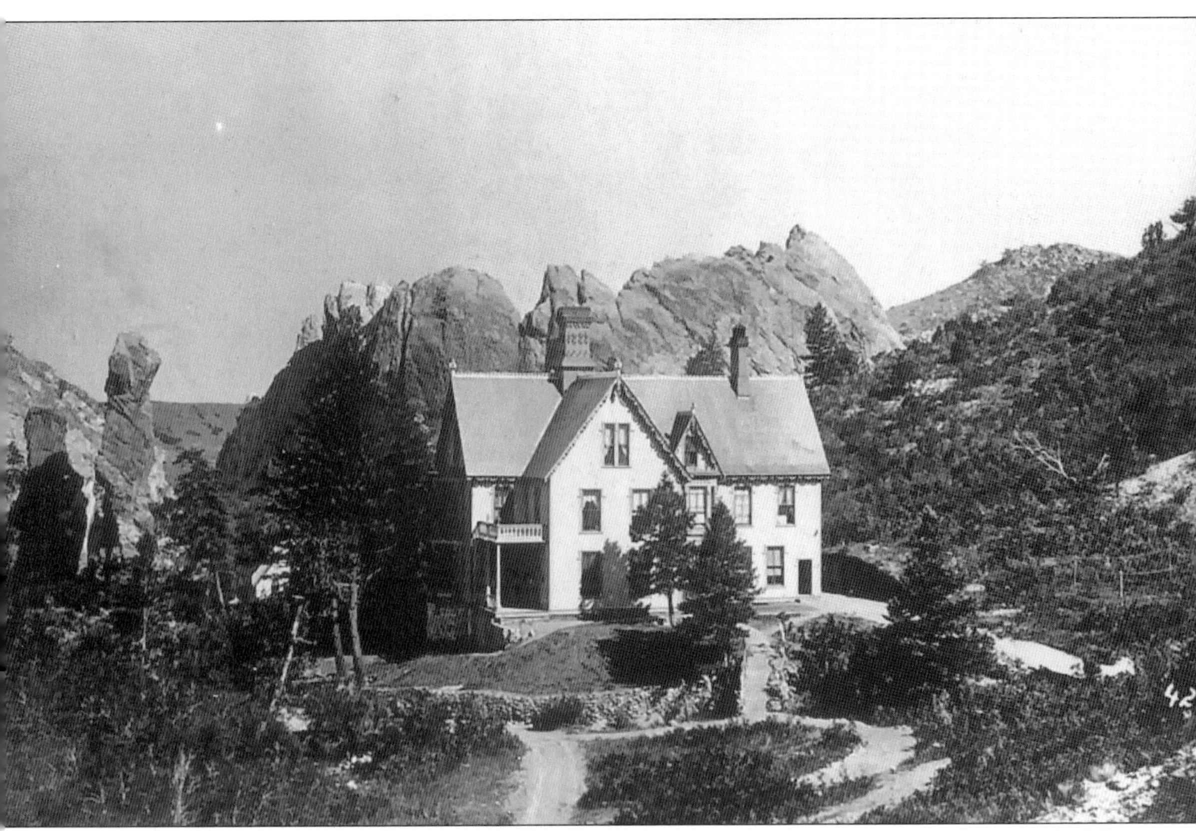

A House Fit for a Queen. (*c.* 1871–1873) In Queen's diary, she mentions the wonderful theatres, beautiful houses in London, and meeting Charles Kingsley, the famous author of *Water Babies* and *Westward Ho.* It was at this time that she met Kingsley's daughter Rose and his son Maurice Kingsley, who would later travel to Colorado Springs and organize lots and membership in the new town. The Palmers camped for a while above the stables at Glen Eyrie during the construction of their home. Miss Kingsley describes a tea party she attended at the stable. " . . . [T]he Palmers are building a most charming large house, but until it is finished, they live in a sort of picnic way, in rooms ten by ten, partitioned off from the loft over the stable! There was just enough room for us all four (General and Mrs. Palmer, Maurice Kingsley and Rose Kingsley) to sit at tea, and we all had great fun. There were four cups, but no saucers, and we borrowed two forks from the restaurant (the Log Cabin) so that we each had one . . . ." (Courtesy Special Collections, Colorado College.)

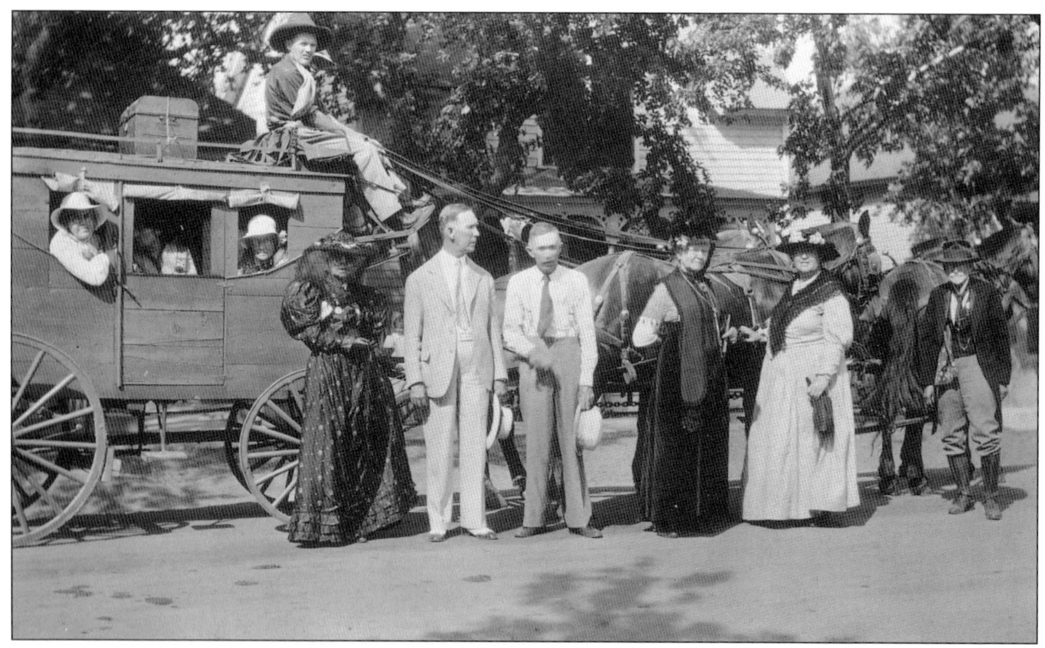

Ladies Peering from the Carriage. (*c.* unknown) These important local citizens are, from left to right, (carriage) Dora Foster, unknown, and Mrs. Edith Earrin; (standing) Jessie Aiken, George Birdsall (probably mayor at the time), Melvin M. Sinton, unknown, and Harriet Laud. The driver is unidentified. (Courtesy Colorado Springs Pioneer Museum.)

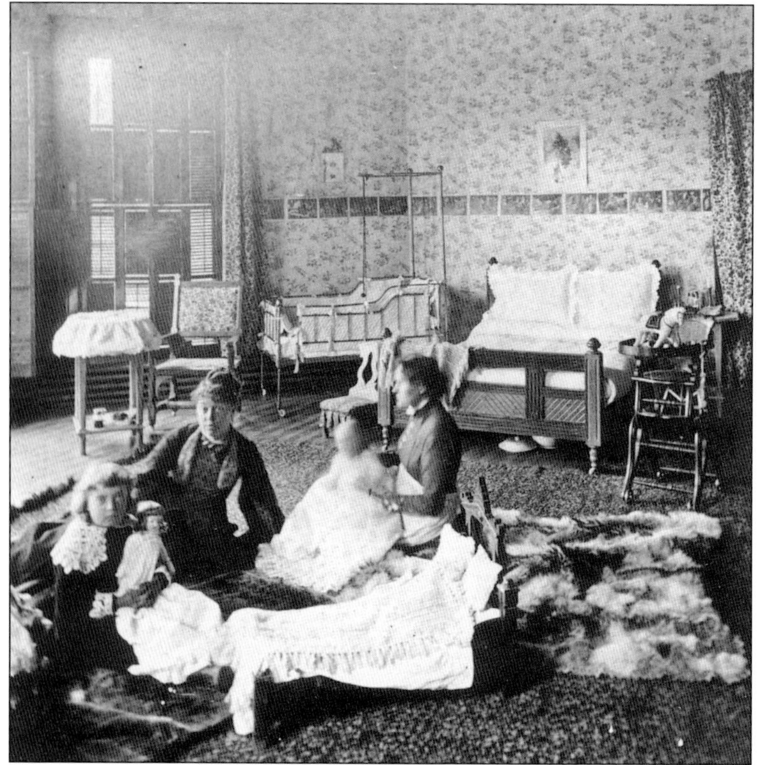

A Personal Look at the Nursery at Glen Eyrie. (*c.* 1880) From left to right are Elsie Palmer, Queen Palmer, Dorothy Palmer, and Tante. Queen sits casually on the floor with Tante, the nanny, who holds Dorothy on her lap. Elsie cradles her doll next to a doll's bed. A child's bed, with a chamber pot underneath, a baby's crib, and a little horse sitting on the tray of a high chair suggest this was a happy and playful room. (Courtesy Colorado Springs Pioneer Museum.)

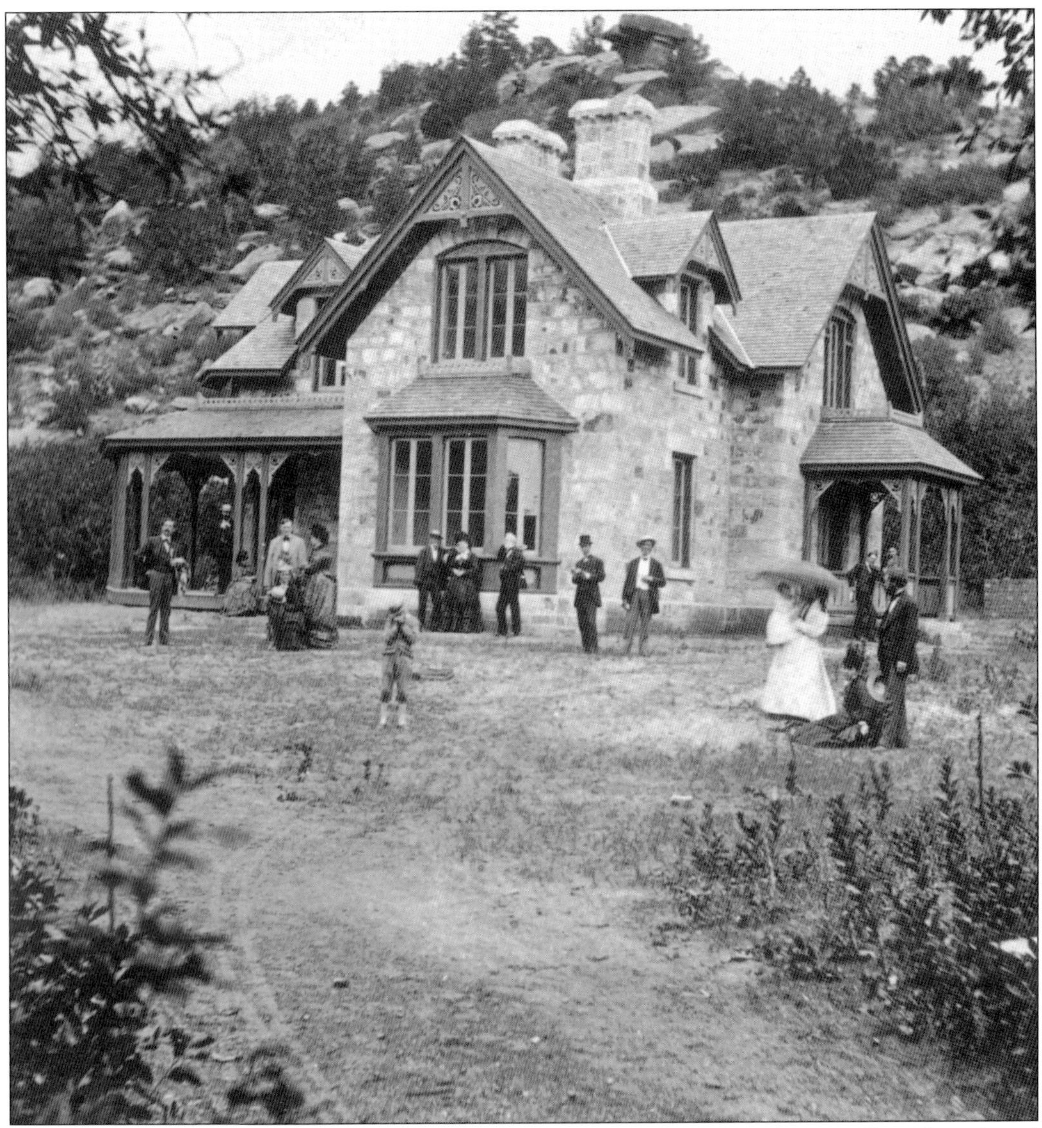

BRIARHURST—DR. BELL'S ENGLISH-STYLE COTTAGE. (*c.* 1873–1886) Dr. Bell, a close friend and business partner of General Palmer, built his delightful home in Manitou Springs. He and his wife hosted Canon Kingsley for a while at their home as he recovered from a bad cold. Kingsley wrote to his wife from Manitou, "Oh my love, your birthday letter was such a comfort to me for I am very home-sick and counting the days till I can get back to you..." Kingsley goes on to be less than favorable about the area describing it as "...like an ugly Highland strath, bordered by pine woods..." Unfortunately, Dr. Bell's home was razed to the ground on January 8, 1886. *The Denver Tribune* reported: " . . . the fire is believed to have originated from burning coals that fell from the fireplace starting the inferno. No lives were lost and much of the furniture, pictures and books were saved. It is estimated the loss of the house and some contents that were on the second floor were between $35,000 and $40,000 . . . " (Courtesy the Denver Public Library.)

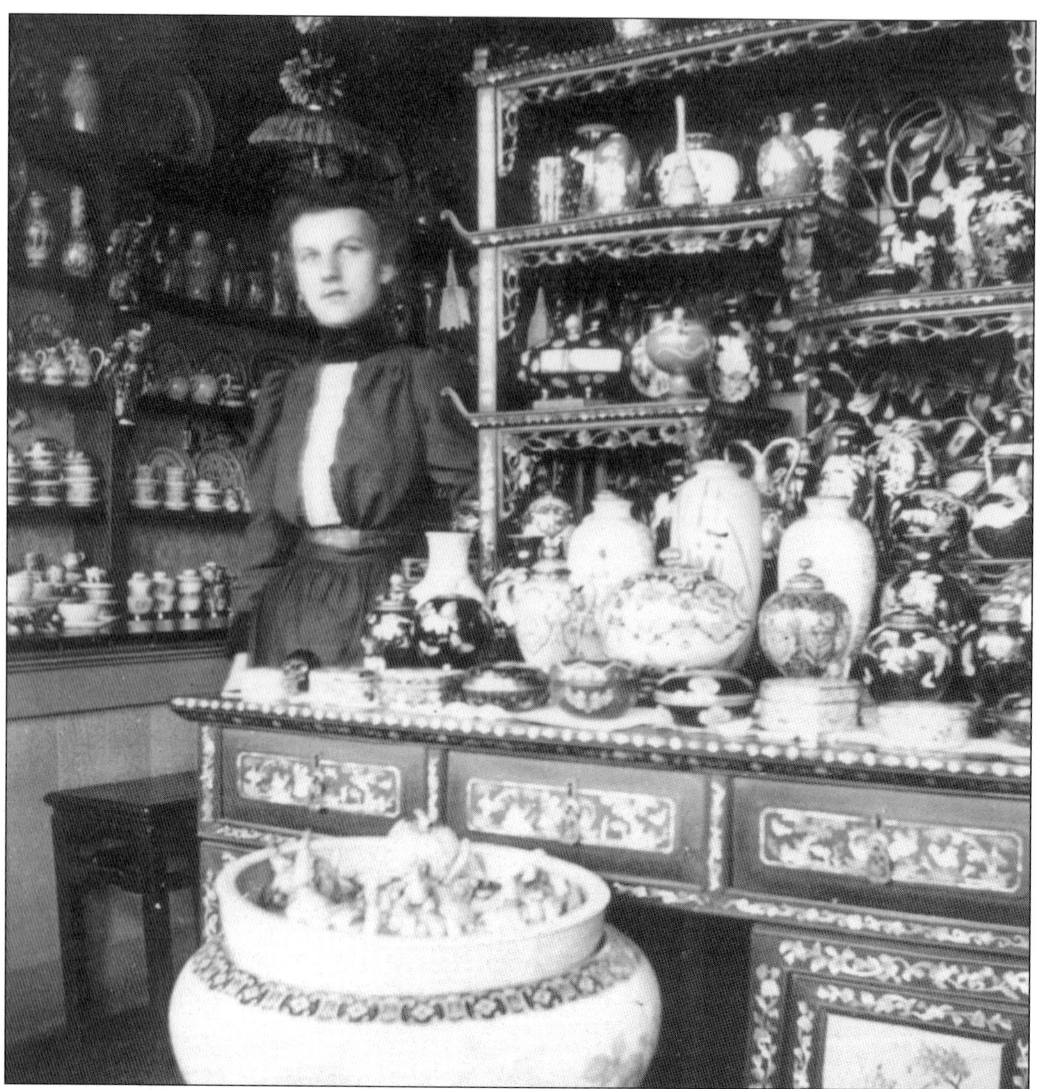

China Jim's Extraordinary Store. (*c.* 1900) An unidentified woman poses in China Jim's curio store. Unlike many of his contemporaries, China Jim (Bo Dun Da) opened a specialty import store where he sold unusual items brought from China. As business flourished, he moved to a more prominent location in Colorado Springs, where he caught the attention of General Palmer and they became friends. Unfortunately, Jim allowed a toothache to worsen over Christmas and was later admitted to Glockner Hospital. He was first treated for blood poisoning and then pneumonia, from which he died. The memoirs of Dorothy Bass Spann, daughter of Jesse Bass, horse trainer at Glen Eyrie, recalls a Christmas Party at the castle where she and China Jim's boy were recognized. "The General called out, I want Jesse Bass's baby and China Jim's little boy to come to the tree first for their gifts." Dorothy remembers the two children clutched hands as they walked toward the General. She recalls that her gift was a fully functioning toy stove but she was unable to remember the gift that Jim's son was given. (Courtesy Pikes Peak Library District.)

Two

Mining and the Wealth it Brought

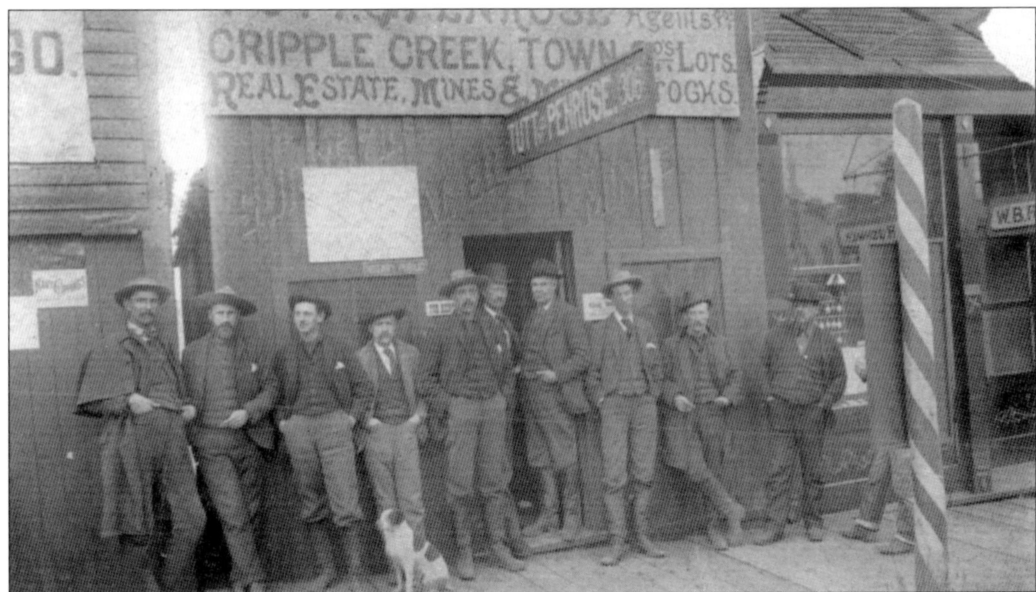

The Dynamic Duo. (*c.* 1892–1899) Charles Tutt took this group photograph with "Spec" Spencer Penrose fifth from left. The other men are unidentified. Charles Tutt and Spec were school friends in Philadelphia and continued their friendship in Colorado, where they pursued mining and real estate ventures. They made an attractive pair, especially Penrose, who was said to be "startlingly handsome." The sign on the building reads: The Tutt and Penrose Agents for Cripple Creek Town. (Courtesy Pikes Peak Library District.)

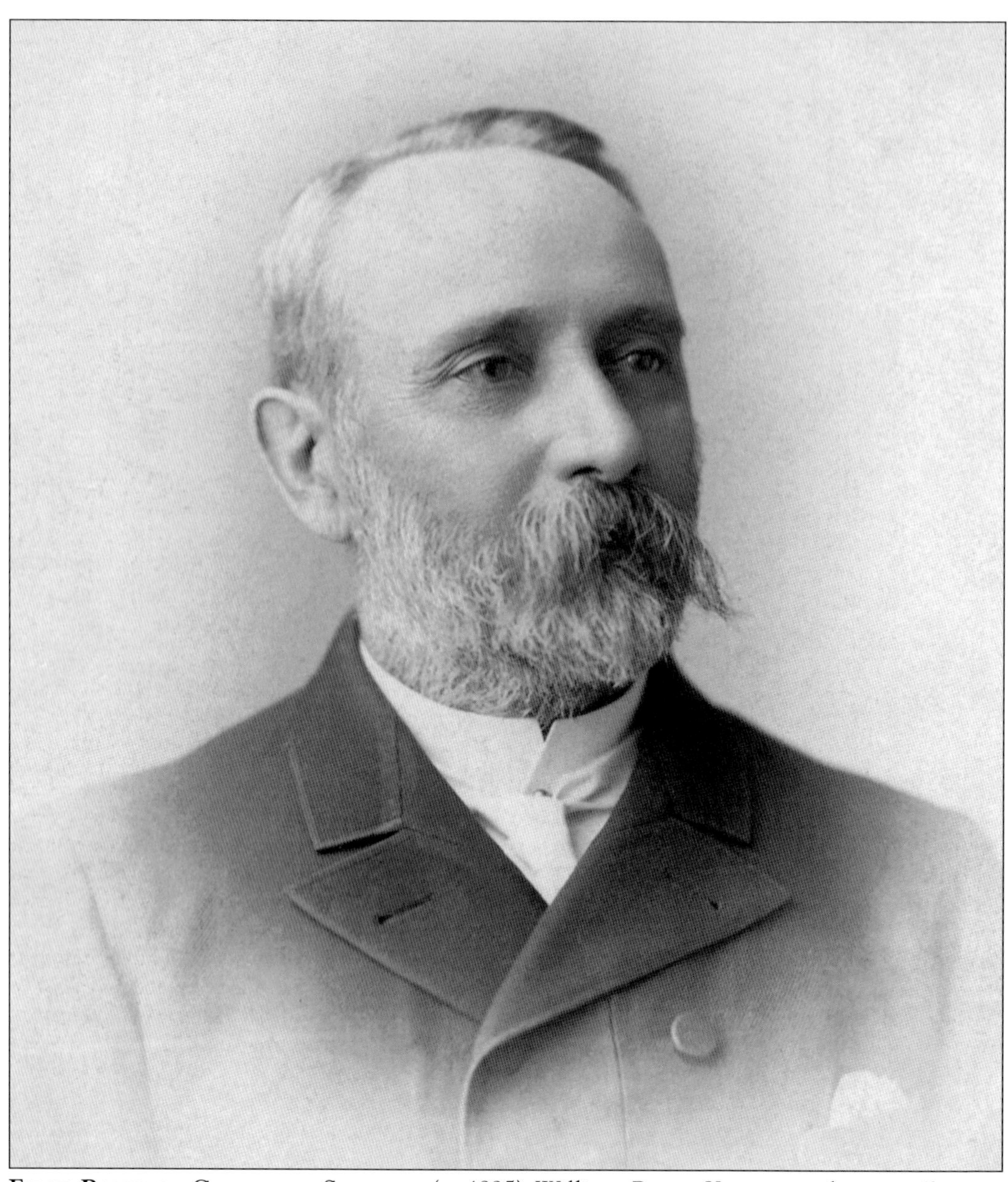

FIRST BANK OF COLORADO SPRINGS. (*c.* 1895) William Bangs Young was born in Boston, Massachusetts in 1832. In 1871, he and his family left Chicago after the Great Fire and traveled west by wagon. William was a bold and ambitious businessman who saw the opportunities available in Colorado through Palmer's narrow–gauge railroad from Denver to Colorado Springs, the gold and silver mines, and the "wealthy lungers" who came from Europe. It was clear to Young that a banking system was needed for the fast growing town. He began a clearinghouse in 1873, a type of banking system, but it failed in October of the same year, leaving some creditors destitute and angry. With murmurs of lynching, he barely escaped town with his life, although his eyes were badly blackened. He returned the following year and redeemed himself by paying back the money that was owed to the creditors. He also started the First National Bank of Colorado Springs, the first to have the endorsement of the U.S. Treasury with $50,000 worth of gold pieces he kept in a buckskin bag. (Courtesy Rogers Davis.)

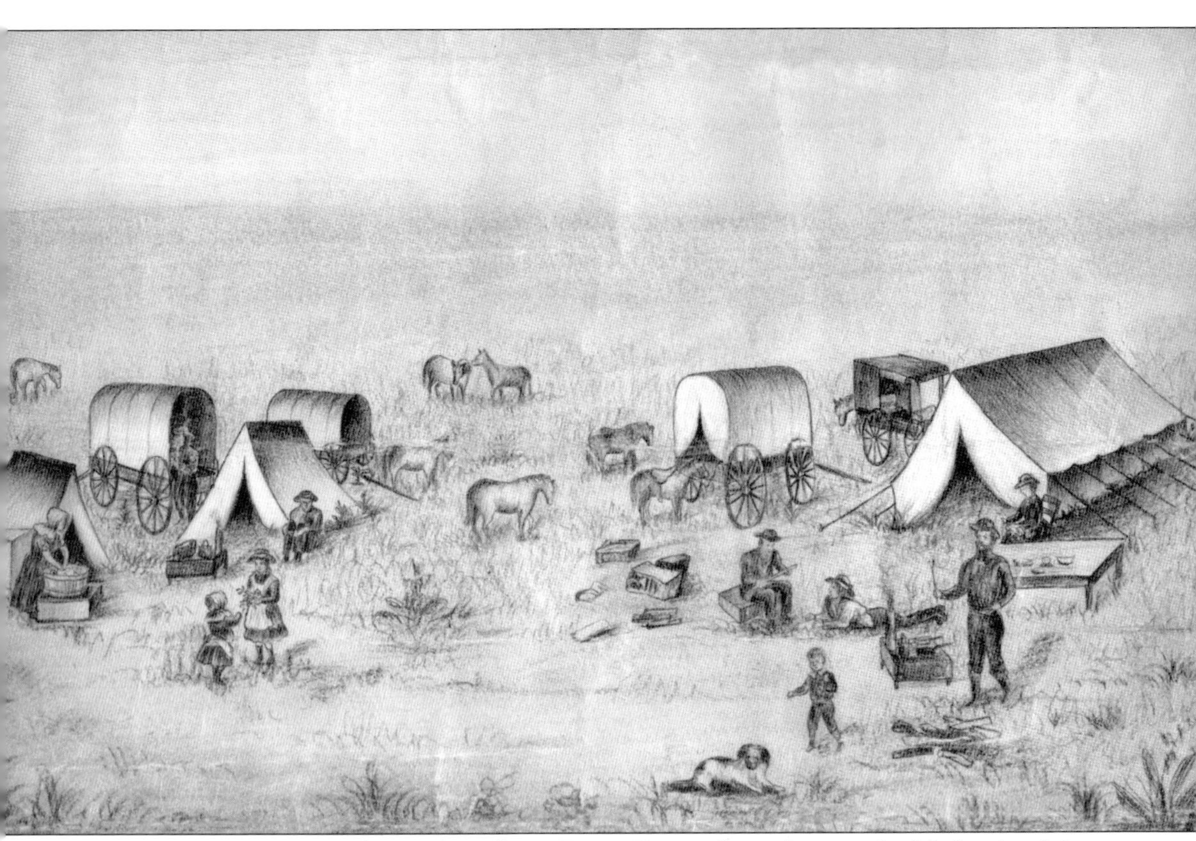

Crossing the Plains. (*c.* 1871) William Bangs Young drew this wonderful sketch of their camp as he and his family traveled west to a new life in Colorado. They traveled with at least one other family by wagon rather than using the railroad: William's wife Mary Elizabeth had a weak heart and the doctor felt the train ride would be "too fast" for her health. The doctor believed a longer journey would give Mary's heart a chance to gradually adjust to the high altitude in Colorado. The drawing depicts a woman washing some clothes in a tub as another woman sits in a chair. A man appears to be stoking the fire and a young girl (thought to be William's daughter Marian) gives flowers to a younger child. William Bangs Young started the First National Bank in Colorado Springs, which was authorized by the U.S. Treasury. He competed against the El Paso and the Peoples Bank, but prided himself that those banks were "private" and not sponsored by the treasury. (Courtesy Rogers Davis.)

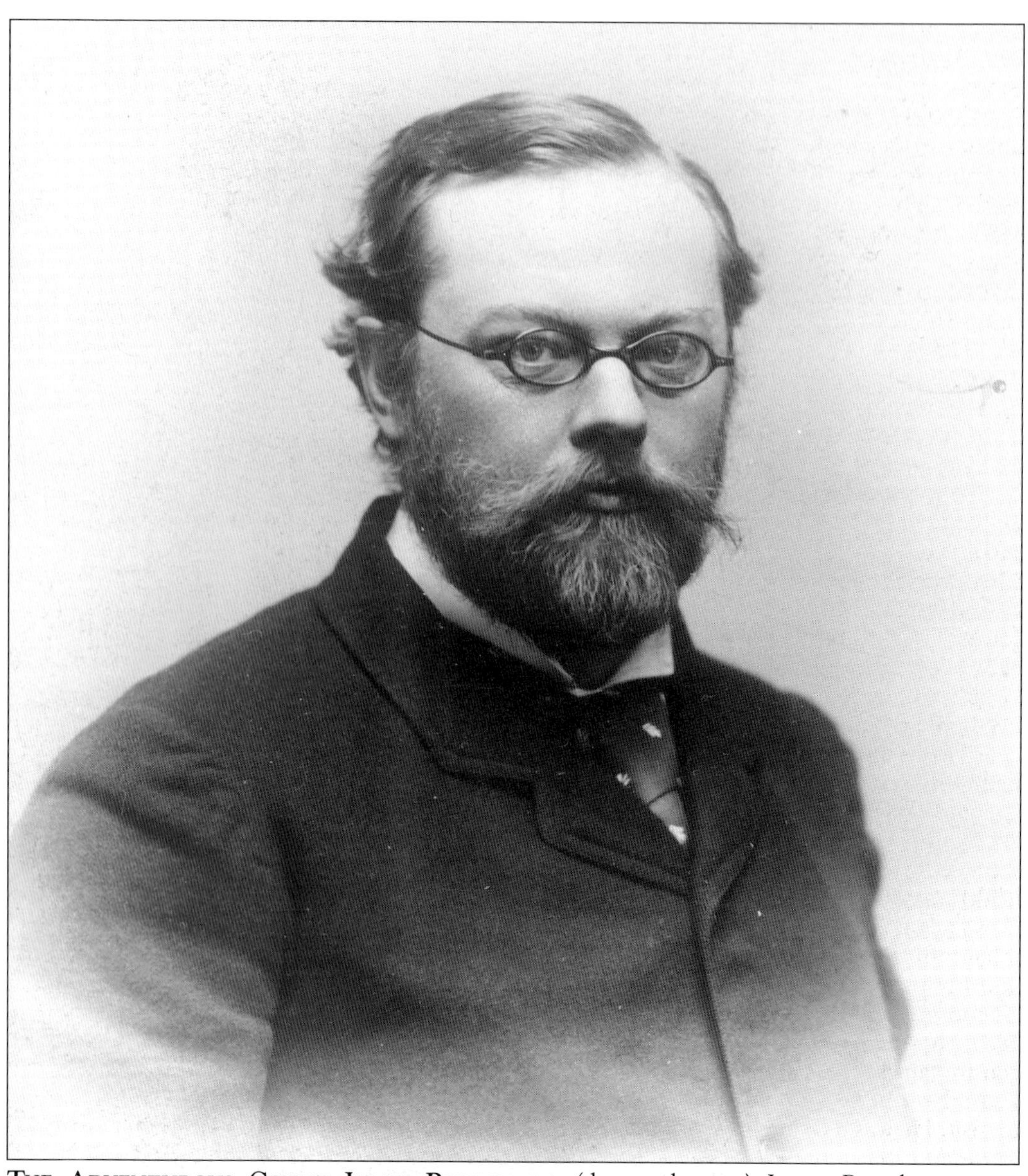

THE ADVENTUROUS COUNT JAMES POURTALES. (date unknown) James Portales was an entrepreneurial man who arrived in Colorado Springs to make his fortune, but instead fell in love with his beautiful cousin, Berthe. Berthe had recently divorced her husband and was living quietly in a small cottage on Pikes Pike Avenue when James proposed marriage and she accepted. James considered himself a good businessman and he formed an alliance with a man called William J. Willcox who ran a dairy farm called the Broadmoor. Before long his influence was seen at the Broadmoor by cross-breeding the cows and providing better food and plentiful water, which resulted in fine dairy products such as the Gilt Edge Crown butter. Other ventures such as his casino and real estate did not produce the wealth needed to sustain his estate in Glumbowitz, Prussia, (now Poland) or keep Berthe in her accustomed lifestyle. He eventually restored some of his wealth from a mine in Arizona called the Common Wealth mine, and he returned to Glumbowitz where he died in 1908, at the age of 55 years. (Courtesy Colorado Springs Pioneer Museum.)

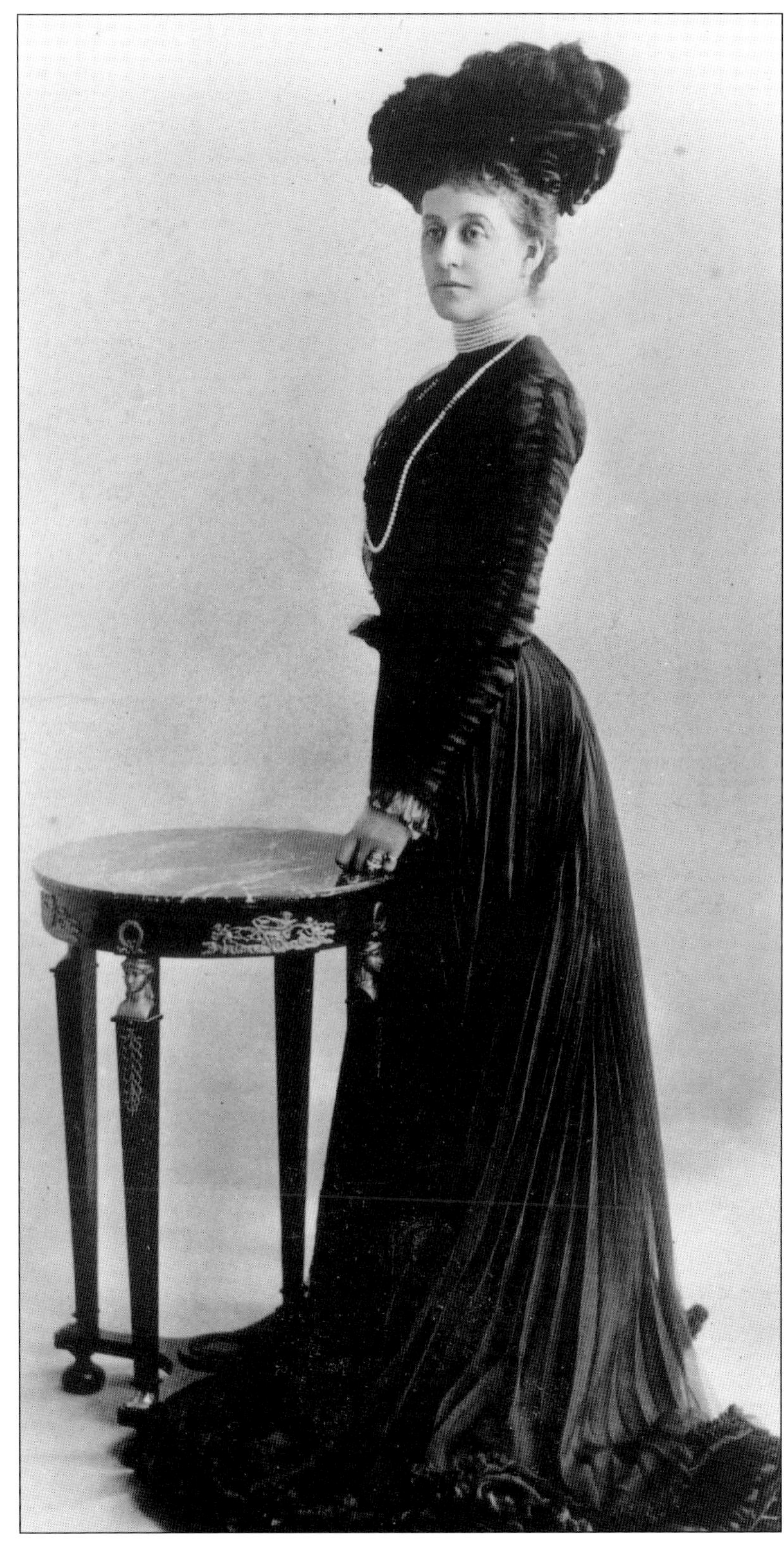

THE BEAUTIFUL BERTHE POURTALES. (date unknown) Berthe de Pourtales grew up in Cambridge, Massachusetts, where it is said her beauty was legendary and her fabulous gowns purchased in Europe brought admiration from the ladies in society. Berthe was a young divorcee with two small daughters when she left the East Coast and traveled west to be with her brother, Louis Otto, who lived on a ranch near Florissant. He had been sent to Colorado by the family physician supposedly for health reasons, but also possibly to curb his habit of drinking champagne. In 1885, another cousin, James Pourtales, came to visit. He was a warm and charming man but was given to grand ideas that never seemed to materialize. After a brief courtship, he and Berthe fell in love, married, and became part of the cream of Colorado Springs society. (Courtesy Colorado Springs Pioneer Museum.)

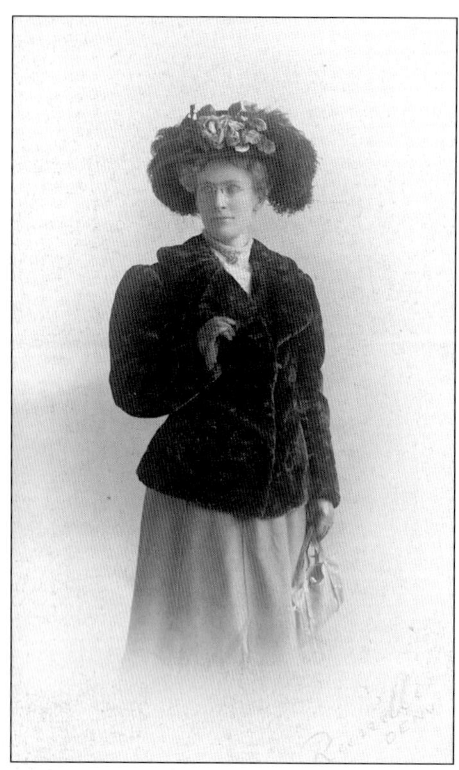

A Lady with Style. (*c.* 1881) The fashionable owner of the Judd Eating House in Palmer Lake poses in a fur jacket and hat. The restaurant was adjacent to the railroad depot. As trains stopped en route to Colorado Springs, passengers alighted and took refreshments. General Palmer, being an astute businessman, purchased hundreds of acres in and around the town that bears his name. (Courtesy the Palmer Lake Historical Society and Lucretia Vaile Museum.)

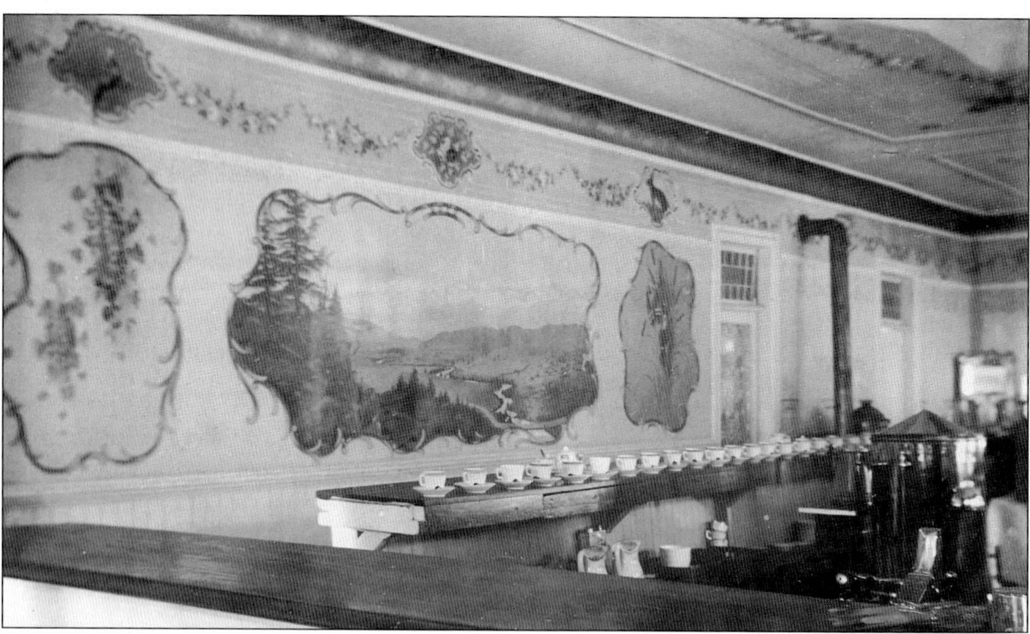

The Judd Eating House. (*c.* 1883) In 1883, Dr. William Finley Thompson began to promote Palmer Lake as a health resort that could be easily accessed by the Denver and Rio Grande Railway. He produced pamphlets describing the beauty of the region and told passengers that they could alight at Palmer Lake and get a wonderful meal at the Judd establishment, "a well kept eating house." (Courtesy the Palmer Lake Historical Society and Lucretia Vaile Museum.)

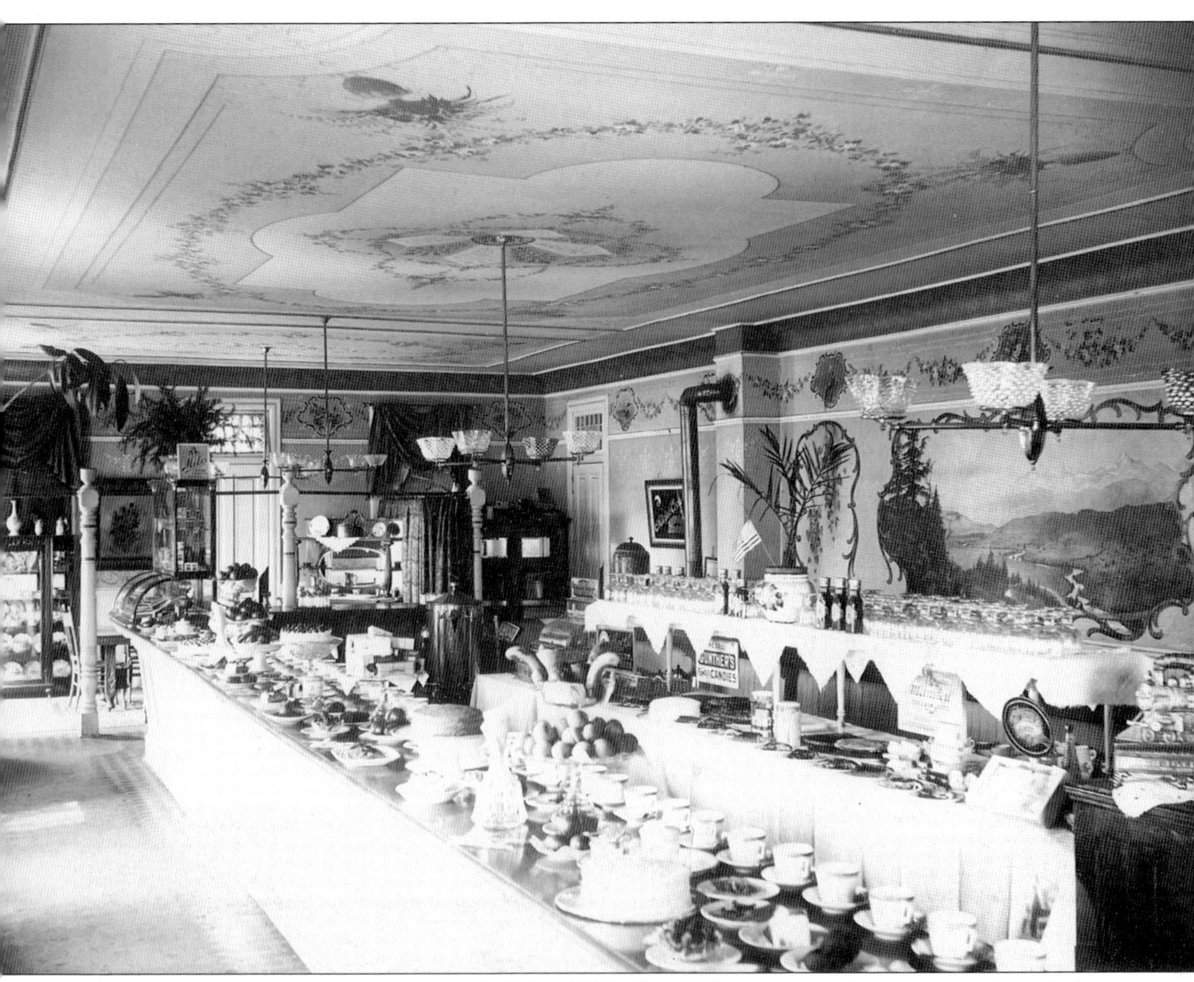

AN ELEGANT PLACE TO EAT. (*c.* 1883) In 1883, Dr. William Finley Thompson platted the town of Palmer Lake and set about promoting it as a health resort. The town hosted the Rocky Mountain Chautauqua in 1887. It began as a spiritual retreat that originally lasted a few days, but developed over the years into a six-week course including Bible study, botanical and bird study, painting, golf, tennis, and the arts. The restaurant was beautifully decorated with colorful murals on the ceiling and walls. The china and silverware are carefully laid out in readiness for visitors to take some light refreshment when the train stops briefly en route to Colorado Springs. Pies, cakes, sandwiches, and fruit are on display on the counter. With its elegant glass light fixtures, curio cabinets, and potted ferns, the Judd Eating House appealed to many sophisticated guests and became a favorite place to stop en route. (Courtesy the Palmer Lake Historical Society and Lucretia Vaile Museum.)

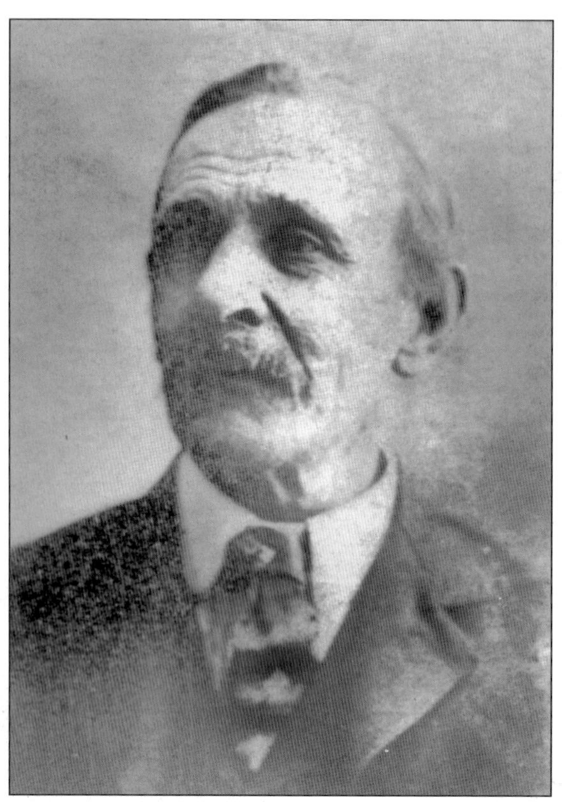

BOB WOMACK, A SIMPLE COWBOY WHO LOST A FORTUNE. (*c.* 1900–1909) Bob Womack of Cripple Creek spent much of his time searching for gold and fantasized about becoming a millionaire. He struck it rich and celebrated so wildly that he lost his senses and sold his Poverty Gulch claim for $500! It reaped millions for the new owners but Womack died penniless on August 10, 1909, at his sister's home. (Courtesy Pikes Peak Library District.)

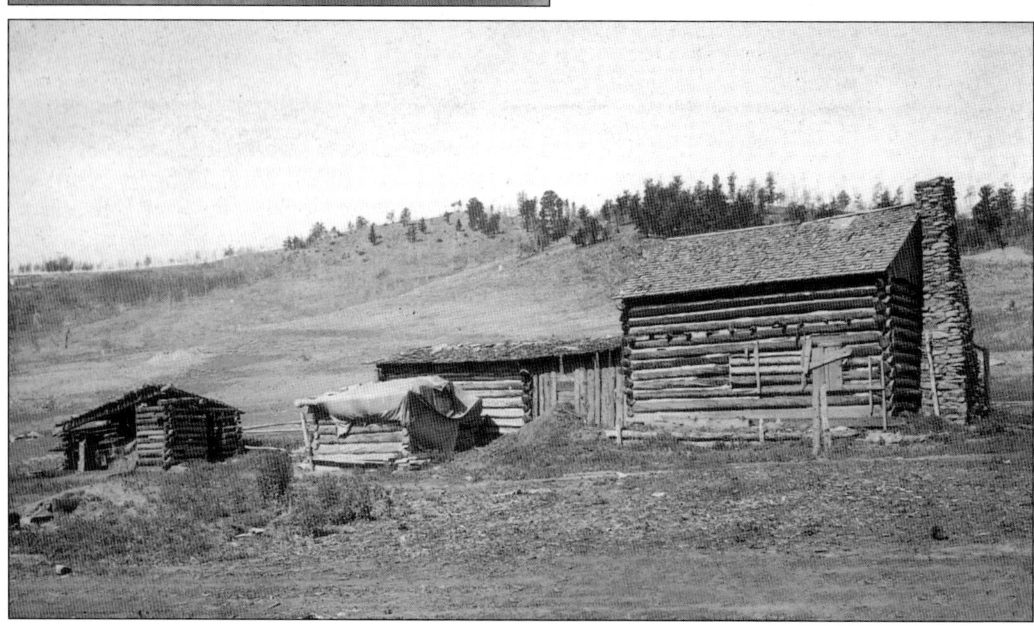

THE WOMACK RANCH. (*c.* 1876–1878) Samuel Womack brought his family to Colorado in 1876. They homesteaded and searched for gold, but it was their daughter Lida who controlled the finances. She was not unattractive, but she had a fine head on her shoulders and therefore young men were intimated by her and respectfully addressed her as "Miss Lida." She never married and nursed her brother Bob until he died. (Courtesy Colorado Historical Society.)

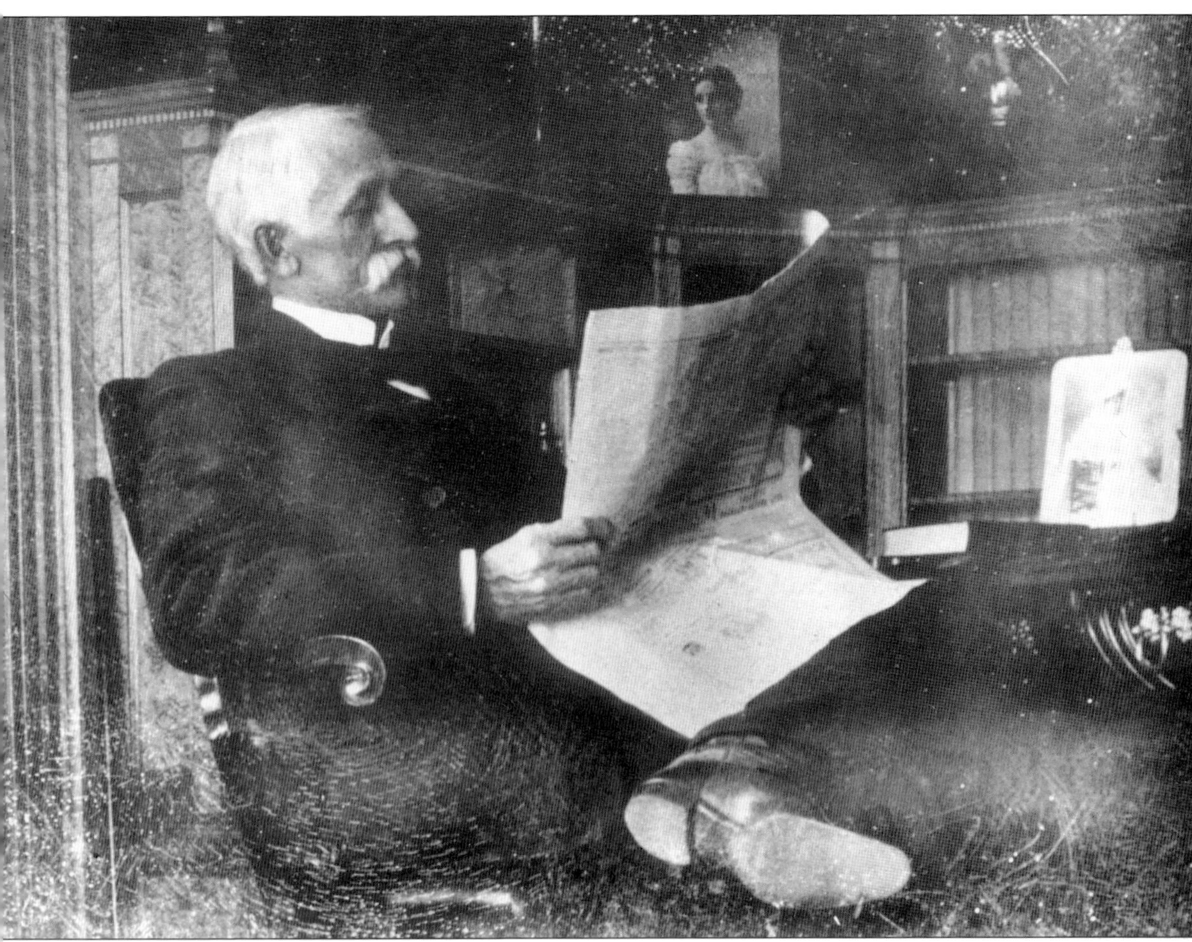

WINFIELD S. STRATTON, A MILLIONAIRE OVERNIGHT. (*c.* 1900) Winfield Scott Stratton arrived in Cripple Creek in 1874, a divorced man and carpenter looking for work. He and a friend invested in the Independence Mine, which made them millionaires almost overnight. The fortune did not sit well with Stratton, who said of his wealth, "Too much money is not good for any man . . . I have too much and it is not good for me." When his wealth was advertised in the newspapers, he was inundated with begging letters and, being a kind man, he gave away much of his fortune to the less fortunate. The young girl who did Stratton's laundry mentioned one day that her deliveries would be faster if she rode a bike. The following day, Stratton purchased a gross of bicycles and distributed them to all the laundresses in the area. In 1901, he purchased Colorado Springs Rapid Transit and also formed the Colorado Springs Suburban Railway, turning it into a successful first-class operation. (Courtesy Colorado Springs Pioneer Museum.)

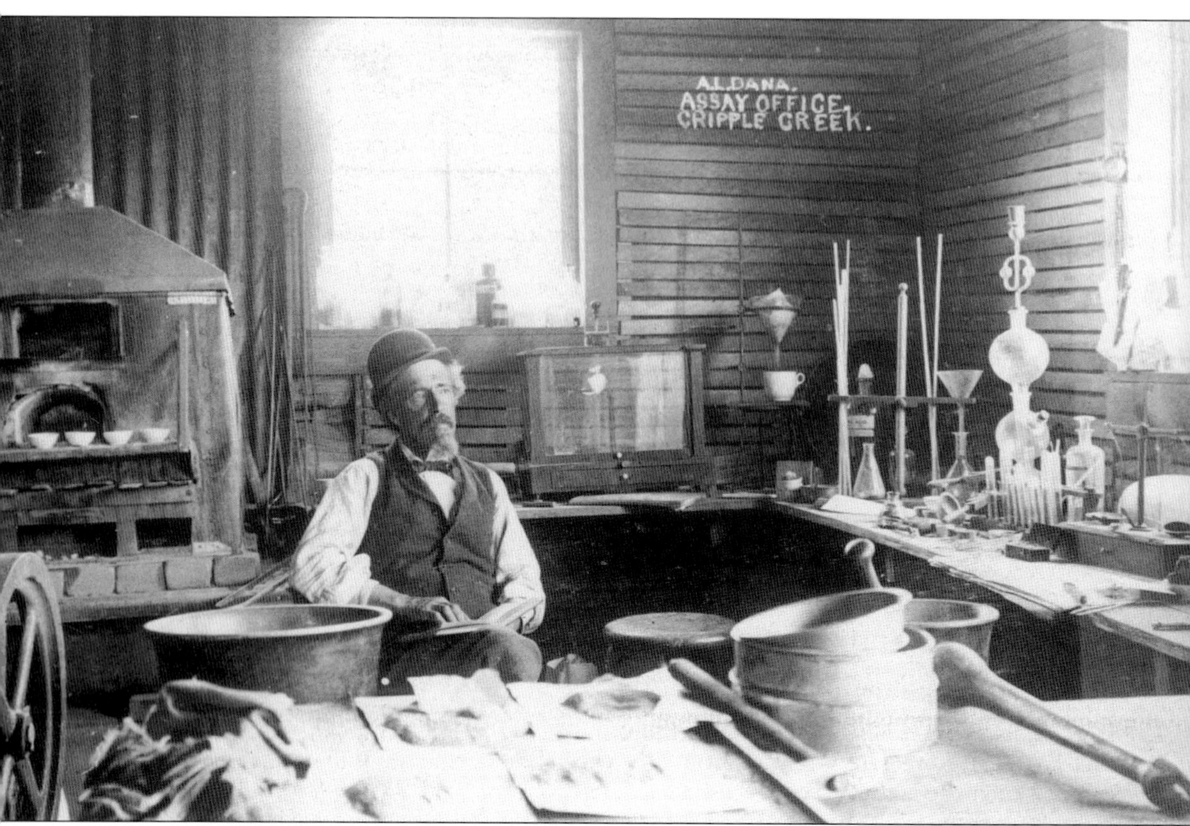

The Most Important Office in Town To a Miner. (c. 1892) The plaque on the office wall reads, "A.L. Dana, Assay Office, Cripple Creek." Discovery of gold or silver by a miner would quickly take him to the assay's office to determine the presence, absence, or quality of the ore specimens found on his claim. Awaiting the results must have been excruciating, and many men found solace in the saloons in Cripple Creek. The quality of ore varied with the lesser grades sometimes used to pave the streets rather than incur the cost at the mill. In 1899, when the town was at its height, it supported 72 lawyers and 39 real estate agents. One of the main thoroughfares was Bennett Avenue, which had every conceivable business from bakeries to blacksmiths. The town also boasted of a large hotel called the National that accommodated over 150 guests. (Courtesy Pikes Peak Library District.)

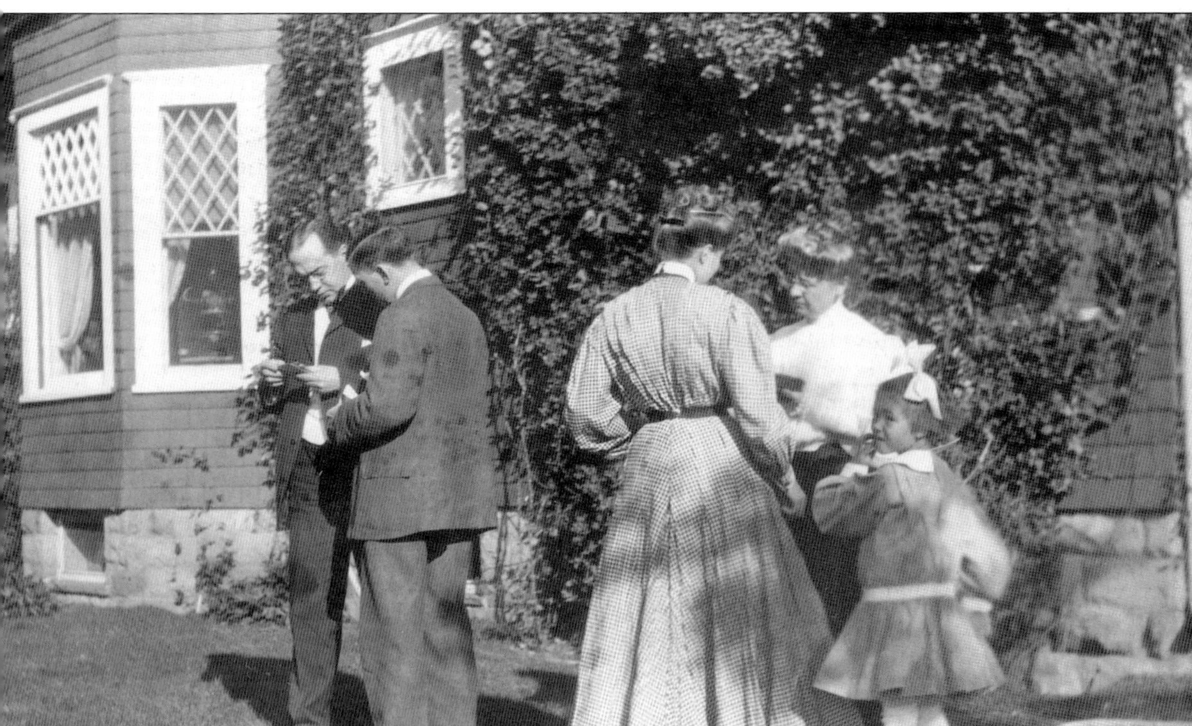

DOLL RECEPTION AT THE WILBUR STORE. (*c.* 1915) Not only did the Wilburs have a successful dry goods company, they merged businesses with Johnson and Sons, another large firm in Colorado Springs, and were then able to offer footwear, millinery, and ready-made women's dresses. Mrs. Wilbur continued her annual Doll Reception during the Christmas season as the local newspaper reported that ". . . there are none finer anywhere and orders are received for them from every part of the United States and the number shipped to every part of the country is phenomenal . . . ." The event was nationally recognized because many of the dolls were beautifully dressed and some had real hair and eyelashes. Mrs. Wilbur supervised the dress design and materials used for the dolls that varied in price from $1.25 to $25.00. To be sure that all children would be able to afford a doll, Mrs. Wilbur also purchased many "factory dressed" dolls that were sold at 25 cents each. The photograph shows the Wilburs at their home on Wood Avenue; a parrot sits in its cage in the latticed window. (Courtesy Colorado Springs Pioneer Museum.)

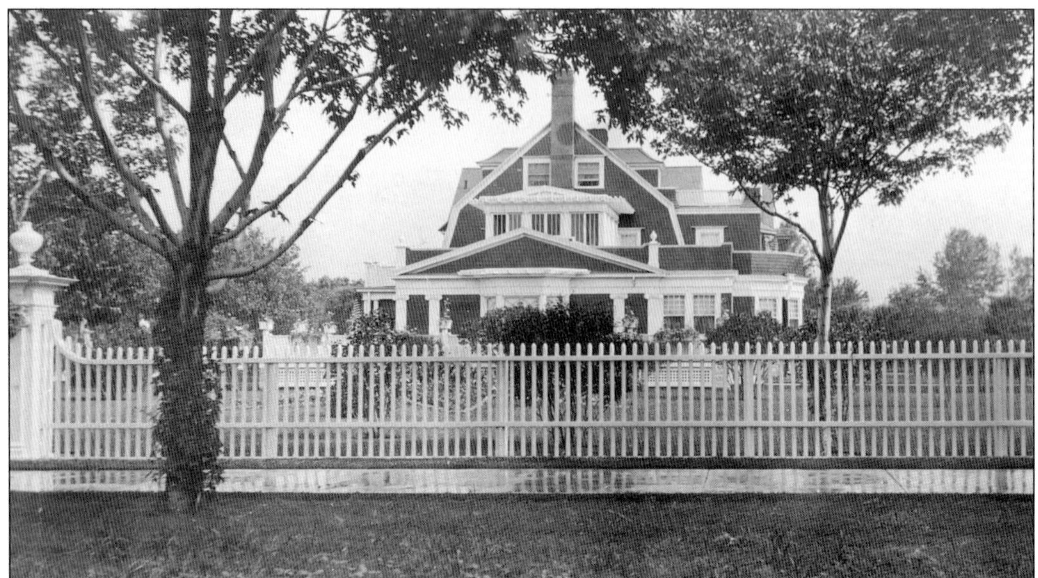

GOLD MINING MILLIONAIRE. (*c.* 1919) Jimmy Burns staked out the Portland Mine with James Doyle on Battle Mountain, just above Stratton's Independence Mine. They struck it rich but kept the find secret until they had enough money to fight the adjacent claims they knew would come. The Burns' splendid home, on the corner of Wood Avenue and San Miguel, was one of many built on the street known as Millionaire's Row. (Courtesy Colorado Springs Pioneer Museum.)

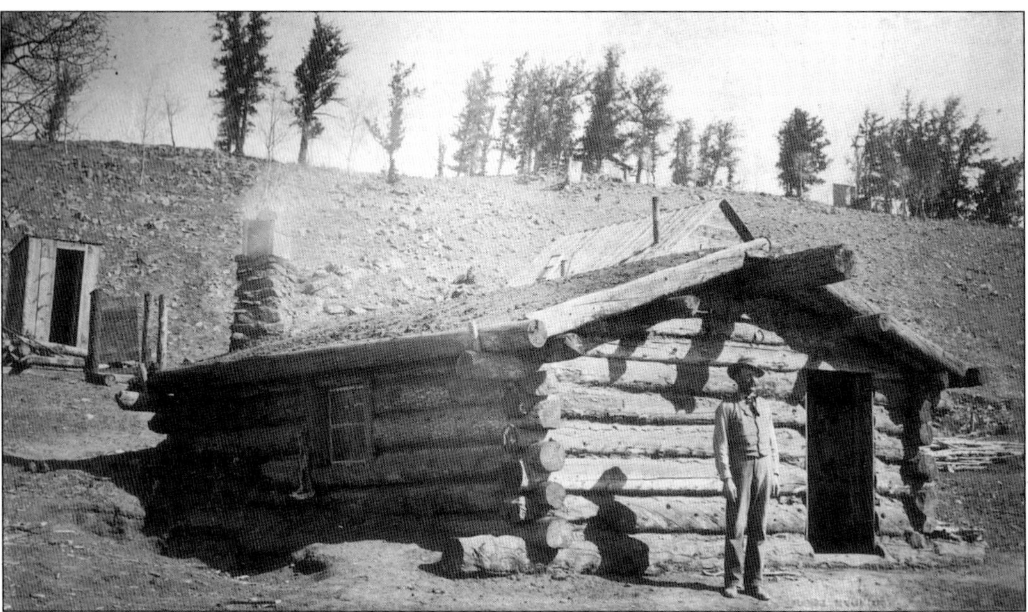

THE FIRST CABIN IN CRIPPLE CREEK. (date unknown) An unknown man stands to attention in a vest, shirt, and tie outside a cabin that is said to be the oldest in Cripple Creek. The cabin appears to be built into the slope of the hill, therefore providing some help in the materials and construction. It also has a dirt/gravel roof with a stone chimney and a privy in the rear. (Courtesy the Colorado Historical Society.)

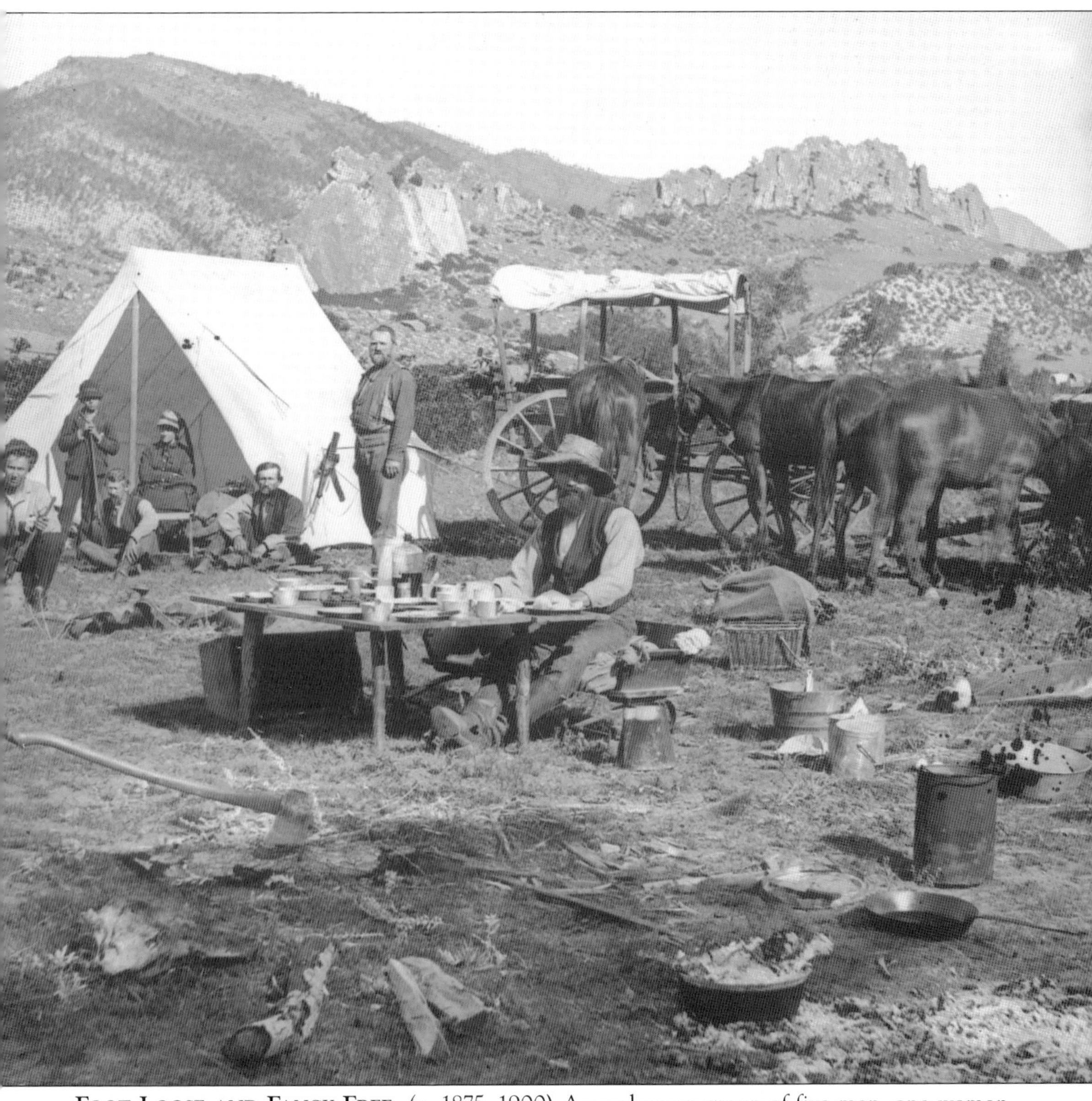

Foot Loose and Fancy Free. (*c.* 1875–1900) An unknown group of five men, one woman, and a young boy make up this party, camping in the foothills with the Garden of the Gods in the background. The woman sits at the entrance to the tent while the young boy stands, leaning on a shovel. The man on the left is holding a rifle and a saddle sits nearby. There are many cooking utensils discarded around the campfire and a large axe sits in a log. Should an accident or sickness occur at one of these sites, the family often took care of the patient themselves. The women usually had a good understanding of homeopathic remedies such as poultices for strains made with mustard, flour, water, and sagebrush tea that seemed to be a favorite for just about anything. Many people barely eked a living from the land as Isabella L. Bird notes in her book *A Lady's Life in the Rocky Mountains*: most men wore shoes or boots, ". . . but they didn't necessarily match . . . ." (Courtesy the Denver Public Library.)

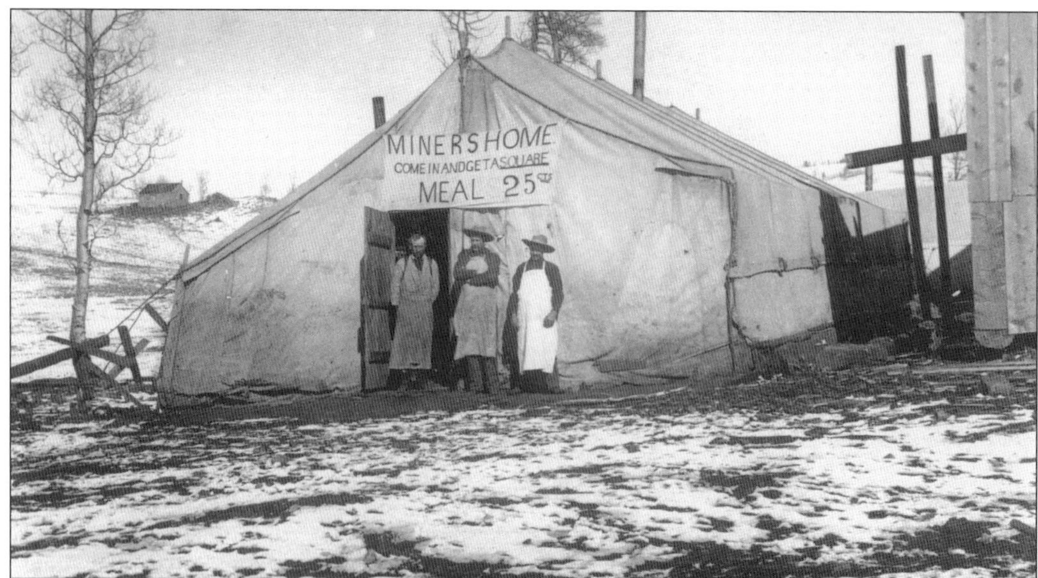

A Home Away from Home. (*c.* 1893) A makeshift restaurant offers miners "A Square Meal for 25 cents." Wherever miners worked, secondary businesses sprang up, such as boarding houses, laundries, saloons, and restaurants. Most meals consisted of a large portion of bacon or beef with biscuits, gravy, and bread, and perhaps a slice of pie. (Courtesy Pikes Peak Library District.)

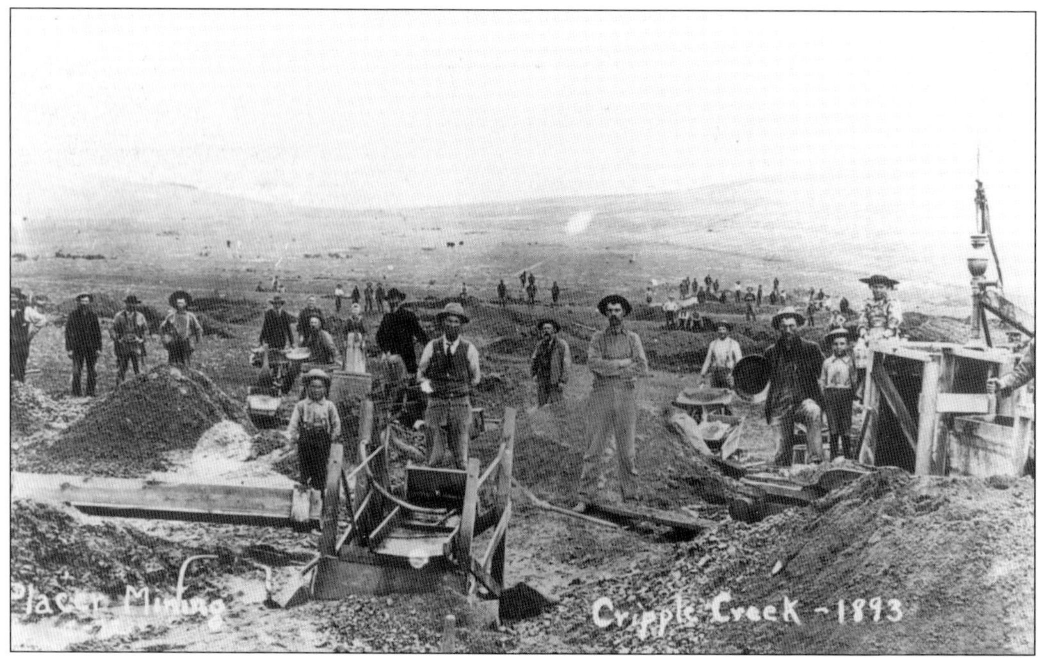

Some Used the Placer Mining Method. (*c.* 1893) Women and girls, some wearing hats and bonnets, participate in the Placer Method. This was a process for mining fine particles of gold and silver from riverbeds. Miners diverted the main stream into side streams to get easier access to the main riverbed. The miners enjoyed dry weather because of the naturally lower water level in streams. (Courtesy the Colorado Historical Society.)

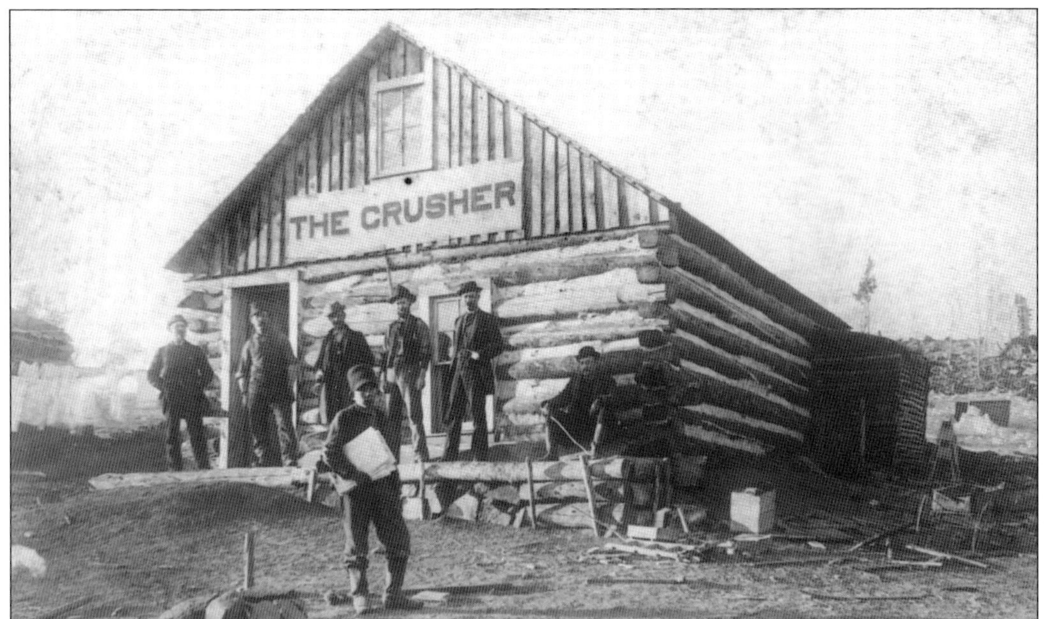

The First Newspaper Office in Cripple Creek. (*c.* 1892) *The Crusher*, Cripple Creek's first newspaper, began in 1891. A young boy stands in front of *The Crusher* log cabin office holding what appears to be a batch of newspapers for delivery as six men pose at the entrance to the office. In 1899, fifteen newspapers were published in the region, eight of which were produced by Cripple Creek. (Courtesy the Colorado Historical Society.)

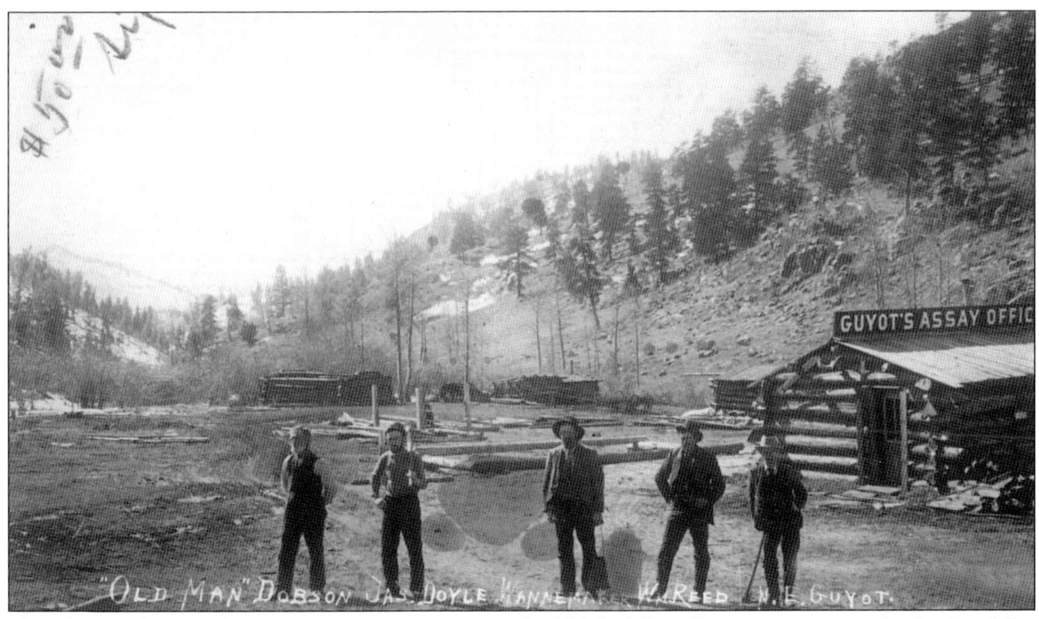

The First Assay Office in Cripple Creek. (*c.* 1891) A handwritten note on the back of the photograph reads: "In this cabin Stratton partook of my hooch, cursed the "trace" results of Jim Doyle. Here slept the first R.R. scouts in 1891. In 1892 W. Stratton presides with a grin at the R.R. meeting. I called it Grand Hotel Pueblo which broke up in a roar of laughter." (Courtesy the Colorado Historical Society.)

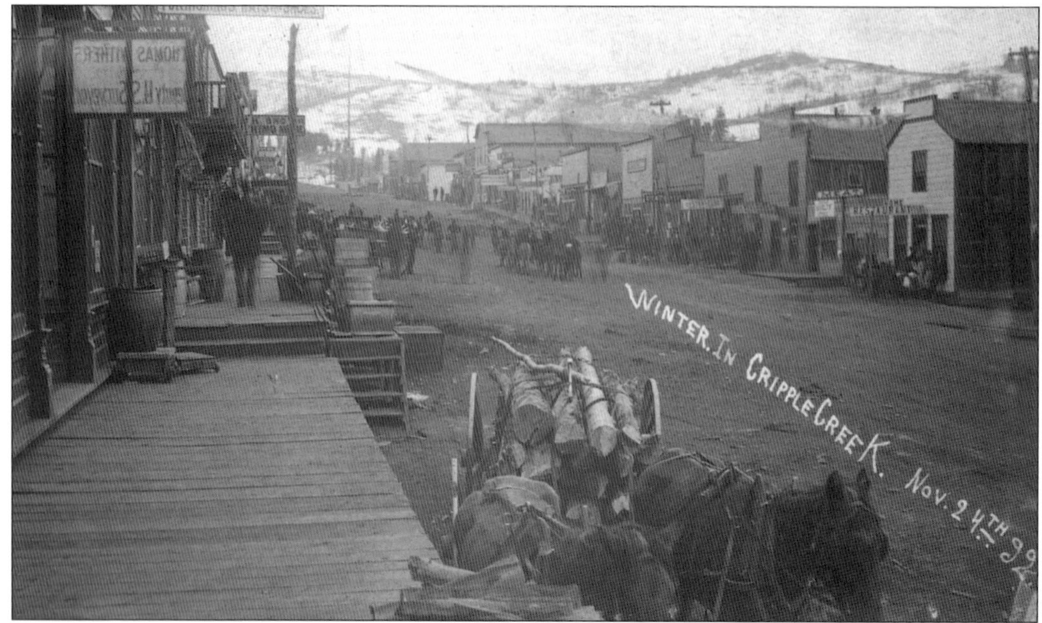

The Beginning of Winter. (*c.* November 24, 1892) An early winter scene in Cripple Creek with snow-capped mountains is pictured here. In 1892, the town was officially incorporated, and this led to two real estate men, Bennett and Myers, to plat an 80-acre township and offer lots for sale. Some people believe the town got its name when a cow was crippled after falling into a nearby creek. (Courtesy the Colorado Historical Society.)

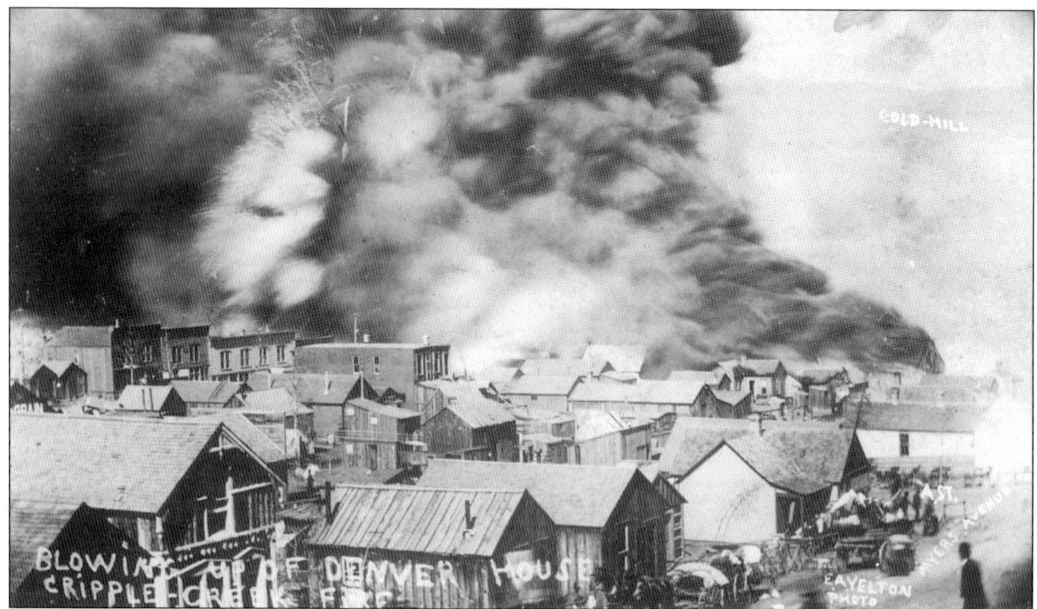

First a Fight—Then a Fire. (*c.* 1896) An argument between a bartender and his lady turned ugly when he slapped her face, and the ensuing fight knocked over a lighted stove that engulfed the room in flames. Fire Chief Allen was called and summoned his men into action. They saved all the "ladies" in the building, including various rabbits, cats, and the ladies' prized possession, laudanum. (Courtesy the Colorado Historical Society.)

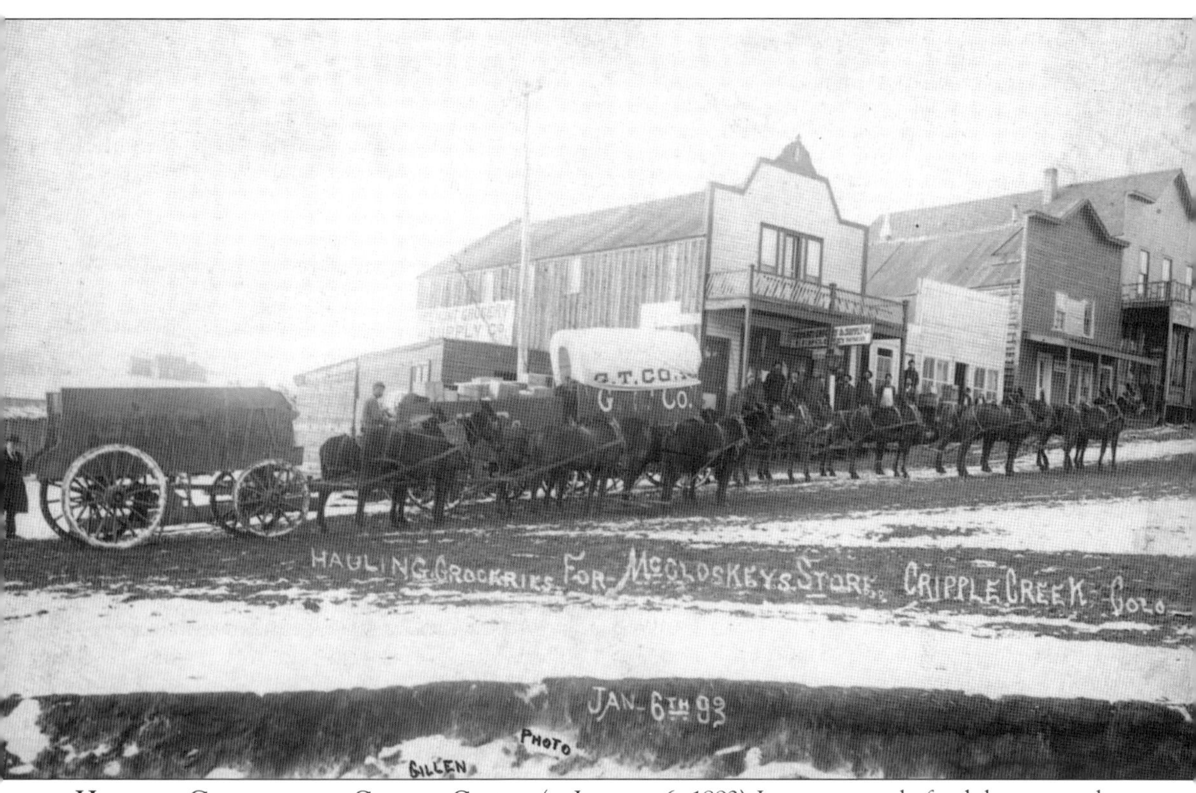

HAULING GROCERIES IN CRIPPLE CREEK. (*c.* January 6, 1893) It was not only food, but general supplies that were needed to develop the Cripple Creek area. One book after another gave pertinent information to those who planned a trip west; one in particular was *The Rocky Mountain Gold Region*, by S.W. Burt and E.L. Berthoud. They recommended a wagon and oxen as the main items necessary for a trip to the gold fields. An outfit consisting of four men should include: 500 pounds of bacon, $50; eighty pounds of coffee, $12; thirty pounds of candles, $7; ten pounds of tea, $5; yeast powders, $4; eighty pounds of salt, $15; five pounds of pepper, $1; and four bushels of beans at $8. The trek westward required many other items, of course, such as sacks of flour, bedding, soap, weapons, and gunpowder. (Courtesy the Colorado Historical Society.)

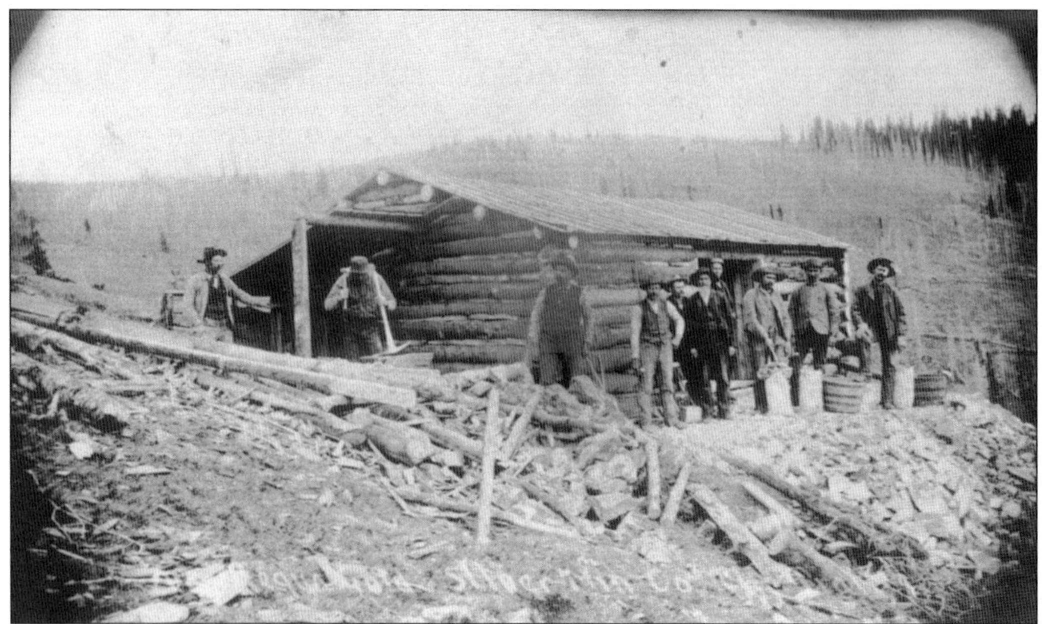

THE LURE OF GOLD AND SILVER MINING. (*c.* 1892) Ten men stand outside a log cabin. The men identified on the back of the print are, from left to right, Mr. Dutron, Edward Russell, Mr. Grimes, C.W. Banta, Aba Banta, Jim Burroughs, unknown, B.A. Banta, Chas. McGowan, and unknown. The name "Requa Gold & Silver Mining Co." is written across the front of the photograph. (Courtesy Pikes Peak Library District.)

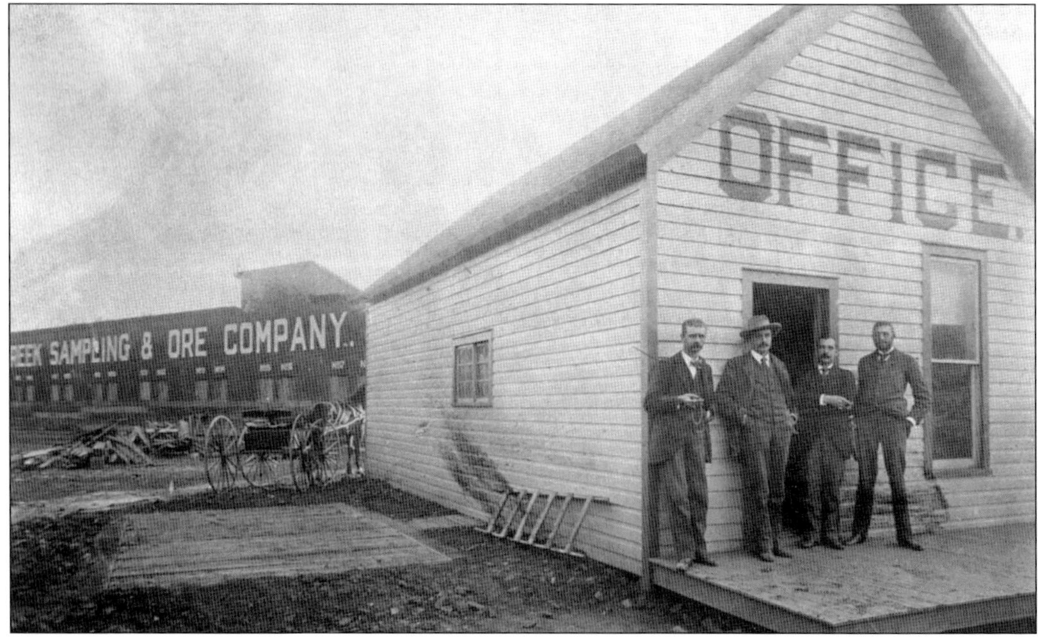

BOOM DAYS IN CRIPPLE CREEK. (*c.* 1874) From left to right are Bela Kadish, Spencer Penrose, Edward Newhouse, and Chas. L. Tutt, Sr. The men stand in front of a wooden building, the sign on which reads: Cripple Creek Sampling & Ore Company. There is a horse and buggy in the rear of the building. (Courtesy Pikes Peak Library District.)

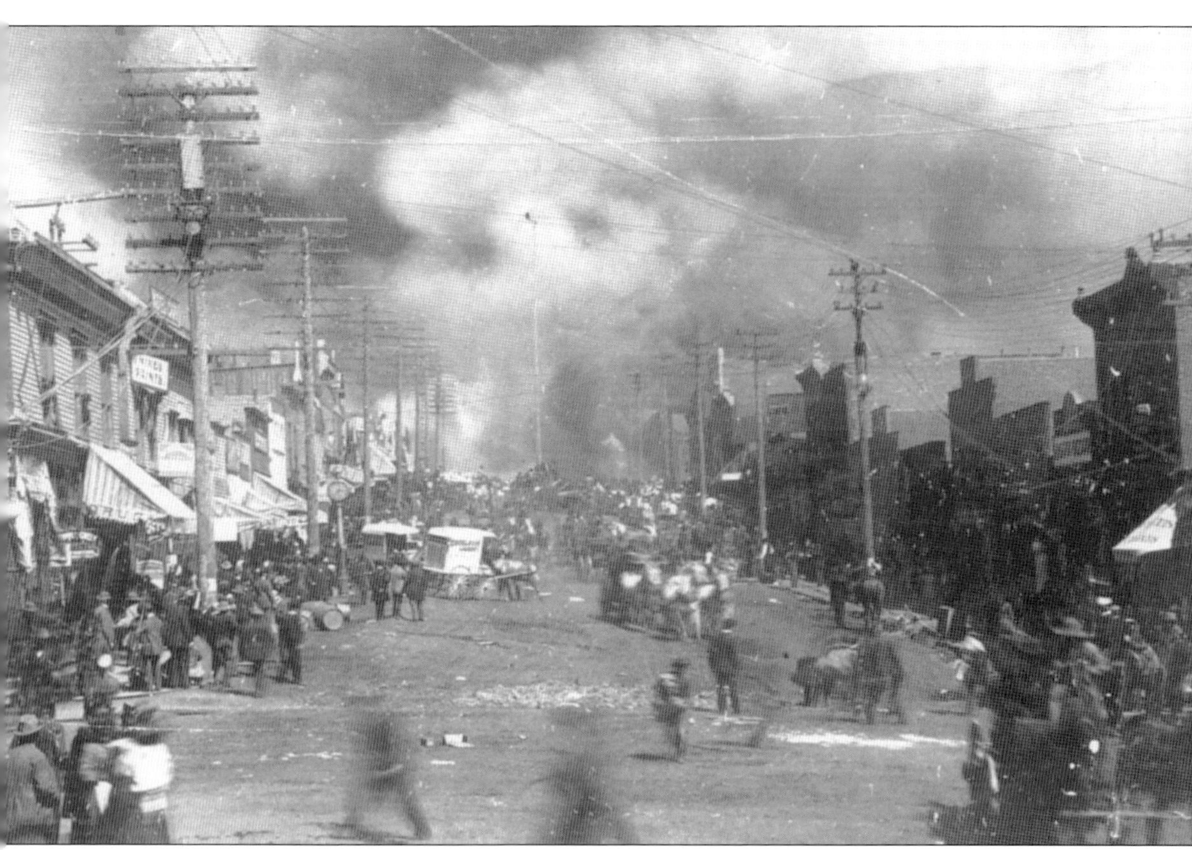

DEVASTATION IN CRIPPLE CREEK. (*c.* 1896) Residents of Cripple Creek rush to and fro as fire consumed the town. There were two fires in Cripple Creek within days of each other. The first fire began on Saturday, April 25th, 1896, after a brawl between a bartender and his girlfriend overturned a lighted stove, spreading flames throughout the second floor of the Central Dance Hall. Then, three days later, just as the town was recovering, Fire Chief Allen once again fired his revolver in the air signaling the volunteer fire fighters into action. This time the fire started in the Portland Hotel's kitchen after a maid had spilled fat on the range. The fire quickly spread as hot embers, helped by the wind, landed on nearby buildings. People in Colorado Springs heard by telephone of the bad luck in Cripple Creek and acted immediately, but it was Winfield Stratton who took charge stating, "We've got to move and move fast! No time to get money pledges. Charge everything to me. We'll divide the bills afterwards." (Courtesy Pikes Peak Library District.)

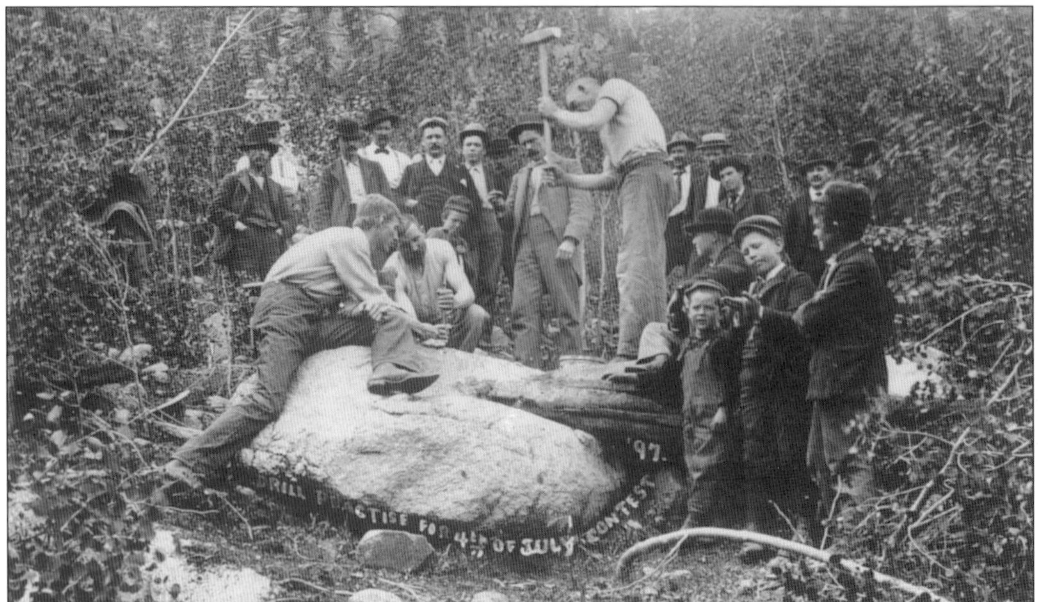

Drill Practice For the July Fourth Celebrations. (*c.* 1897) Two men hold onto a drill as one man hammers it home. The men are practicing for the 4th of July contest as eleven men and five boys watch them. The photo is labeled: "Drill practise for 4th of July Contest '97." Other competitions were played out during the 4th of July celebrations and Thanksgiving. (Courtesy Pikes Peak Library District.)

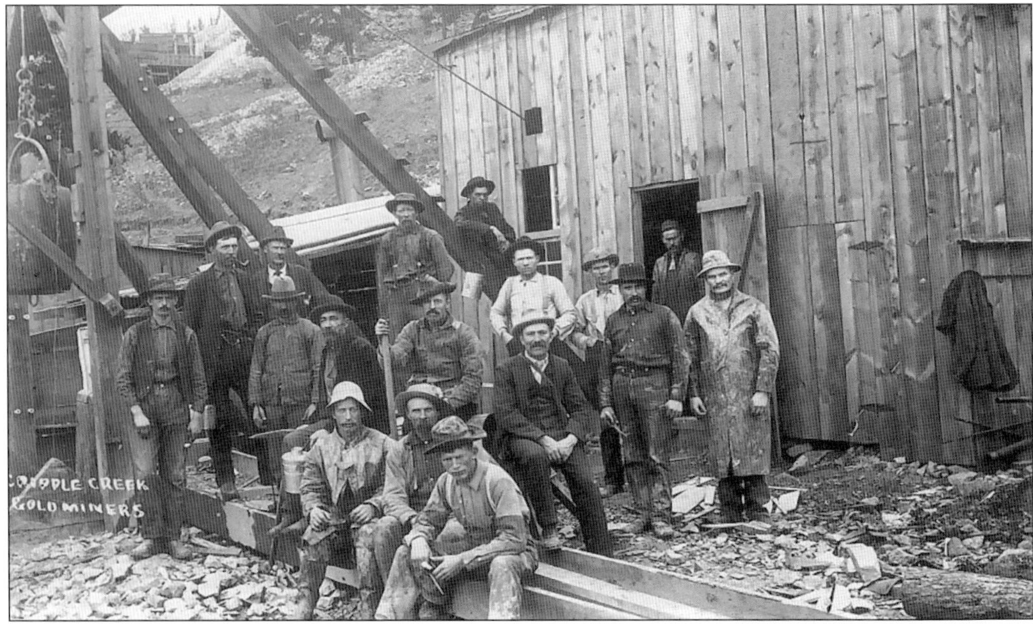

The Gold Strikes Produced Millions. (date unknown) Cripple Creek was called the World's Greatest Gold Camp with good reason, because some men like Winfield S. Stratton and Jimmy Burns became millionaires, but most just eked a living. Still they came, seeking wealth, and the small town grew from 500 people in 1891 to almost 2,500 one year later. (Courtesy Special Collections, Colorado College.)

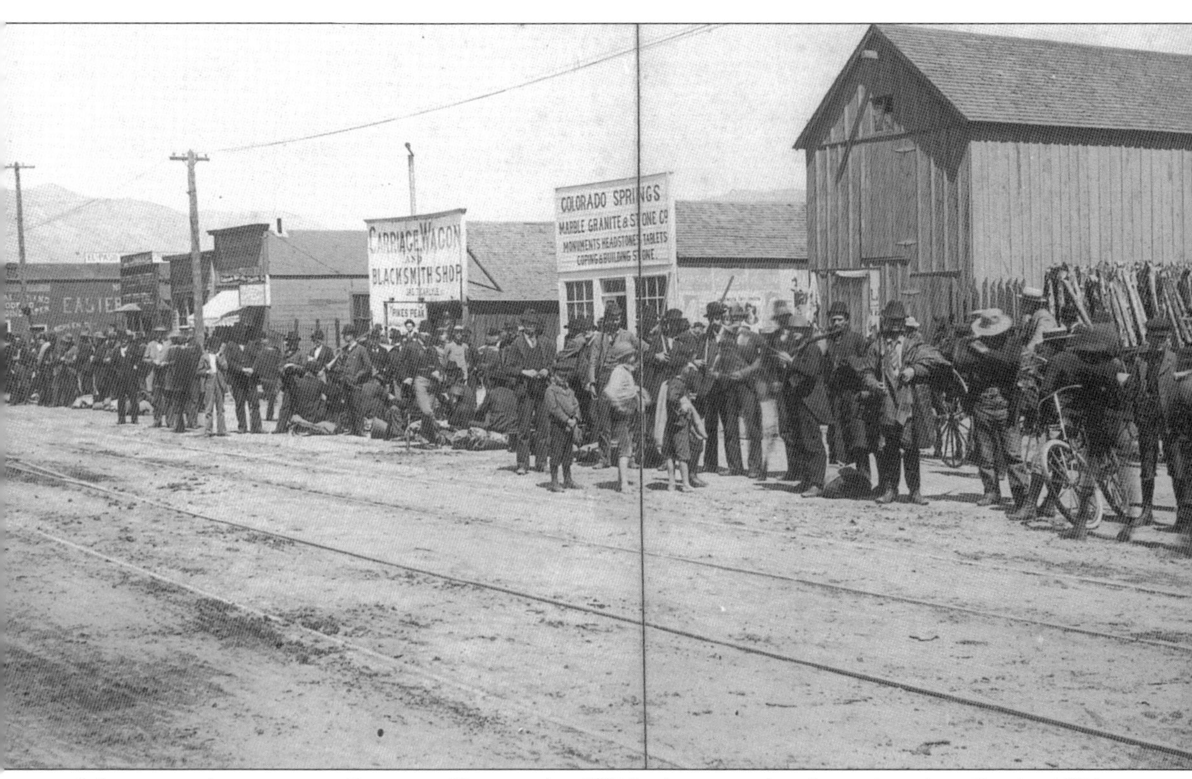

MILITARY ACTION IN CRIPPLE CREEK. (*c.* 1904) As a result of a miners' strike in 1894, mine owners and workers agreed to a $3.00 per 8-hour working day with no discrimination between union and non-union workers. But in 1904, 45 union members were discharged from the Standard Mill in Colorado City. Suspecting prejudice against union workers, the dispute quickly spread to Cripple Creek. It began as a verbal battle in the press, but soon escalated into threats, intimidation, and finally civil disobedience. Military law intervened under the auspices of General Bell, who brought in deputized men to gain control of the situation. Before the conflict was over, men lost their lives and others were banished from homes. Bell later said, "So we arrested the worst men in camp; gave them a fair hearing; picked the sheep out from the goats, loaded the latter into a special train, put aboard guards...ran 'em down to within two miles of the Kansas line; unloaded 'em and marched 'em to the state line . . . they disappeared over the prairie. And that was the end of the Western Federation of Miners and the reign of terror in Cripple Creek. . . ." (Courtesy Special Collections, Colorado College.)

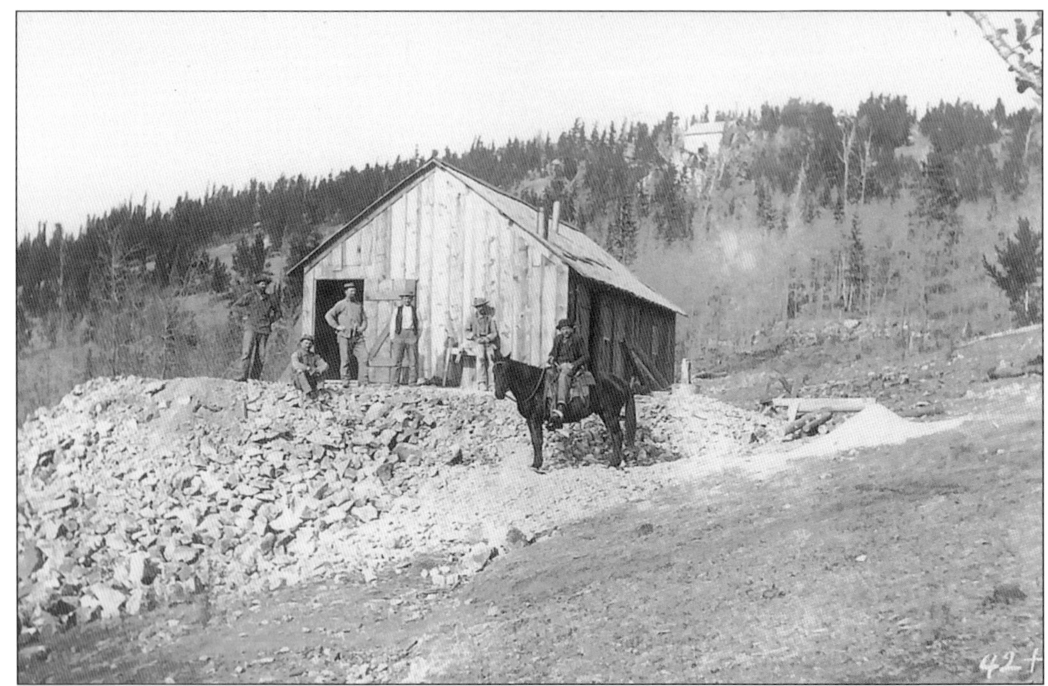

Men Working a Mine. (date unknown) Six unknown men are pictured at Cripple Creek mine, one riding a horse. Although the towns of Cripple Creek and Victor were basically "gold towns," they were remarkably sophisticated with all manner of businesses and shops. The neighboring town of Victor used low-grade ore from their mines to pave the streets, giving Victor the reputation of having "streets of gold." (Courtesy Special Collections, Colorado College.)

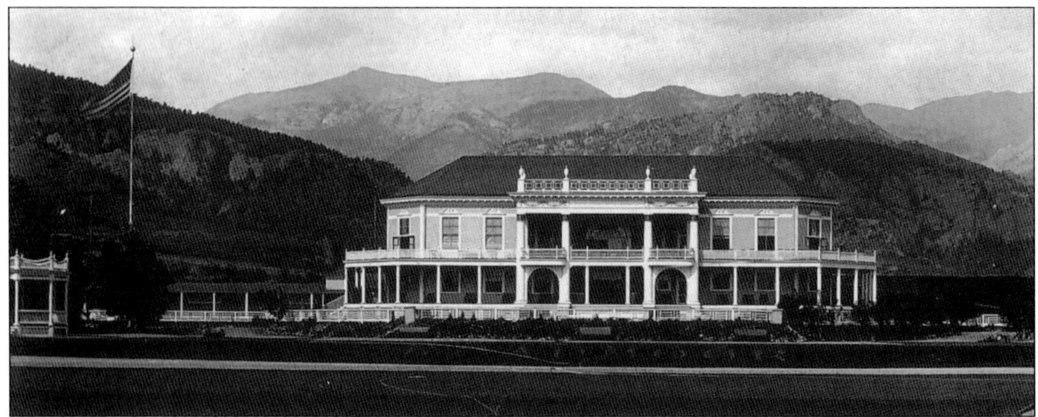

The Broadmoor—an Exceptional Hotel. (*c.* 1918) In 1918, a letter from W.S. Dunning, manager of the Broadmoor, to Manly D. Ormes of Colorado College describes the hotel and suggests Manly pay a visit to see "the center of gaiety, life and action . . . you know its fine orchestra—how it lends such an atmosphere of good cheer and how quickly a few so delightfully spent hours go by . . . the service and cuisine are irreproachable. . . . " (Courtesy Special Collections, Colorado College.)

Three

Cowboys, Indians, and Pioneers

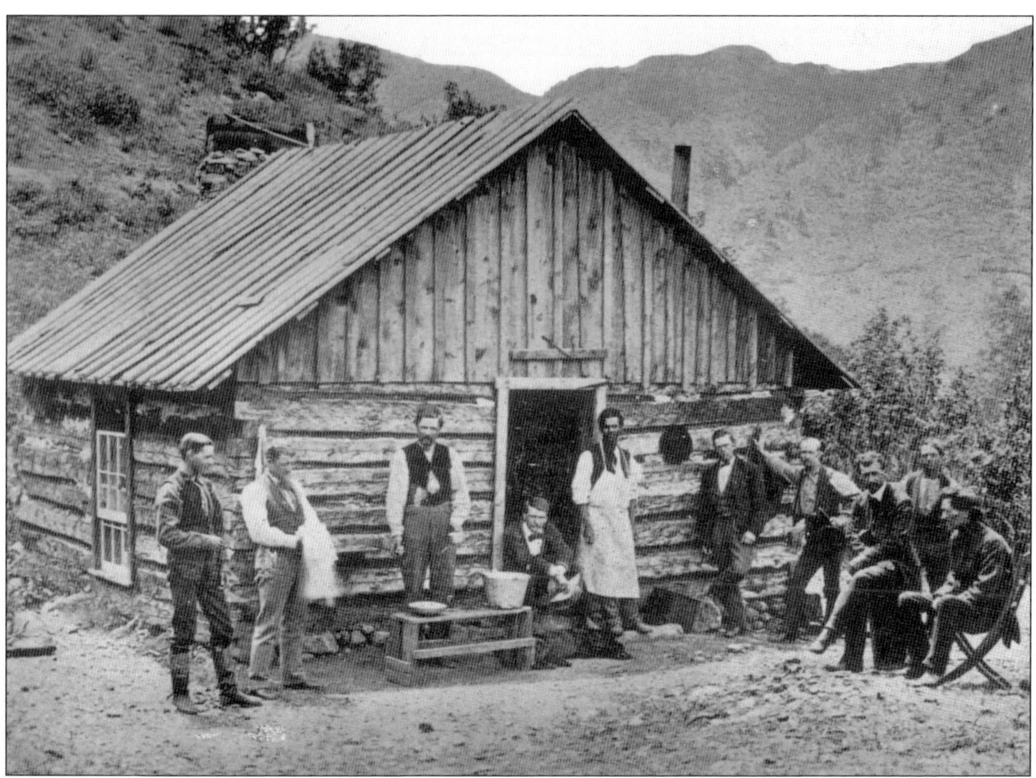

A Man's Home is His Castle. (*c.* 1870–1880) Ten men are photographed outside a square, gable-roofed, hewn log cabin in Manitou. A hand-written note on the back of the photograph states: "Marks, Hutchinson, Munday, Natson, The Cook, Jim Rayner, Jennison." The others are unidentified. One man appears to be wiping his hands while another has a ladle or serving cup in his hands. (Courtesy the Denver Public Library.)

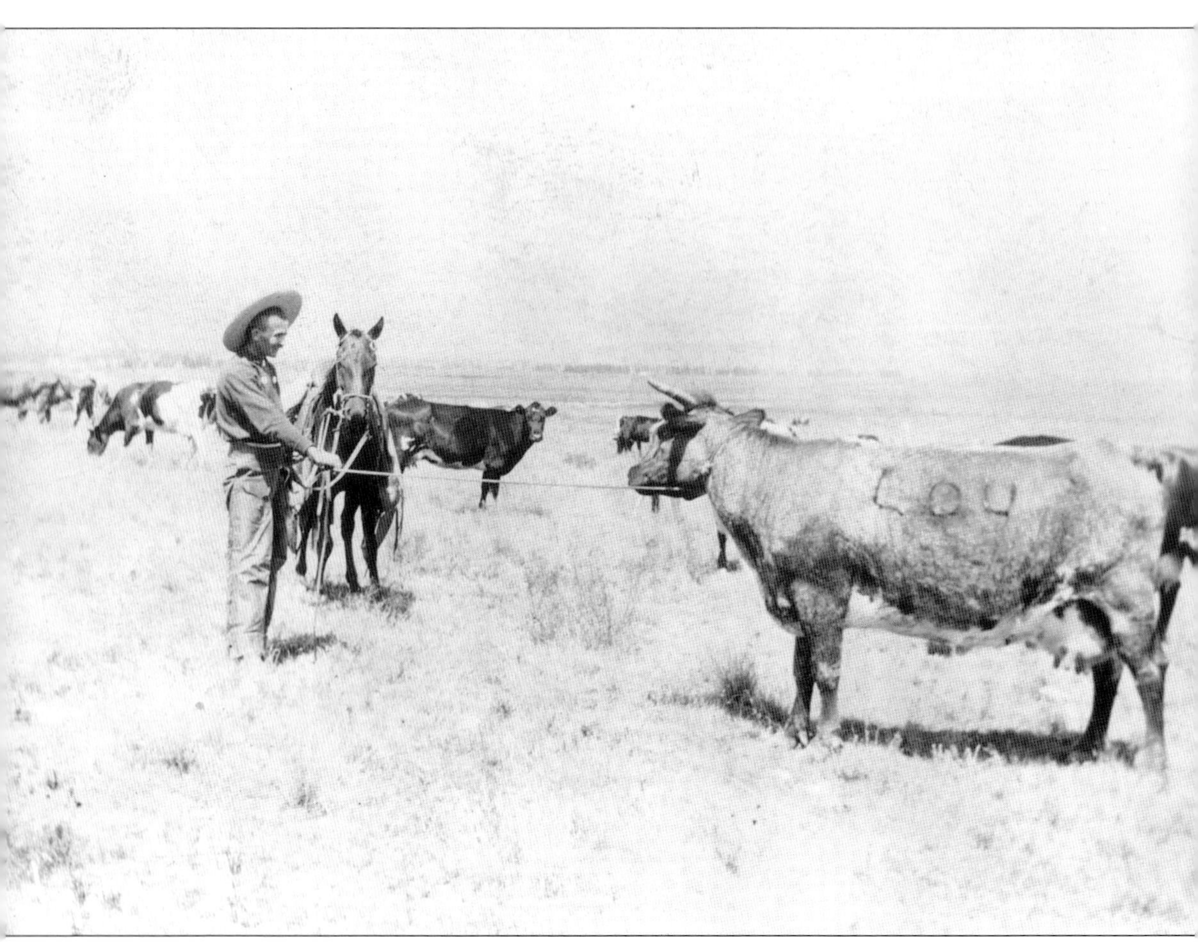

George Sinton—A Cowboy at Work. (*c.* 1891) Mary Sinton kept a journal from the day she married on December 30th, 1880. In her diary she describes her wedding dress of brown silk that was trimmed in brown satin and her husband's suit of black broadcloth. The wedding guests were served chicken and beef and five different types of cake. As the journal continues through their lives, a baby girl was born too soon and died. Heartbreakingly, Mary writes, "I did not hold the baby that afternoon nearly as much as I wanted to, it made George feel so badly." Soon, Mary is expecting another child and she writes in her journal, "How thankful I shall be if it is placed in my arms alive." The Sinton family began a very successful dairy farm as well as other businesses. The photograph shows George Sinton with a cow called Lou but it was brother Melvin who took charge of the ranching while George managed the financial side of the business. (Courtesy Colorado Springs Pioneer Museum.)

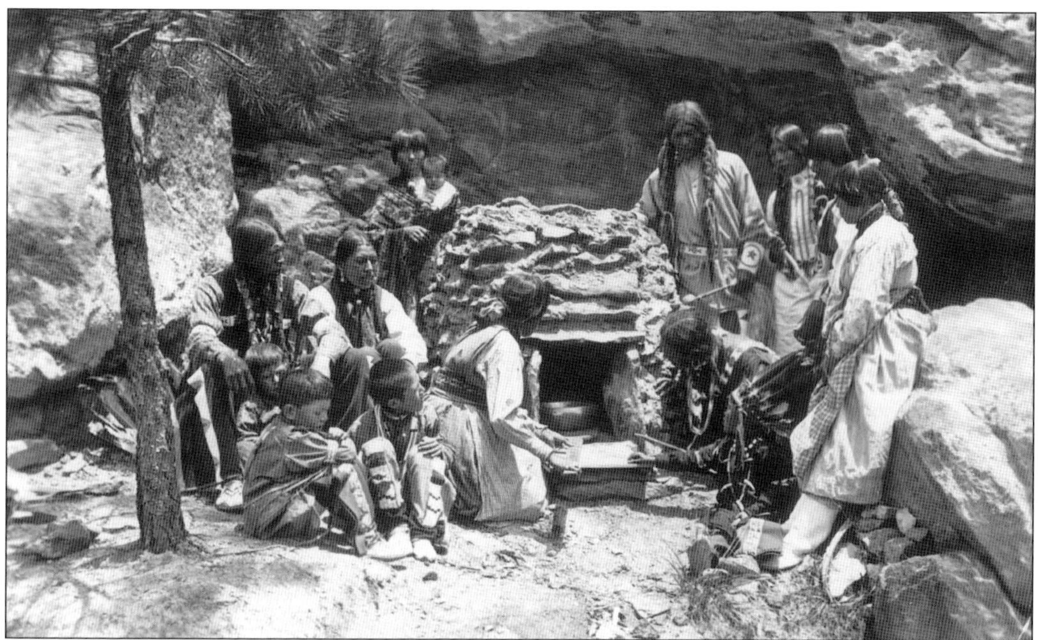

Indian Family Pose at the Manitou Cliff Dwellings. (*c.* 1920) A hand written note on back of the print reads, "Utes, *c.* 1920." The photograph shows an extended family posing for a photograph, presumably as a meal is prepared and cooked. The men wear traditional cotton shirts, beaded leggings, and moccasins. The women also wear leggings, mantas, and moccasins decorated with beads. The native women's quill and bead work were highly prized possessions that displayed the skills passed down through generations. (Courtesy the Denver Public Library.)

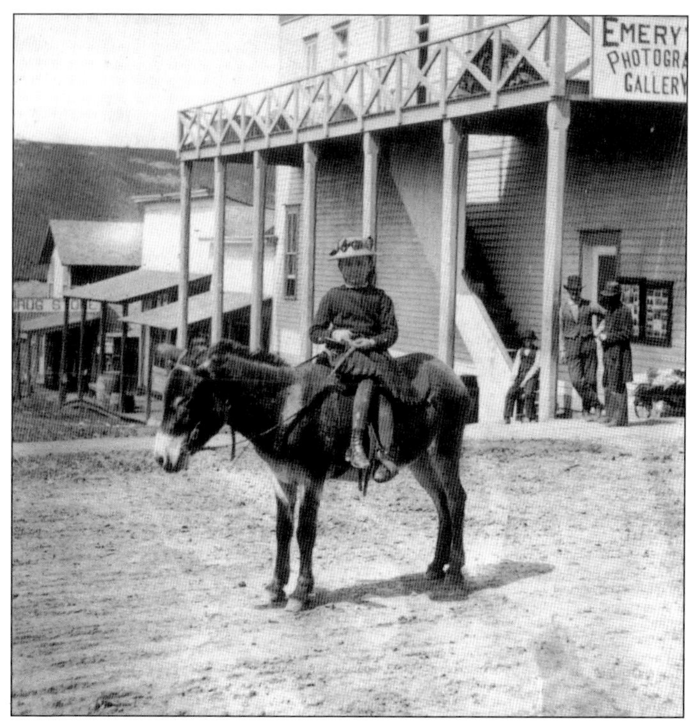

A Pretty Young Girl Sits Side-Saddle on a Burro. (*c.* 1884) Many children had burros of their own. This child is sitting side-saddle on a burro in Manitou Springs. She wears a pleated skirt and a straw hat, possibly decorated with flowers, and poses outside Emery's Photograph Gallery. Photographs are displayed outside the gallery as two men and a young boy watch the photographic session. (Courtesy the Denver Public Library.)

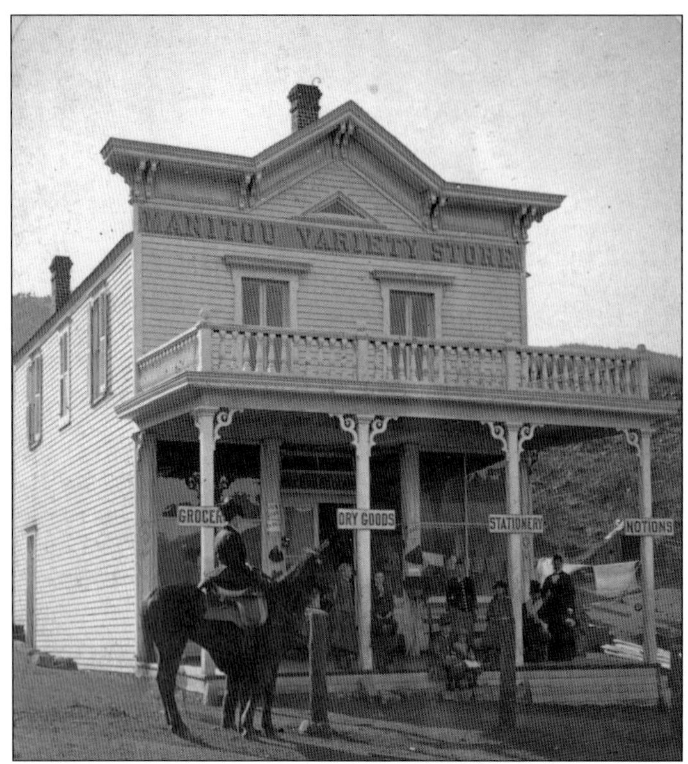

A WOMAN STORE OWNER. (date unknown) Mrs. Myra Baxter started the Manitou Variety Store after she became a widow. Mr. Baxter had been one of the early owners of Cliff House, an impressive hotel catering to 150 influential guests. A woman sits sidesaddle in front of the store that advertises groceries, dry goods, stationery, and notions. Washing is seen blowing in the wind at the side of the store. (Courtesy the Colorado Historical Society.)

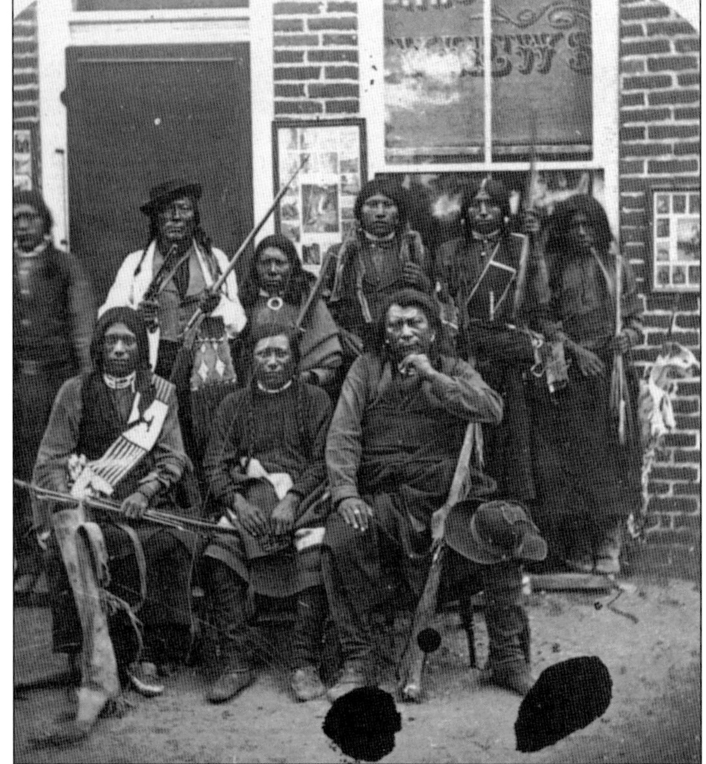

A SMALL GROUP OF UTES. (date unknown) The Ute believe their tribe has always lived in Colorado. Traditionally, they were hunter/gatherers, a nomadic tribe who moved with the season and game. Curious of the white settlers, they often looked in windows and doors and asked homesteaders for food. Mrs. Young, a settler, was about to discard some biscuits in which she had used too much soda. Instead, she gave them to the Indians who thought them to be delicious. (Courtesy Special Collections, Colorado College.)

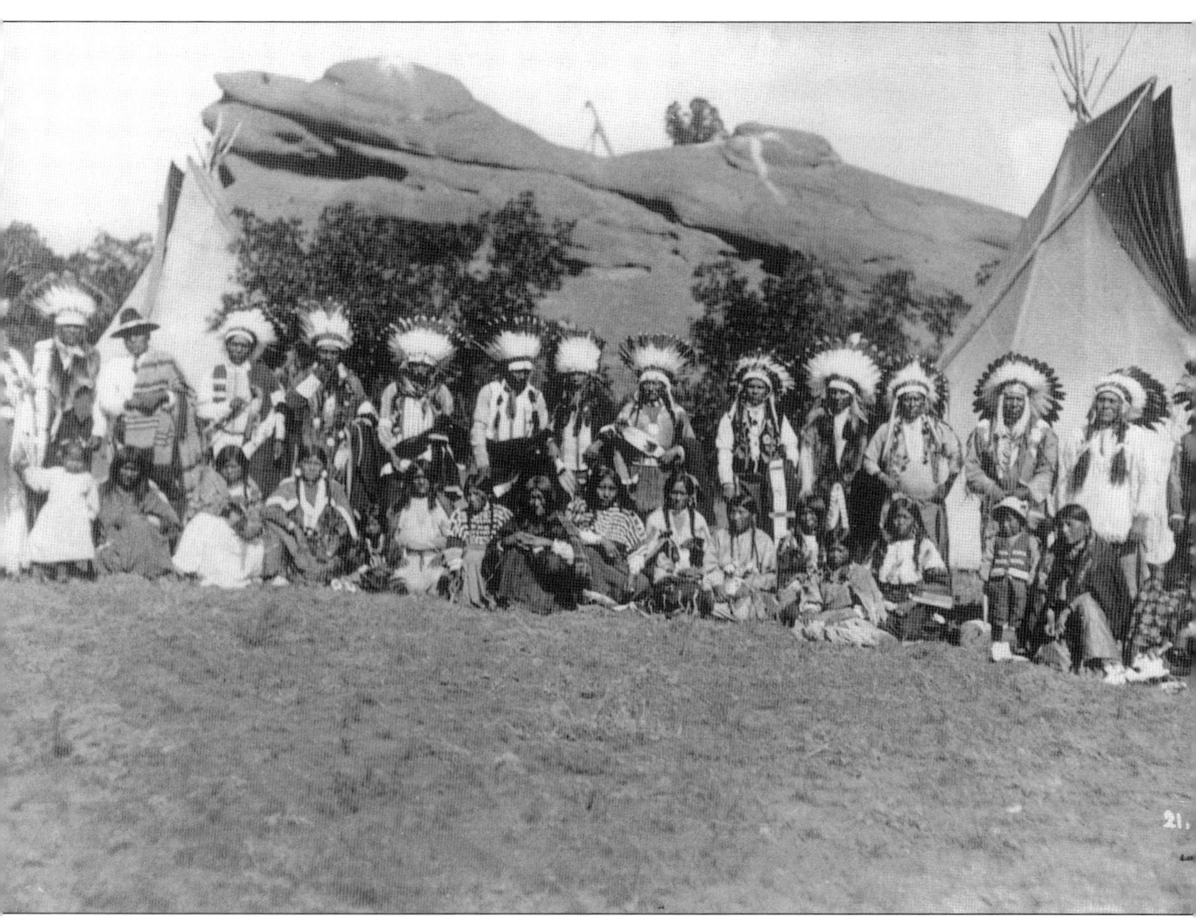

An Assembly of Ute Chiefs at Shan Kive. (*c.* 1913) A wonderful group of Ute Chiefs display their traditional headdresses of eagle feathers and their fine clothes made of elk, deer, and antelope. The Ute women were especially noted for their skill of hide-tanning and produced the softest, whitest buckskin for their families. They did not share their expertise with other tribes but kept it a closely guarded secret. The men wore a buckskin shirt, breechcloth, and leggings that were tied to a belt. The Ute women favored doeskins for their dresses. Usually, two doeskins were needed for a shift type of dress but for a more complicated design with a yoke, three were required. Beads, claws, and elk teeth were used to decorate the finished product. The Ute's were hunter/gatherers traveling at will and were mostly friendly to homesteaders who, at times, helped provide food during harsh winters. After being exiled to reservations in Utah, the Ute's were allowed back to the Garden of the Gods in 1911 to celebrate the ceremony of the Ute Trail Pass. (Courtesy Pikes Peak Library District.)

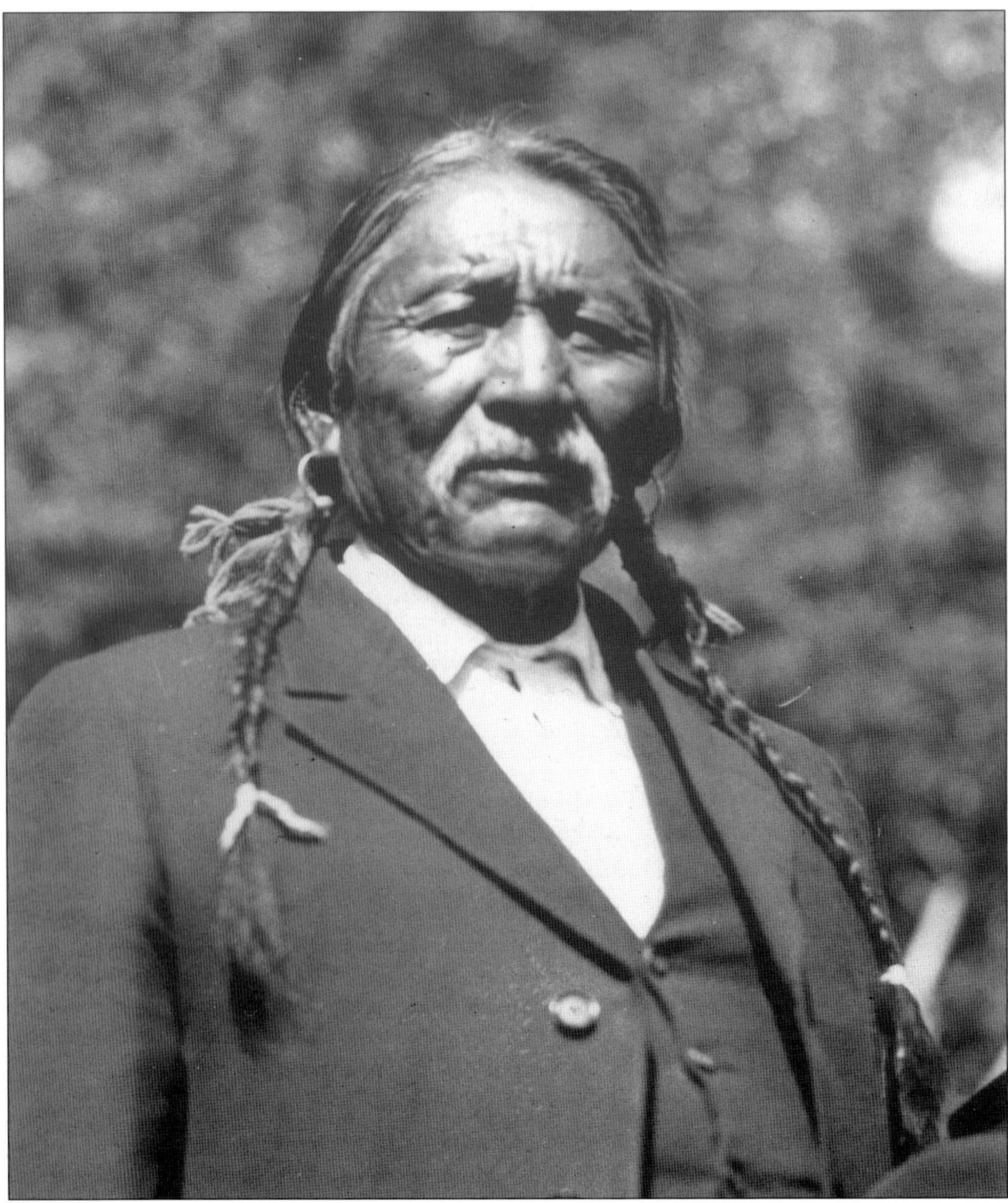

BUCKSKIN CHARLIE IN A THREE-PIECE SUIT. (*c.* 1900 1930) Although he donned a three-piece suit, hat, shirt and tie, he always kept his braids. He was a proud man, known for his pleasant disposition and humor. During the celebrations of the Shan Kiva in 1913, Dorothy Bass, daughter of Jessie Bass who was head of General Palmer's stables, remembered an incident in which her grandfather, Charlie Robinson, and Buckskin Charlie recognized each other. She describes in her memoirs, "I was standing with my grandfather and heard the two speak casually in Spanish. A few minutes later they began to recognize each other as the young strangers who became friends many years before when Grandfather crossed the plains in a covered wagon with the Regiment. The Chief, in full regalia, beads, bells and sweeping feathered headdress, didn't bother to go around the tables, but leaped upon one, crossed quickly and jumped down in front of my grandfather. The two shook hands warmly and embraced." (Courtesy Pikes Peak Library District.)

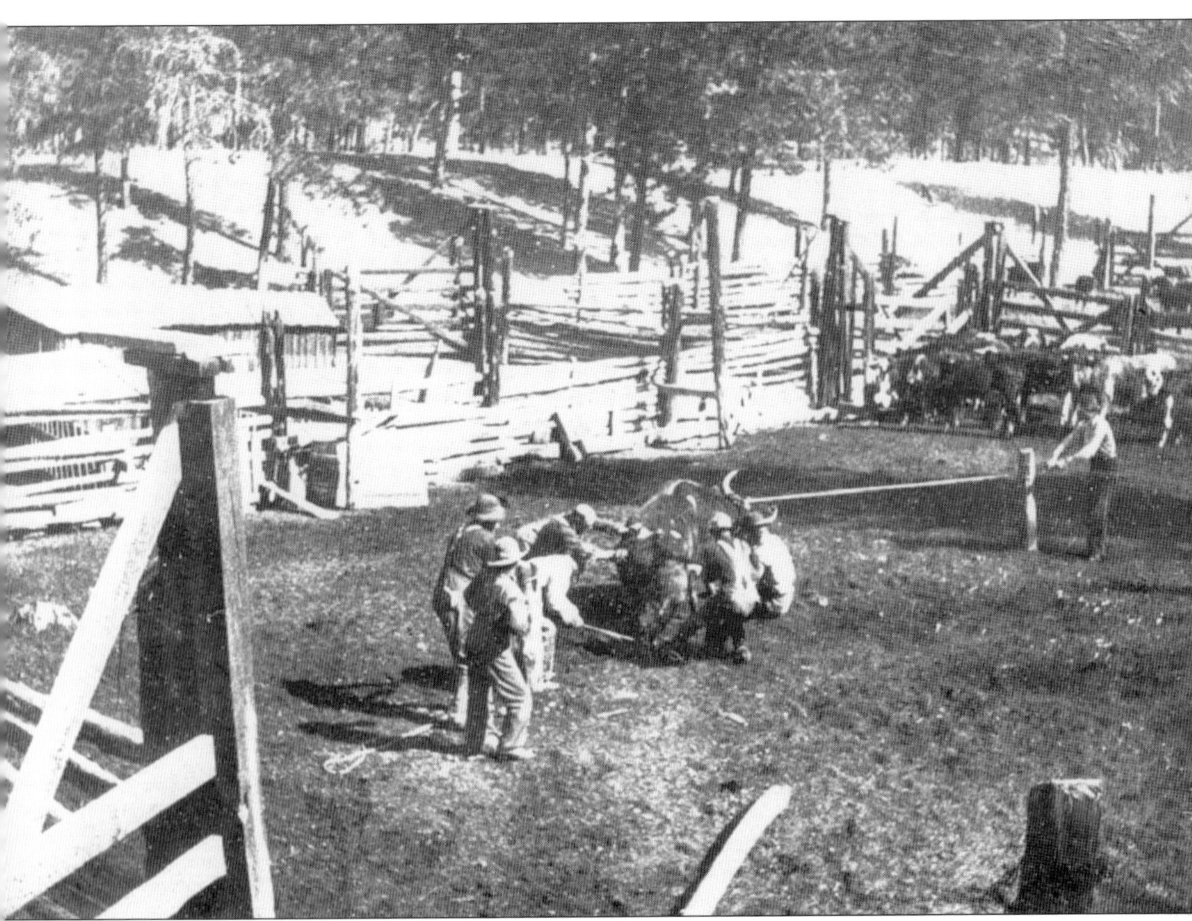

RANGE PIRATES' LIVESTOCK WERE SET FREE. (*c.* 1900) Many ranches began with 640 acres of land obtained by the Desert Land Act of 1873, where a rancher could get a preliminary title for 25 cents an acre. After three years of ownership and proof of some irrigation to the land, another dollar would be charged per acre for the land. Livestock roamed freely on the open range but each bore the owners' brand clearly marked. Most ranchers belonged to the local Livestock Association, if one was available. All members of the association were required to make water on their land available to all roaming livestock. Those men who did not comply with these requirements were called "range pirates" and frowned upon. The livestock were collected in roundups that usually began in September and finished at Thanksgiving. The men (and women) in the roundup lived outside and slept in little tents called "pups." They slept directly on the ground with sugans (a type of quilt) laid underneath and on top. Once the herds were gathered, branded, sorted, and returned to their rightful owners, any that belonged to the "pirates" were turned loose on the open range. (Courtesy Pikes Peak Library District.)

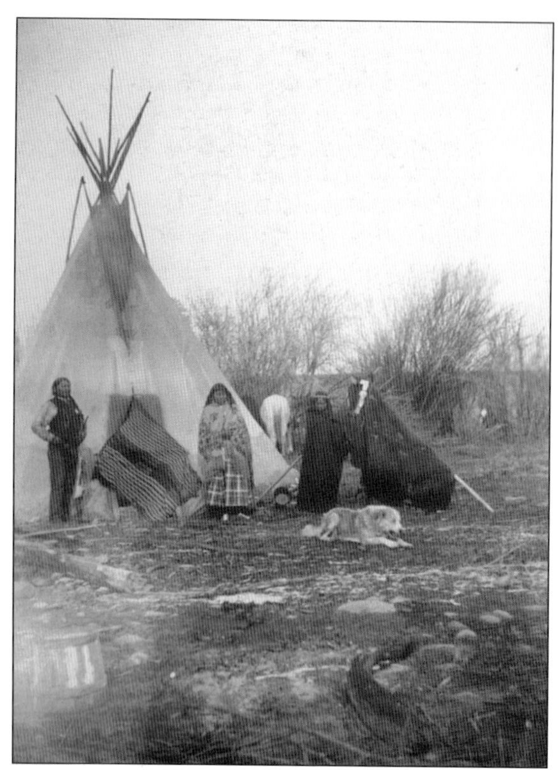

CHIEF IGNACIO AND HIS FAMILY. (*c.* 1890) Early in 1878, Nathan Meeker became Indian agent for the Northern Utes. He tried unsuccessfully to convert the Indians to the customs of the white settlers, and they rebelled in what is known as the "Meeker Massacre." After this terrible incident, the Utes were exiled to reservations and did not return until 1911, when they camped in their beloved Garden of the Gods. (Courtesy Pikes Peak Library District.)

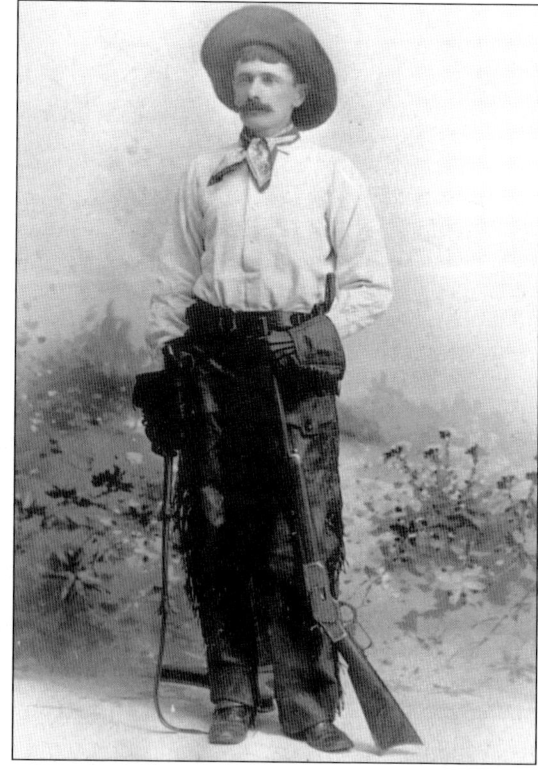

DR. CHARLES FOX GARDINER DRESSED AS A COWBOY. (*c.* 1885) The physician strikes a pose dressed in fringed leather chaps and gloves, sporting a rifle and whip. The unfortunate death of Dr. Edwin Solly in 1906, a well-known physician and originator of the Cragmore Sanitarium in Colorado Springs, gave Dr. Gardiner an opportunity to excel in his field of treating tubercular patients. (Courtesy Pikes Peak Library District.)

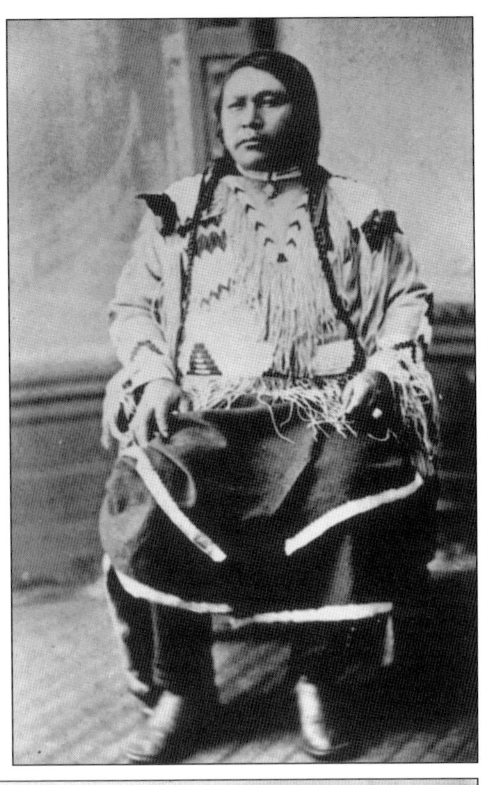

OURAY, CHIEF OF THE UTES. (*c*. 1880) Chief Ouray was an exceptionally gifted man known for his diplomacy and wisdom. Born to Ute-Apache parents, he was fluent in Spanish, English, and several Indian languages. He negotiated the Brunot Treaty in 1873 that was broken by the U.S. when gold was discovered in the San Juan Mountains. President Hayes said of Ouray that he was "the most intellectual man [he had] ever conversed with." (Courtesy Pikes Peak Library District.)

BACON & SON LIVERY STABLE. (*c*. 1879–1900) The first telephone directory in Colorado Springs is dated 1879-1880 and has a full page advertisement by Bacon and Son stating, "Carriages in readiness at all hours at lower prices than any other stable in the city. Orders taken by telegraph will receive prompt attention." (Courtesy Special Collections, Colorado College.)

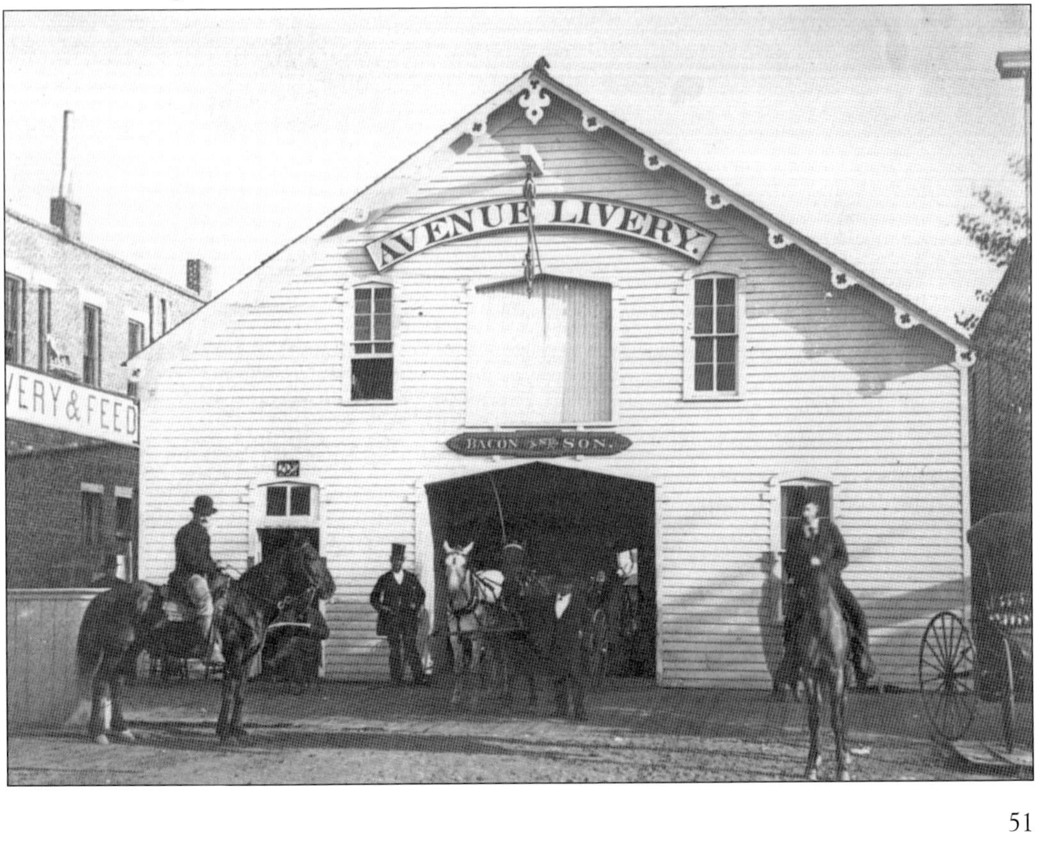

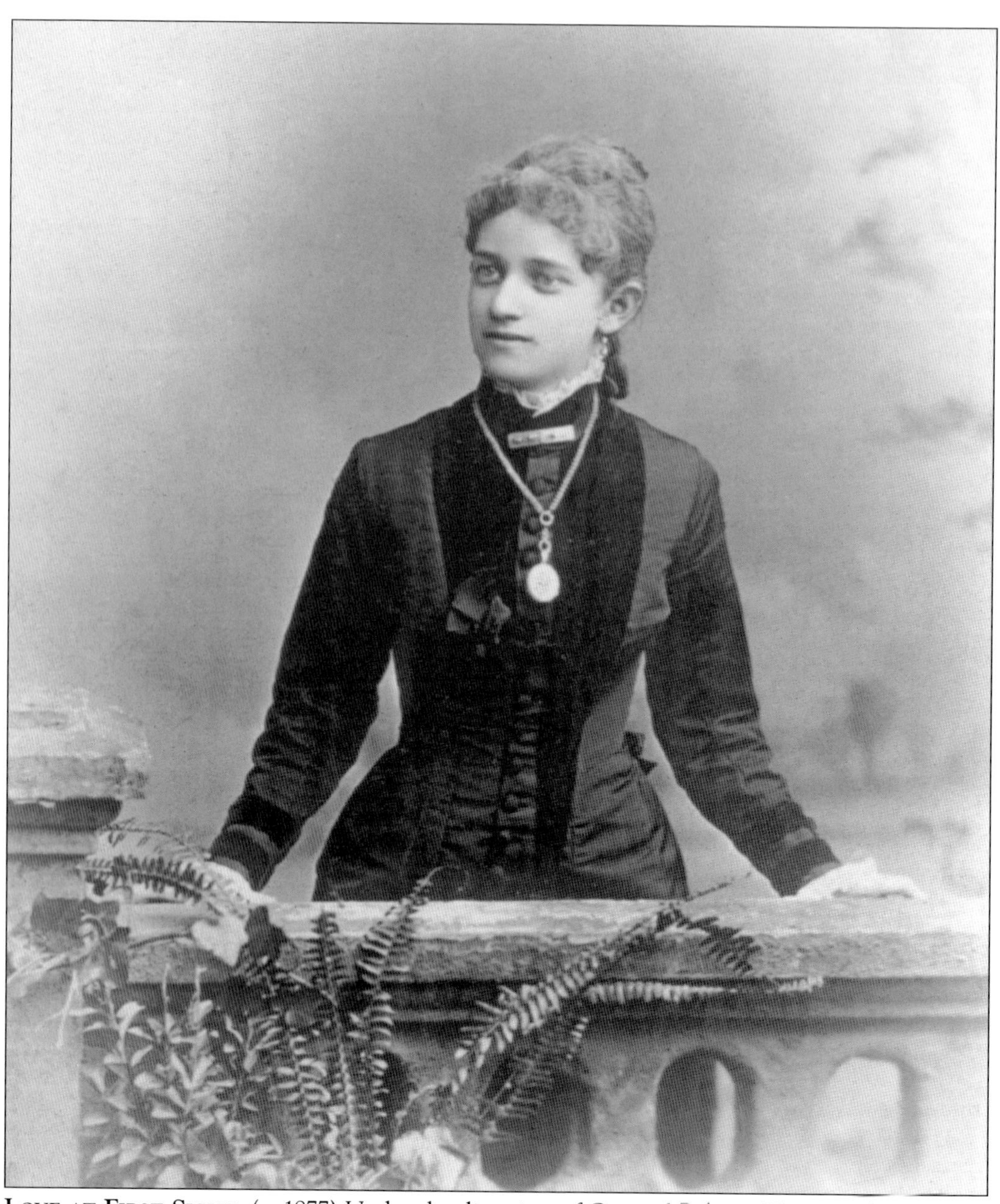

Love at First Sight. (*c.* 1877) Under the direction of General Palmer, Henry Azle McIntyre became sole proprietor and manager of the first Colorado Springs Hotel. McIntyre first set eyes on Marian B. Young at the reception desk as she stood with her parents. Marian was just a child of fourteen years and far too young to be courted, but Henry was smitten with the lovely young girl and decided to make her his bride. The two became friends first and then courted for several years before marrying on May 13, 1877. They had two children together, a boy, Newell, and a girl called Marian Dorothy. It was Marian who later transcribed her father's handwritten journal called *The Diary of a Tenderfoot, Denver and Rio Grande Survey of 1871*. Henry wrote the journal for his mother in New Jersey believing it would be easier than writing individual letters. The journal provides valuable insight into the daily lives of people as they traveled westward and the kinds of obstacles they encountered along the way. (Courtesy Rogers Davis.)

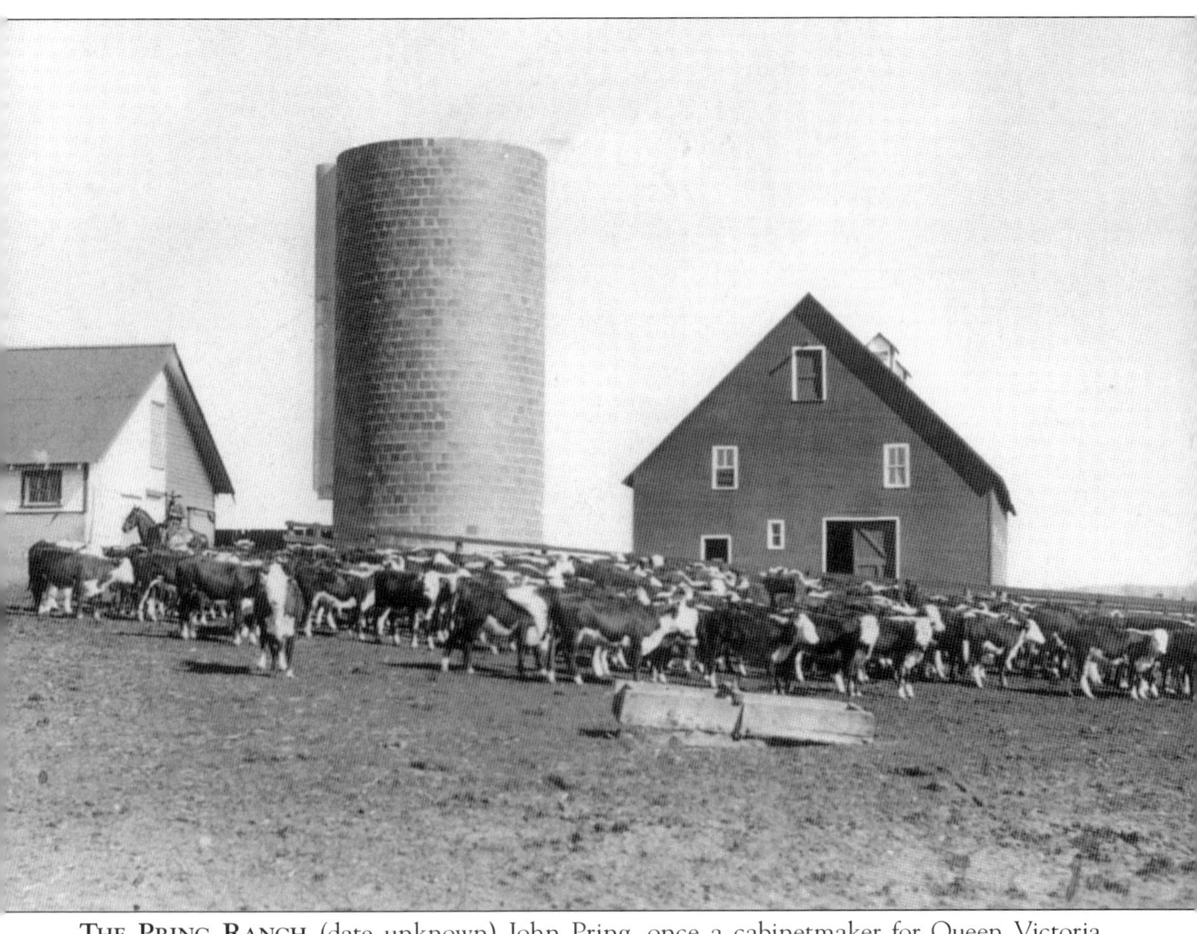

The Pring Ranch (date unknown) John Pring, once a cabinetmaker for Queen Victoria, emigrated from England in 1871 after marrying Mary Jane Thorne in London, England. He, his wife, and three children settled in Illinois where he purchased the Utilities Works in Rock Falls, Illinois. He changed course in 1876 and decided to move to Monument, Colorado, where he purchased 240 acres of land without actually seeing the property. Since he was a good carpenter, he built a large house and barn for his family, using wooden pegs rather than nails, and then began farming and raising livestock. John and Mary Jane eventually raised a family of seven children, one of whom, Ed Pring, went on to purchase several ranches in the Pike's Peak region. The photograph shows a herd of cattle standing in front of a barn and silo with note on back that reads: "Pring Ranch East of Prospect Lake where Valley High Country Club is. Clarence Shemwell on horse." (Courtesy Pikes Peak Library District.)

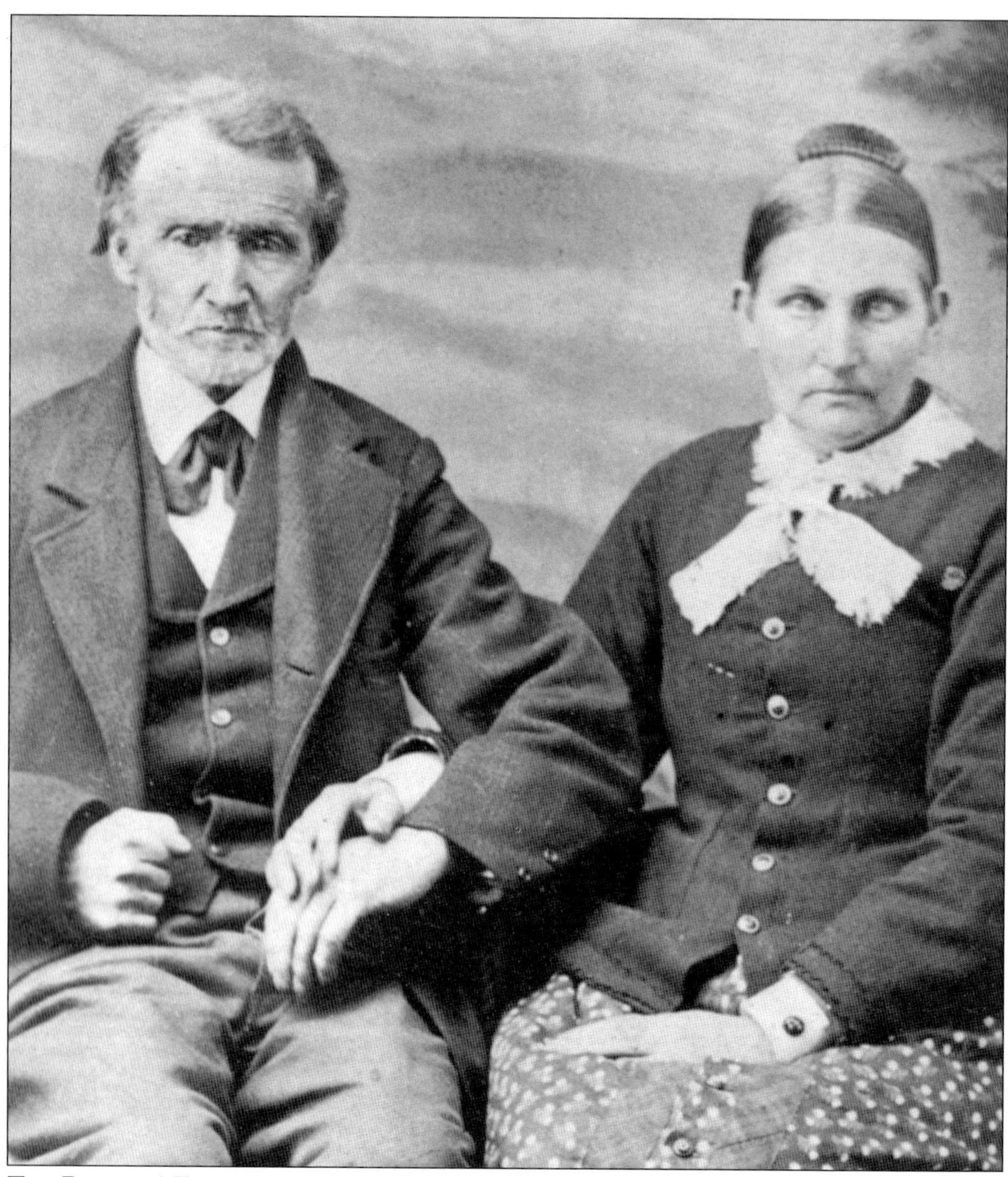

The Roberts' Family Took Shelter in a Fort. (date unknown) The Roberts' family felt so threatened by a band of Indians who camped nearby, they stole away during the night in their stocking feet and walked almost a mile to a fortified development called the Welty Fort. The evening began just like any other. The Roberts' had just finished their evening meal when a band of Indians came by the homestead and demanded food. After they had eaten, a large Indian brandished a gun and told the family to stay inside their home. Fearing for their lives, they devised a plan. After the Indian had checked on the family one more time, they did as they were told and went to bed but instead of sleeping, they lay fully dressed with their shoes ready at their sides. While the Indians slept, the Roberts family escaped, but all the time feared their young child would wake up and cry out in surprise and alert the Indians. The Roberts and other families took refuge at the Welty Fort for several weeks until the Indians moved from the area. (Courtesy the Palmer Lake Historical Society and Lucretia Vaile Museum.)

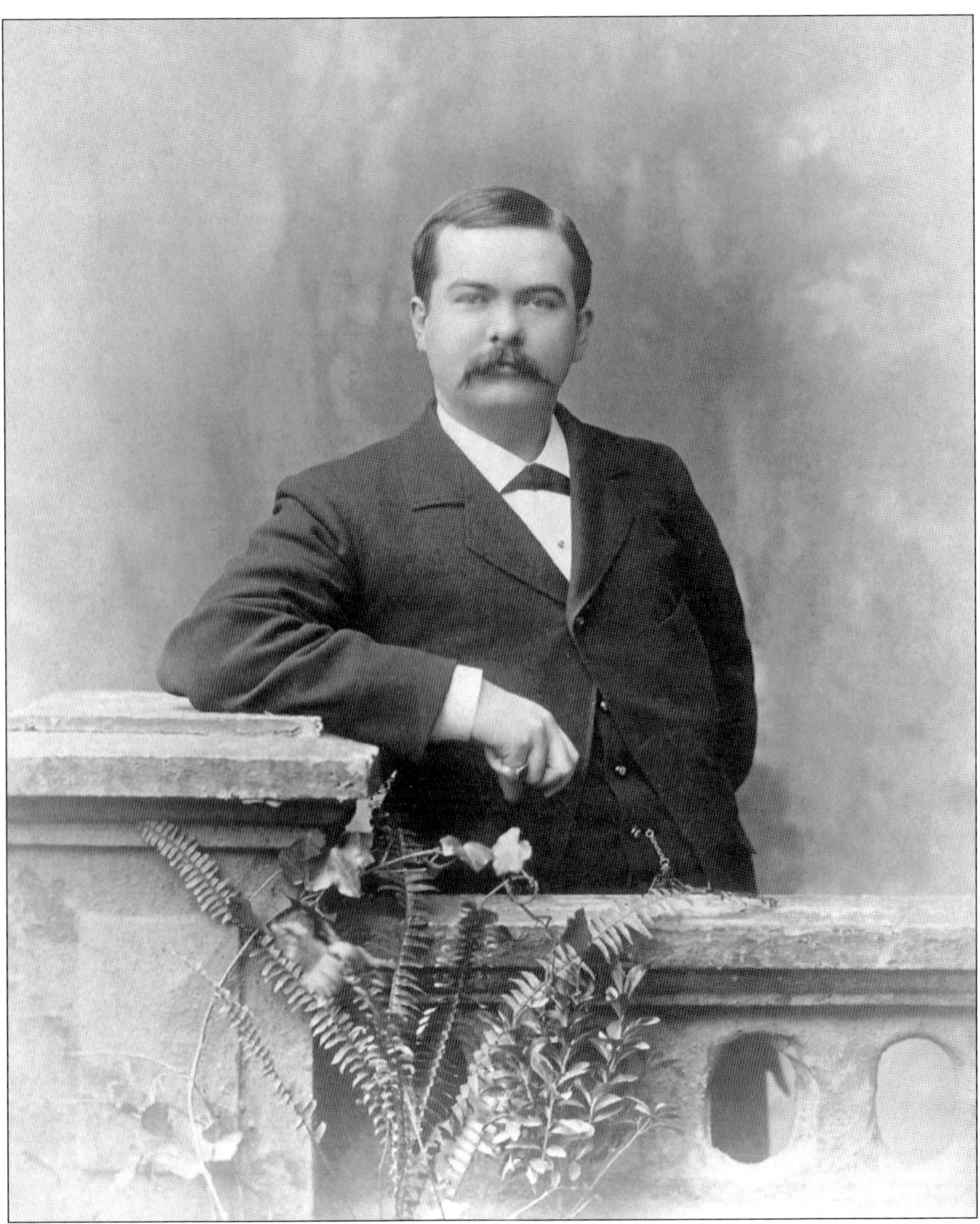

Diary of a Tenderfoot. (*c.* 1871) D. Henry Azle McIntyre kept a journal of his travels west while on business for Palmer as part of the Denver and Rio Grande Railway survey. McIntyre kept the diary because it was easier than writing individual letters to his mother in New Jersey. The journal was called *The Diary of a Tenderfoot, Denver & Rio Grande Survey of 1871*, and was later typed in full by his granddaughter Marian McDonough. The diary gives good insight to the life and times as McIntyre recalls, "We made a good morning run. When we returned to a camp at 12:30, we found a man armed with a rifle and Bowie knife. He demanded pay for the wood we took off his fence yesterday. I felt rather ticklish as they think nothing more of putting a bullet hole through a fellow than they do of eating. . . . " (Courtesy Rogers Davis.)

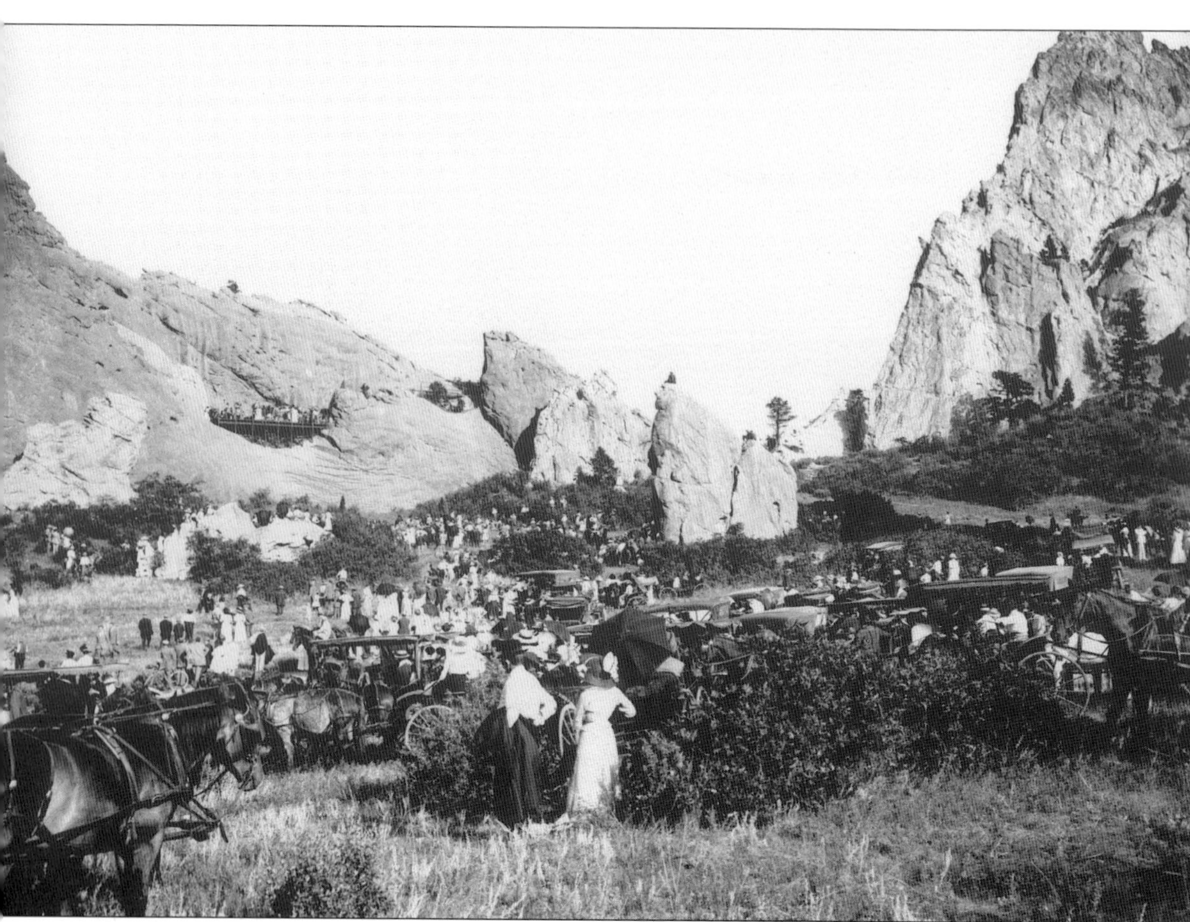

A Crowd Gathers at Shan Kive. (*c.* 1912) A special wooden platform was erected so that spectators could watch the Indians dressed in their full regalia of feathered headdresses, beads, and bells performing their ancient dances. Dorothy Bass recalls a Shan Kive celebration where her grandfather, Charlie Robinson, cooked for the Ute Indians at the Shan Kive. Dorothy remembers her grandfather and Buckskin Charlie, a famous Ute chief, recognizing each other after spending years apart. The two men spoke fluent Spanish and reminisced as they embraced. The following evening, Dorothy was included in the celebrations as Buckskin Charlie removed his daughter's beaded belt, purse, and silver bracelet and gave them to Dorothy. Princess Maria wore only a plain dress with a string around her waist. Dorothy remembers, "I shall never forget how we stood there—hand in hand, as the tribe chanted and danced around us. This event was one of the never-to-be-forgotten moments of my life . . . I still own the belt—a precious souvenir." (Courtesy Pikes Peak Library District.)

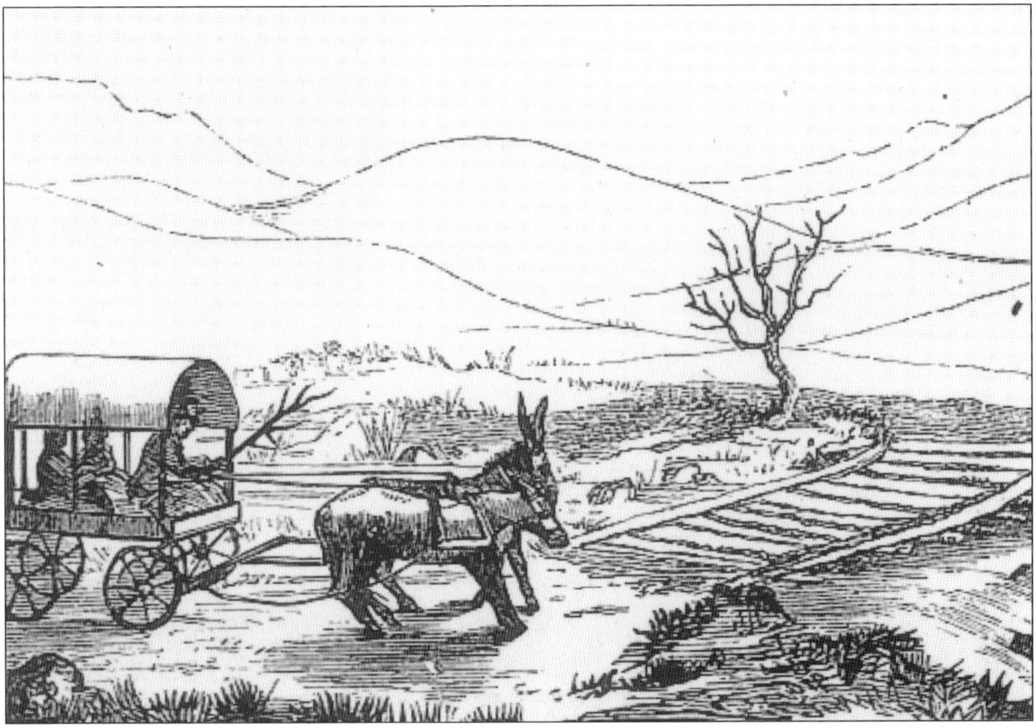

ROSE KINGSLEY, ARTIST. (date unknown) Rose Kingsley did several sketches after she arrived in Colorado Springs on November 1, 1871. She and her brother Maurice met the Palmers when they were in London visiting Rose's father, Charles Kingsley, author of *Westward Ho* and *The Water Babies*. Rose sent letters to her father describing the growth of Colorado Springs: "I find it difficult to keep pace with all the new arrivals, or the new buildings that spring up as if by magic." (Courtesy Special Collections, Colorado College.)

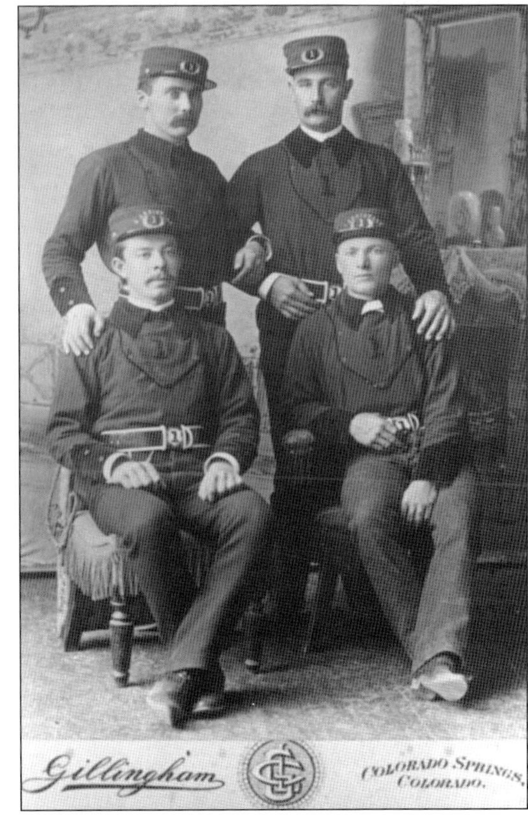

MATT FRANCE, THREE TIMES MAYOR. (date unknown) Pictured, from left to right, are: (front row) A.B. Curry and Nels Johnson; (back row) unknown and Bill Moffatt. Matt France served as mayor for three terms and had been a member of the Board of County Commissioners when he decided the town needed to have a water system that was owned by the city. (Courtesy Dr. Lester L. Williams Museum.)

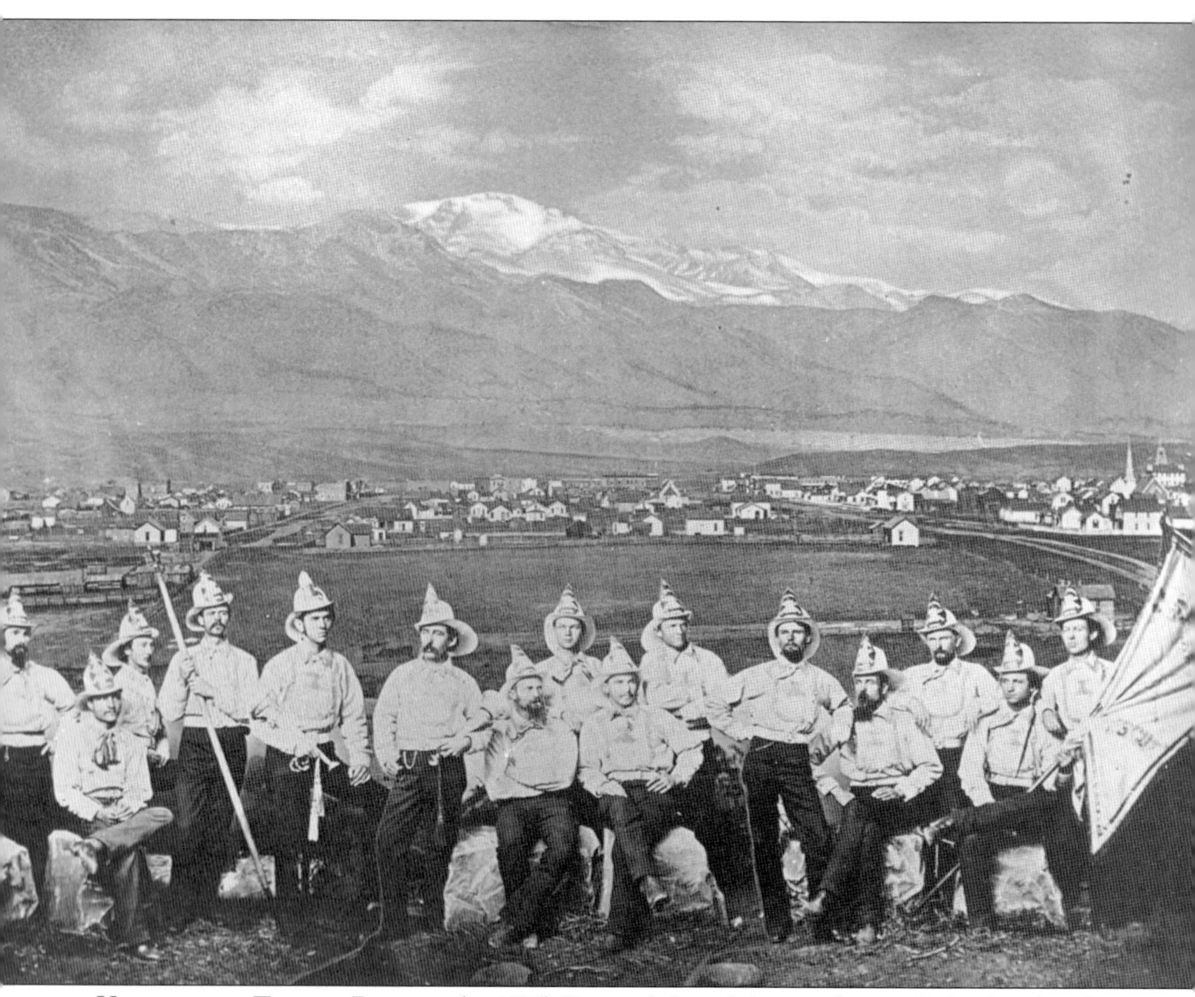

VOLUNTEERS TO THE RESCUE. (*c.* 1875) Pictured from left to right are Delos Durfee, Gus House, Sam White, John Clark, Fred Huggins, Capt. T. H. Burnham, Millard Stone, Joe Barker, Johnny Stone, Miller, Perry Downing, Bradbury, E.R. Taylor, and Lewis Brosius. The brave men of the Hook and Ladder Company of Colorado Springs pose before the town and Pikes Peak. The volunteer fire company was formed on January 29, 1875, with Thomas Burnham elected as foreman. Burnham took his responsibility as foreman seriously and researched various kinds of equipment and apparatus. After a visit to the Denver Fire Department, he proposed the purchase of a Babcock Hook and Ladder truck, and sturdy, attractive uniforms for the men. The town's trustees agreed to the proposal and the required equipment and apparatus were purchased and being used by the summer of 1875. The men trained well and participated in the Annual State Tournament in November 1875, taking the grand prize. Most fire departments competed against each other in contests called the Wet Test and Hub-to-Hub races with prizes of money, brass trumpets (bullhorns), and equipment. (Courtesy Dr. Lester L. Williams Museum.)

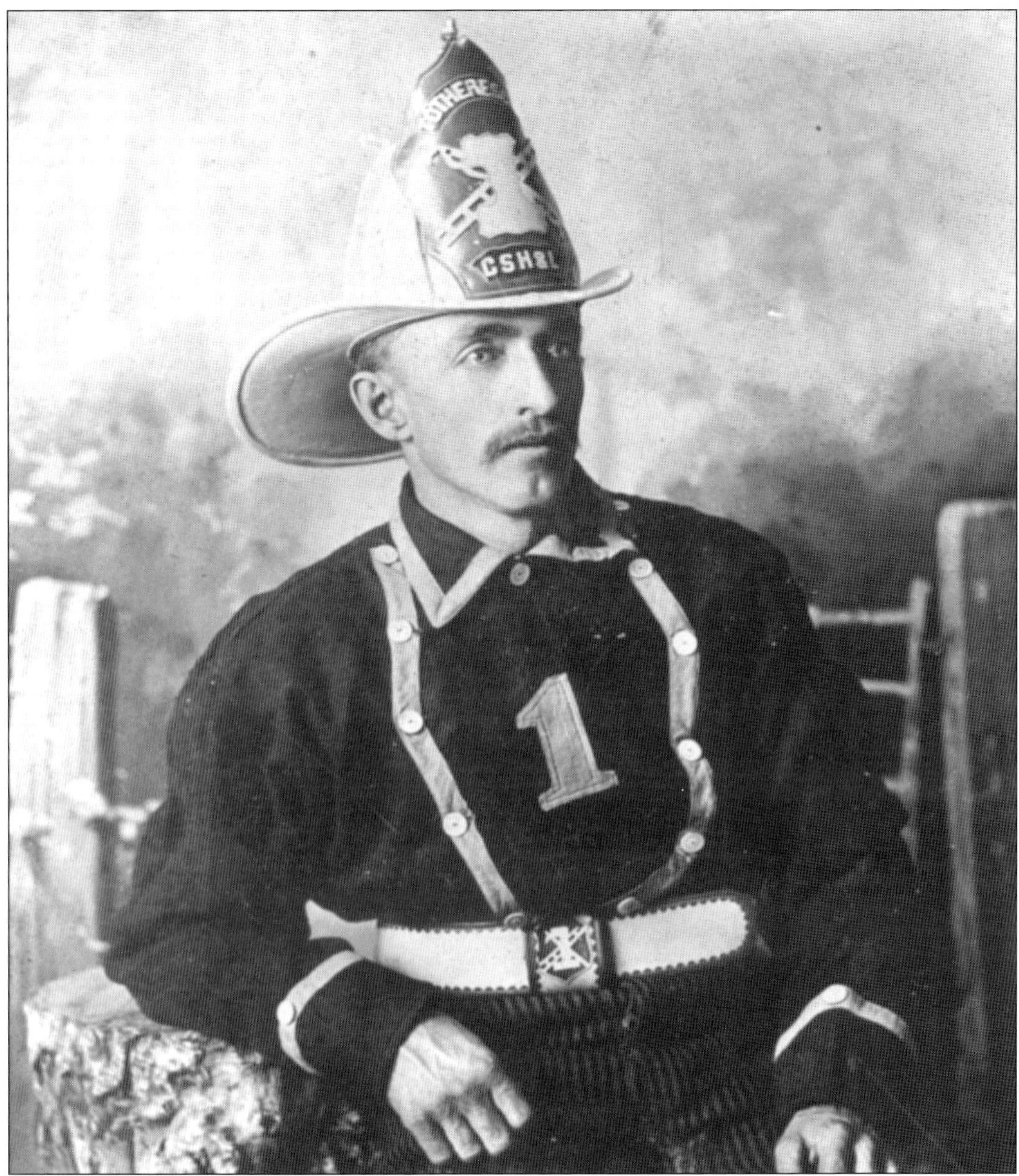

A DASHING FIREFIGHTER. (date unknown) This photograph suggests was likely taken soon after the Hook and Ladder Company was formed on January 29, 1875. The uniforms of Fire Company #1 consisted of a white leather helmet, white belt, and a white flannel shirt. The hat and belt buckle had the emblem of a ladder and pike pole (used to pull down burning buildings) while the leather belt was elaborately trimmed in a scallop effect around the edges. The concept of protecting homes from fires began in England in the 1700s by insurance companies. When a home or business paid a premium to the insurance company, a fire mark displaying the insurance company's emblem was placed above the doorway. If a competing fire station answered a call to a burning house, they would let it burn rather than help and were known to kick over their opponent's leather buckets. Brave, yet boisterous and proud, they would fight each other while the house or building they were supposed to be attending burned to the ground. (Courtesy Dr. Lester L. Williams Museum.)

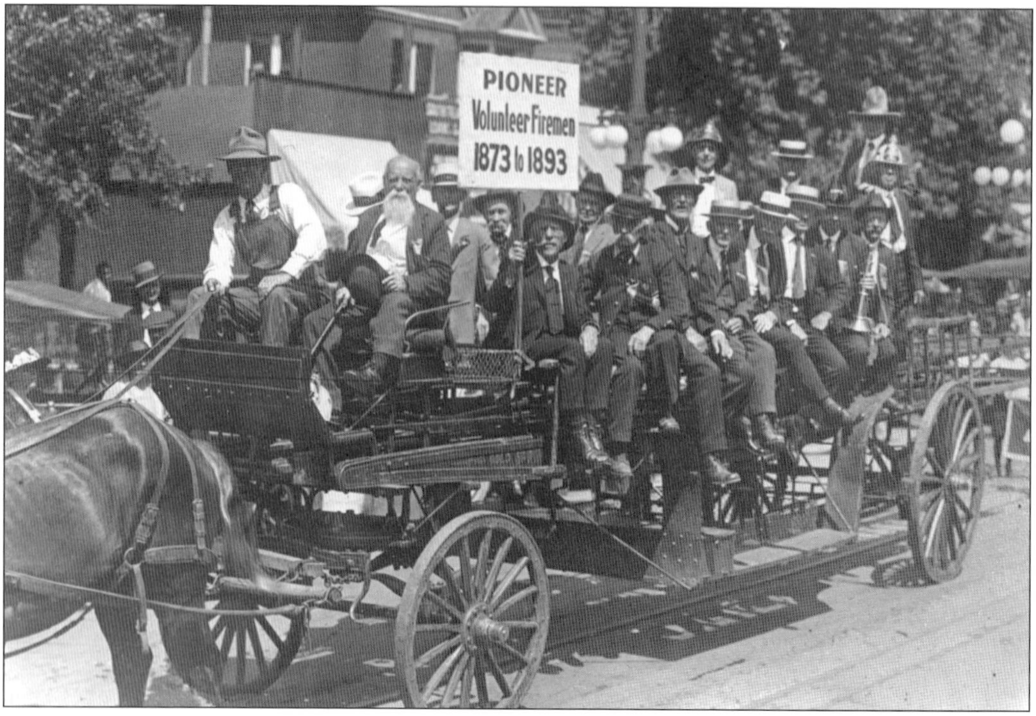

PIONEER VOLUNTEER FIREMEN. (*c.* 1920) A secret meeting on January 29, 1894, led to the end of the volunteer fire department and the first paid fire department in Colorado Springs. A group of veteran firefighters pose for the camera at a parade. Tom Hughes (seated second from left) sports a fine set of whiskers; one man is holding a speaking trumpet, and another is wearing a bib overall. (Courtesy Dr. Lester L. Williams Museum.)

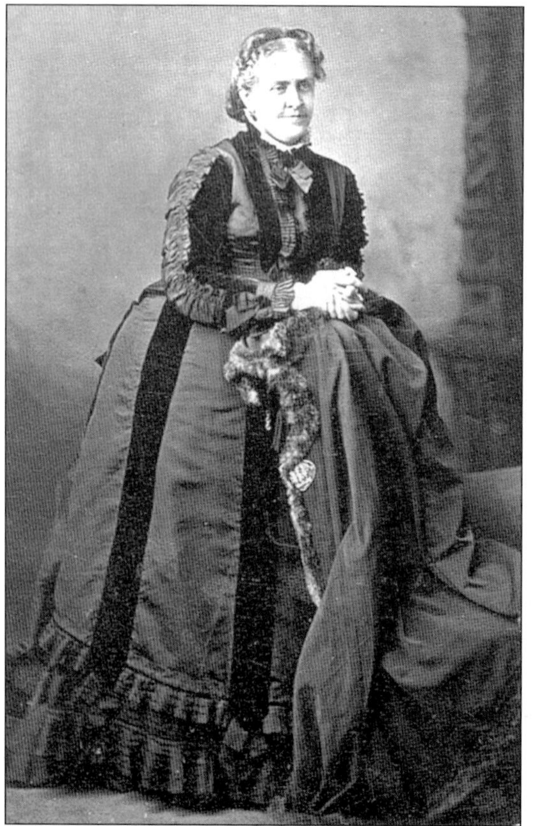

AN ADVOCATE FOR INDIANS' RIGHTS. (*c.* 1877) Helen Hunt arrived in Colorado Springs not only on her physician's advice but also to marry a prominent citizen, William Jackson. Although a wealthy man, Jackson purchased a small home for his new wife on the corners of Weber and Kiowa streets, and they began their married life in 1875. She was a feisty woman and fought against the Indians' mistreatment by the government. (Courtesy Special Collections, Colorado College.)

Four

Life and Times in the Shadow of Pikes Peak

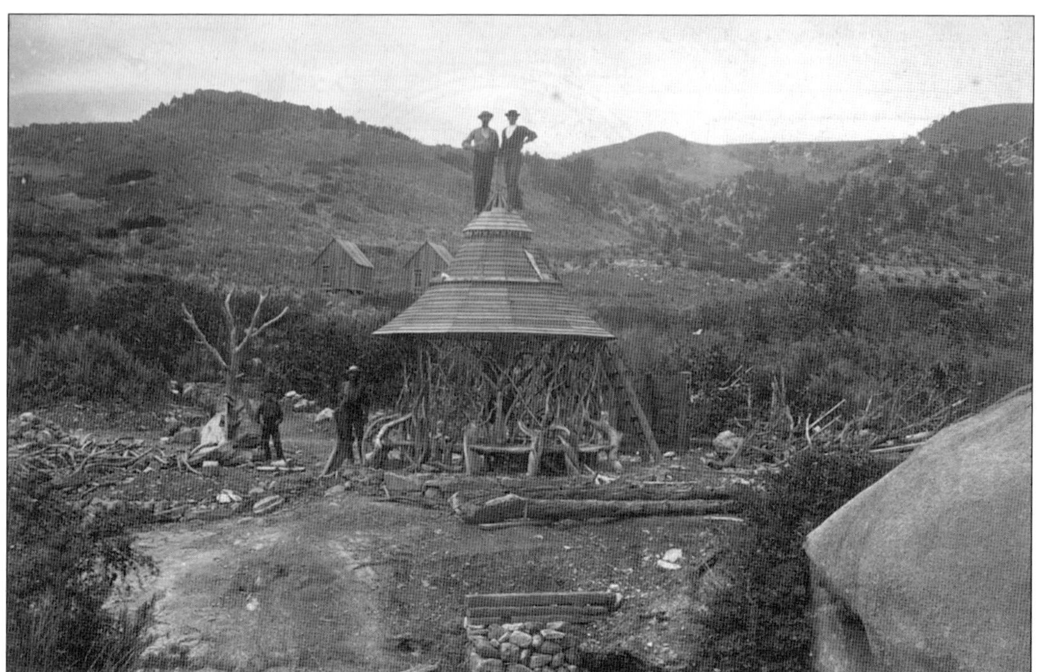

THE CONSTRUCTION OF THE NAVAJO SPRINGS GAZEBO. (*c.* 1871–1880) The photograph shows the men taking a moment to pose during the construction of the gazebo that has a conical, many-faceted roof. Two men on the roof strike a similar pose, while the other two men, one wearing what looks like a boater, appear to be less staged. (Courtesy the Denver Public Library.)

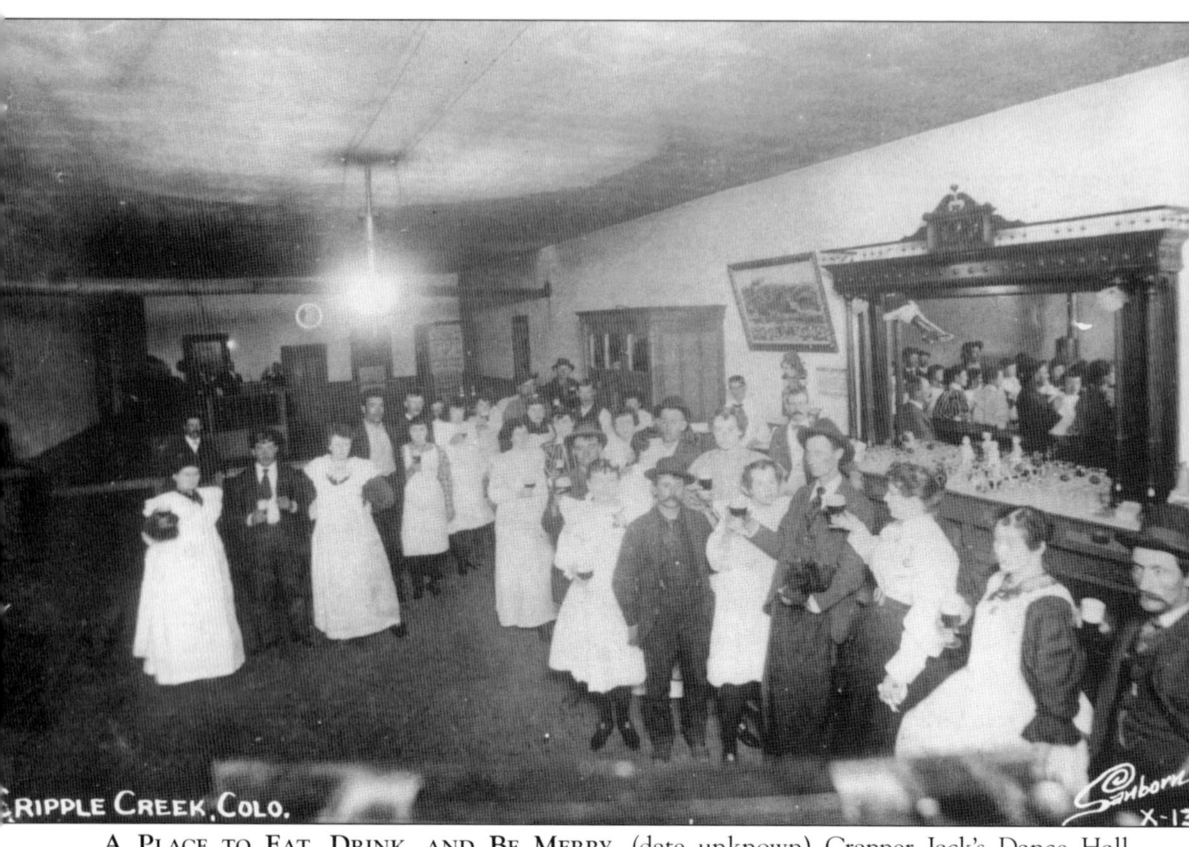

A Place to Eat, Drink, and Be Merry. (date unknown) Crapper Jack's Dance Hall was only one of several places in town that catered to the carefree needs of the miners and businessmen. Other halls such as the Topic, Bucket of Blood, and the Red Onion all played a part as well. The development of Cripple Creek railway brought the inevitable ladies of the night. Pearl DeVere was one of the most notorious madams, known for her choice of beautiful women in her parlor. Her customers were wealthy men whose contributions ranged from $50 to $250 per visit. Unfortunately, Pearl died from an overdose of morphine after entertaining a wealthy man from Denver. Pearl's sister was advised of her death and soon arrived from the east to claim the body. When she saw her sister's occupation recorded on the death certificate, she refused the body and returned home empty-handed. The citizens of Cripple Creek from poor to wealthy all contributed to and attended Pearl's funeral. She is buried in the town's cemetery where some still leave flowers on her grave. (Courtesy Pikes Peak Library District.)

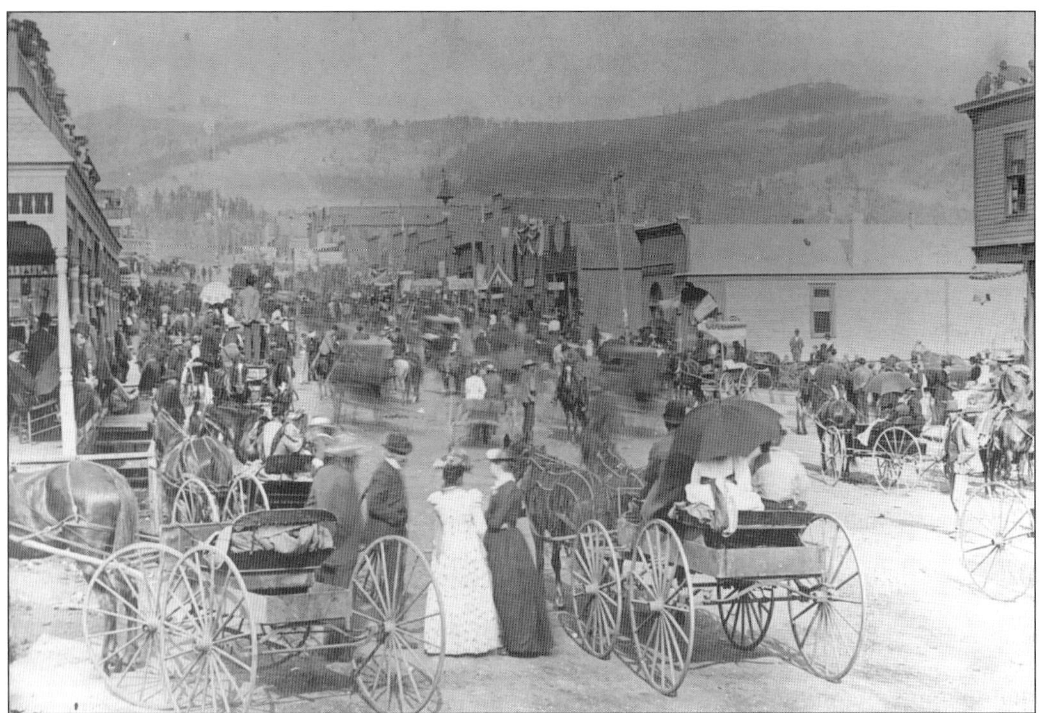

Fourth of July Celebrations on Bennett Avenue. (*c.* 1893) The town of Cripple Creek was built on land owned by two Denver real estate men called Myers and Bennett. When the town was platted, they each named a street after themselves. The photograph shows Bennett Street during the celebrations as women shield themselves with parasols. Men are seen atop the pharmacy building on the right as carriages crowd the street. (Courtesy the Colorado Historical Society.)

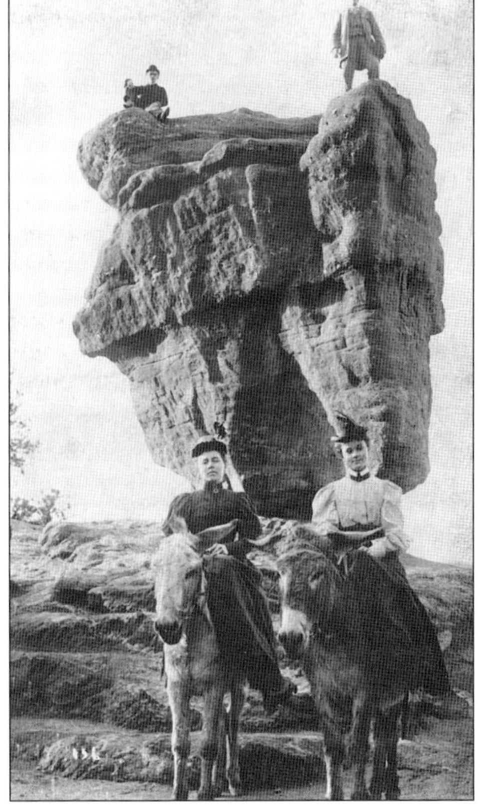

Balanced Rock. (*c.* May 1, 1897) It is said the name Garden of the Gods originated when Melancthon Beach, one of the founders of Colorado City, was showing the area to a friend, Rufus Cable, when Beach stated, "Don't you think Cable, that this would be a great place for a Milwaukee beer garden?" Cable was stunned by the comment and replied, "Beer garden! Why this is fit for a Garden of the Gods!" (Courtesy Colorado Springs Pioneer Museum.)

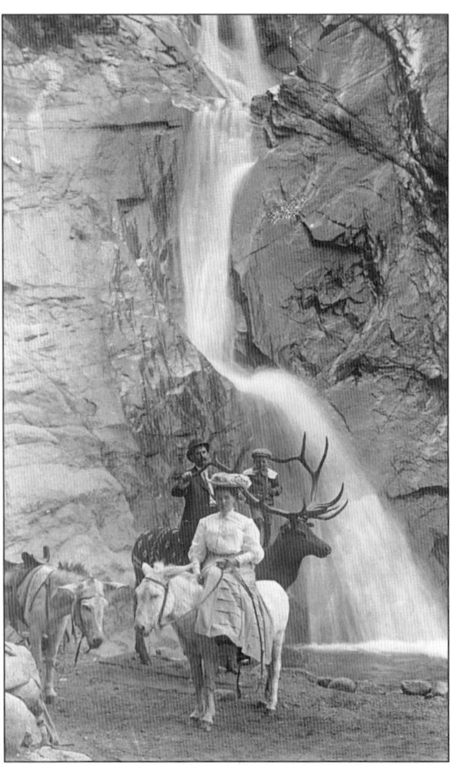

The Seven Falls. (date unknown) The Seven Falls have been a great tourist attraction since Mr. Hull purchased the falls and much of the surrounding area between 1882 and 1885. The staged photograph shows a man sitting astride a fake deer while a young boy stands on its back. The woman sits sidesaddle on a burro dressed in a tuck-pleated panel skirt, delicate white blouse with leg-of-mutton sleeves, and a little cameo at the neck. (Courtesy Colorado Springs Pioneer Museum.)

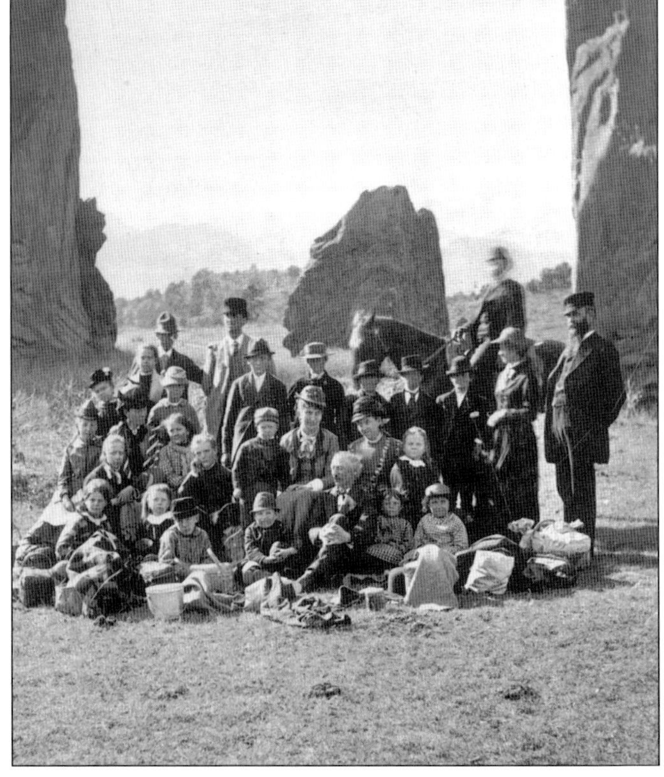

A Picnic Lunch Near Manitou Springs. (*c.* 1880–1890) A picnic lunch as children and adults pose with their lunch pails, baskets and blankets close to the Garden of the Gods. The men wear a variety of hats from conductor styles to bowlers. Some women and girls wear decorations such as flowers or brooches on their hats while three girls wear similar checked fabric dresses. (Courtesy the Denver Public Library.)

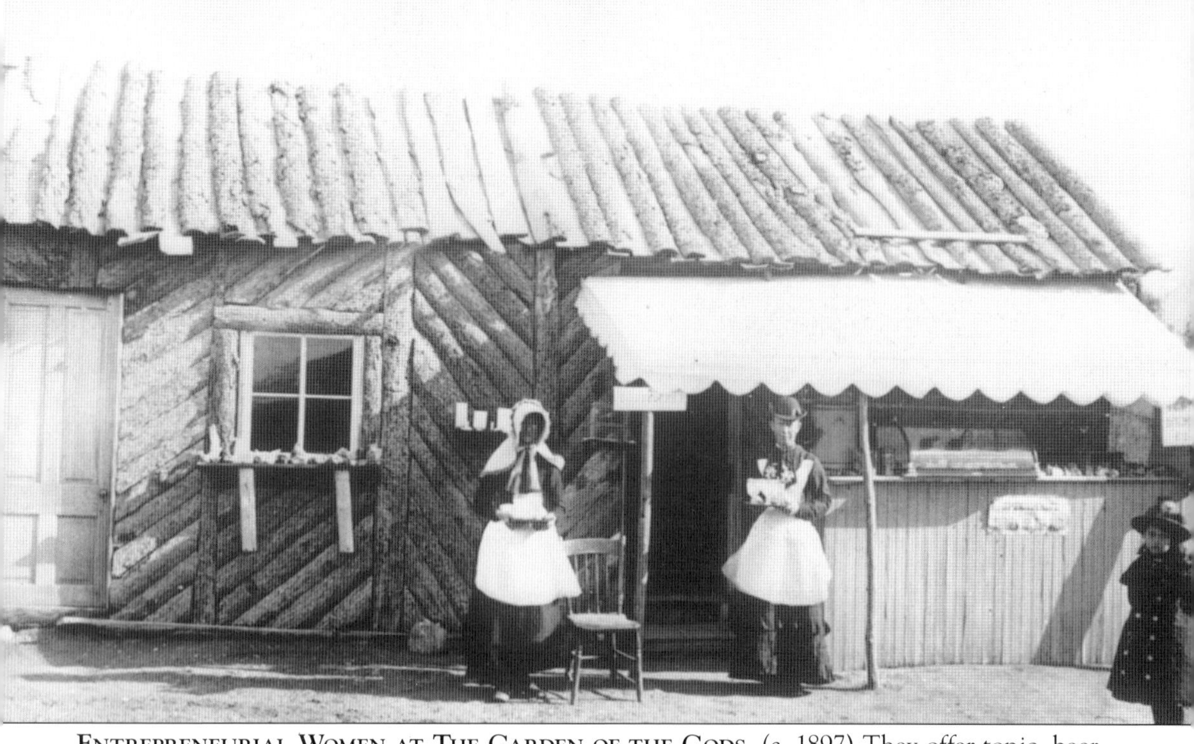

Entrepreneurial Women at The Garden of the Gods. (*c.* 1897) They offer tonic, beer, iced milk, lemonade, and cigars as well as specimens from The Garden of the Gods. As the area developed, so did the need for refreshments and souvenirs shops. One of the most famous characters to eke a living from the garden was P.D. Rice, who purchased four lots close to the Gateway Rocks. He set about building a beer hall and souvenir shop and called it "the best sparklin' place in El Paso County." Rice was a large, colorful character, weighing almost 300 pounds, and it was only natural that his beer hall would be known as Fatty Rice's Place. In 1879, Charles Perkins, a railroad developer, purchased hundreds of acres in the Garden but never built a property, preferring to leave the area unspoiled. On his death, he bequeathed the land to the City of Colorado Springs "where it shall remain free to the public, where no intoxicating liquors shall be manufactured, sold, or dispensed, where no building shall be erected except those necessary. . . ." (Courtesy Pikes Peak Library District.)

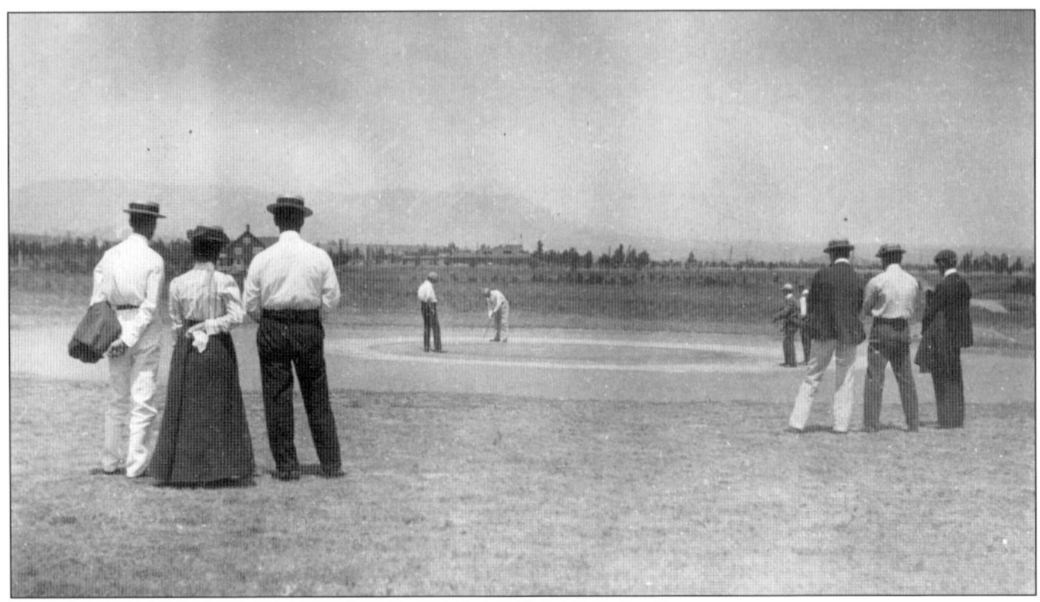

THEY GOT TOGETHER AND FORMED A CLUB. (c. 1901) Mrs. Jewett and other spectators watch golfers and a referee on the seventh hole. In 1889, a tract of land 300 by 600 feet was donated by the Austin Bluffs Company and the Cheyenne Mountain Country Club was born. Membership was limited and consisted of businessmen and professionals, although their humor shows in the name they gave themselves, "The Grizzlers." (Courtesy the Denver Public Library.)

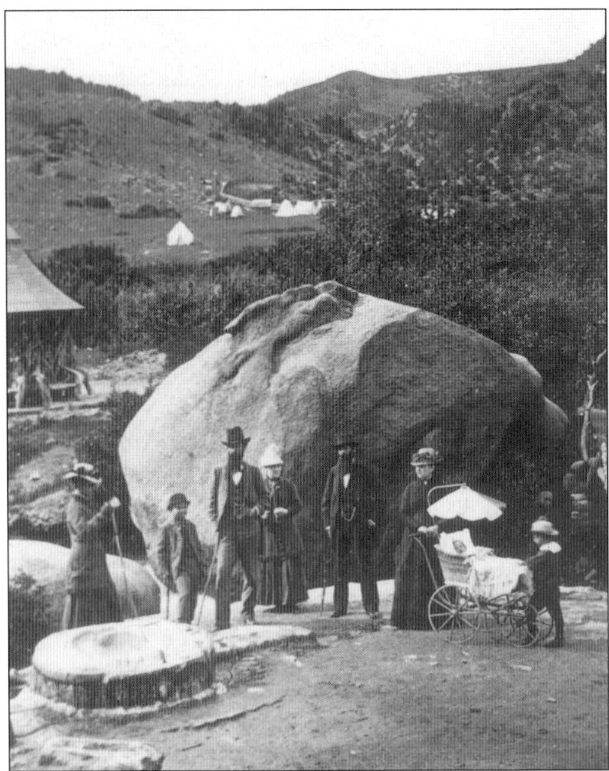

A THIRSTY CROWD VISIT THE NAVAJO SPRINGS. (date unknown) A group of visitors pause at the Navajo Springs in Manitou. The men sport long dark beards, hats, and watch-chains in their vests. The baby carriage has large wheels and a canopy. A young boy stands in front of the carriage wearing a "sailor suit" type of dress. Several tents can be seen in the background. (Courtesy the Colorado Historical Society.)

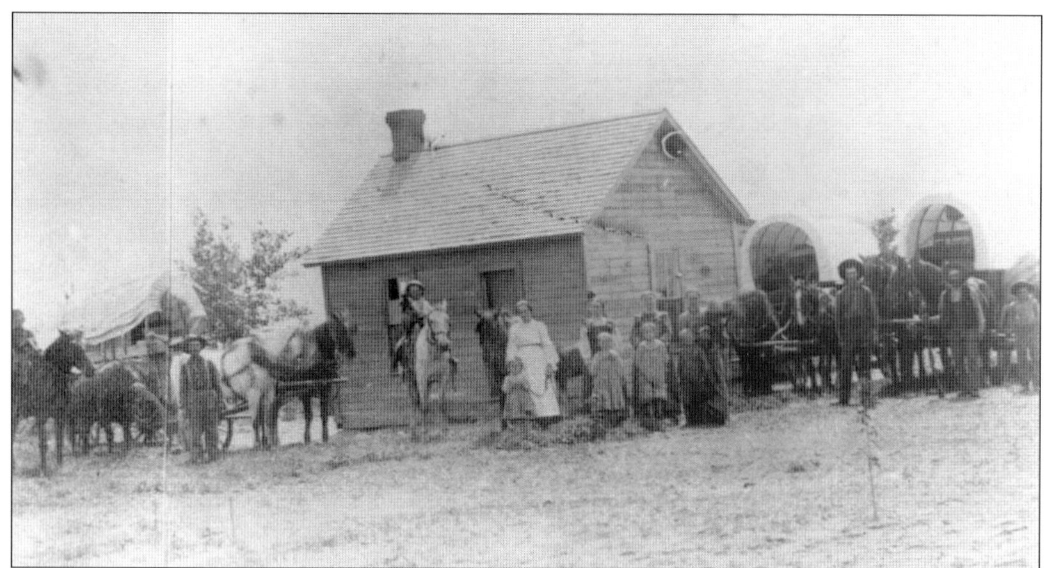

A Week in the Garden of the Gods. (*c.* 1899) A group of men, women, and children pose in front of a small wooden building with three covered wagons and teams of horses. The note on back of photograph reads: "May 23, 1899—Aug.28, 1899, Cherokee Oklahoma 1899 taken just before the trek to Colorado camped in the Garden of the Gods for a week—Aug. 28th, 1899." (Courtesy Pikes Peak Library District.)

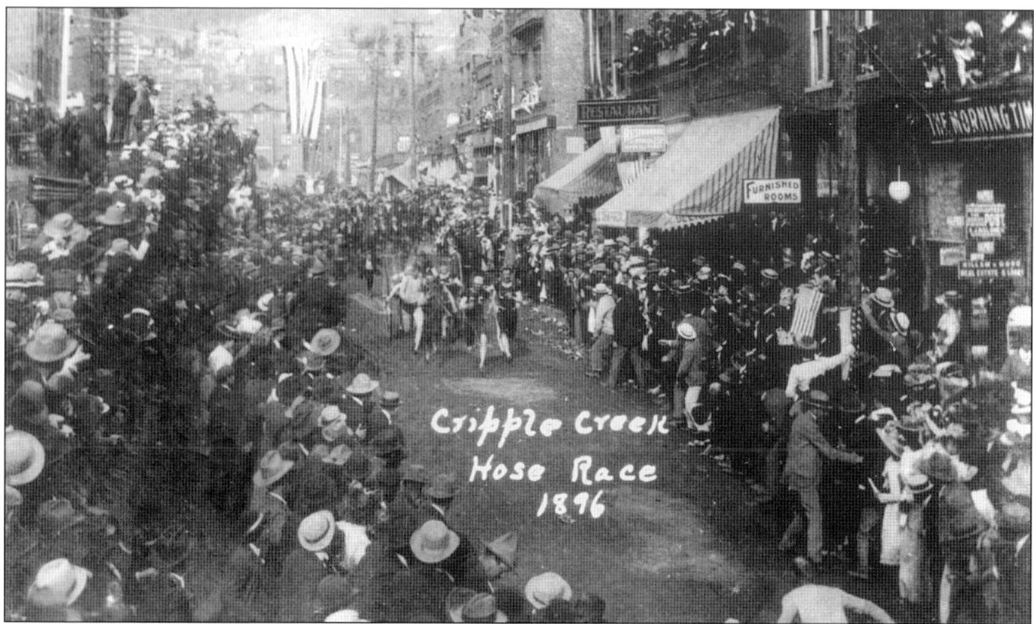

A Chance to Show Their Mettle. (*c.* 1896) The residents of Cripple Creek crowd on the street and from balconies to watch the Hose Race. Traditionally, men in the volunteer fire department were strong and gregarious fellows, both attributes needed to deal with dangerous situations. The Hose Race shows the ability, strength, and courage of the local firefighters as they pull their equipment behind them at a fast run. (Courtesy the Colorado Historical Society.)

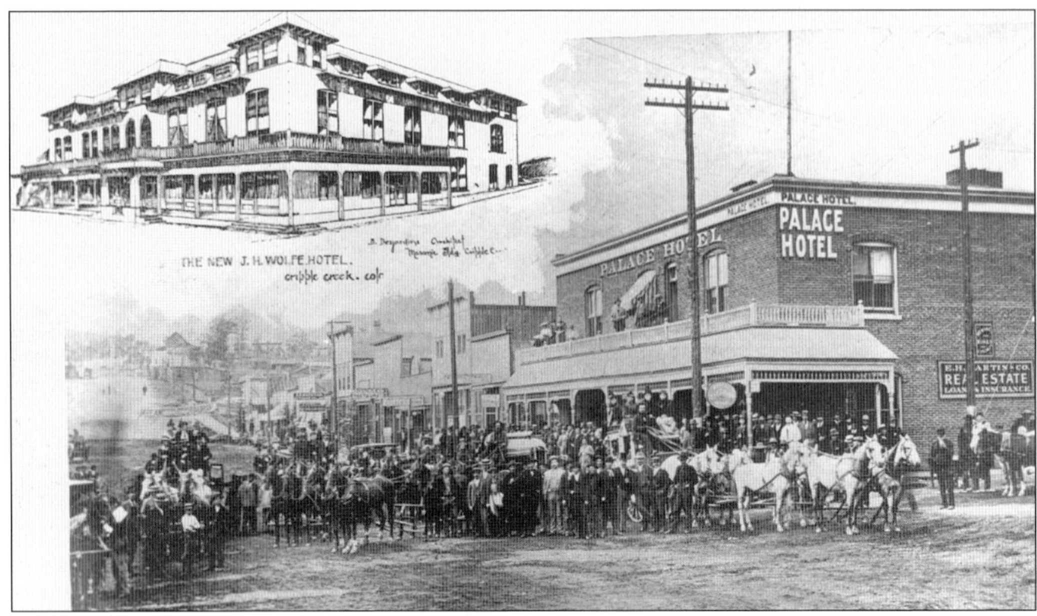

A Huge Crowd in Front of The Palace Hotel. (*c.* 1891) People stand on the balcony of the Palace Hotel while hundreds pose in the street. Several stagecoaches are in the street with teams of horses, one with a team of six matching white horses. A note on back of photograph reads, from "*Cripple Creek & Colorado Springs Illustrated*, 1896. Page 20." (Courtesy the Colorado Historical Society.)

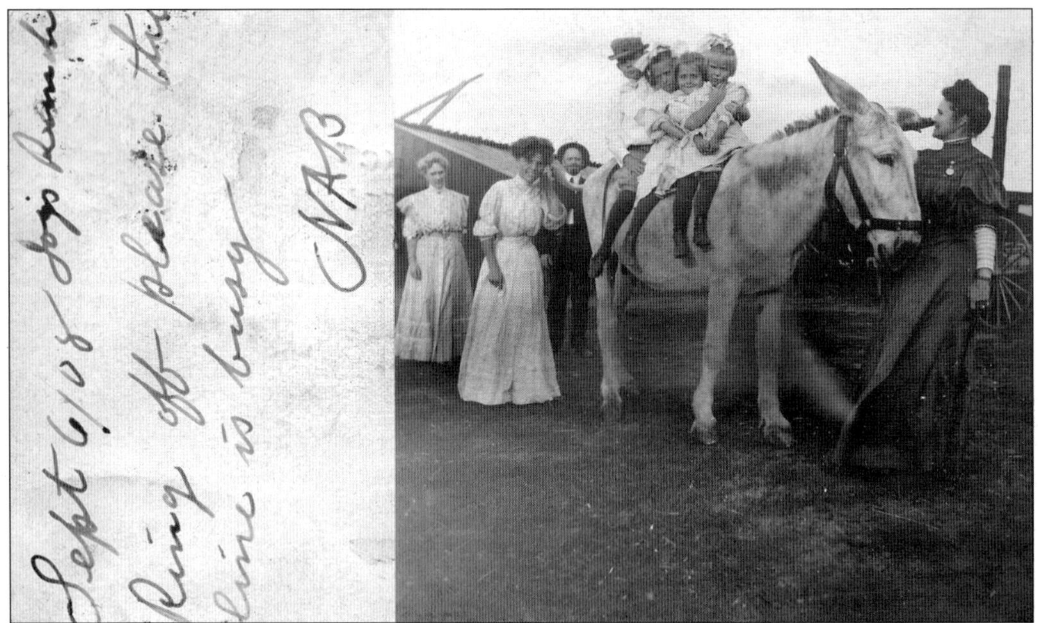

Ring Off Please! (*c.* September 6, 1908) The woman in the rear takes the donkey's tail and pretends it's a telephone line. The note next to the photograph reads, "Ring off please, the line is busy." The woman standing next to the donkey is wearing a dark dress with leg-of-mutton sleeves, dark lace gloves, a high collar, and a pendulum type of brooch or watch. (Courtesy the Palmer Lake Historical Society and Lucretia Vaile Museum.)

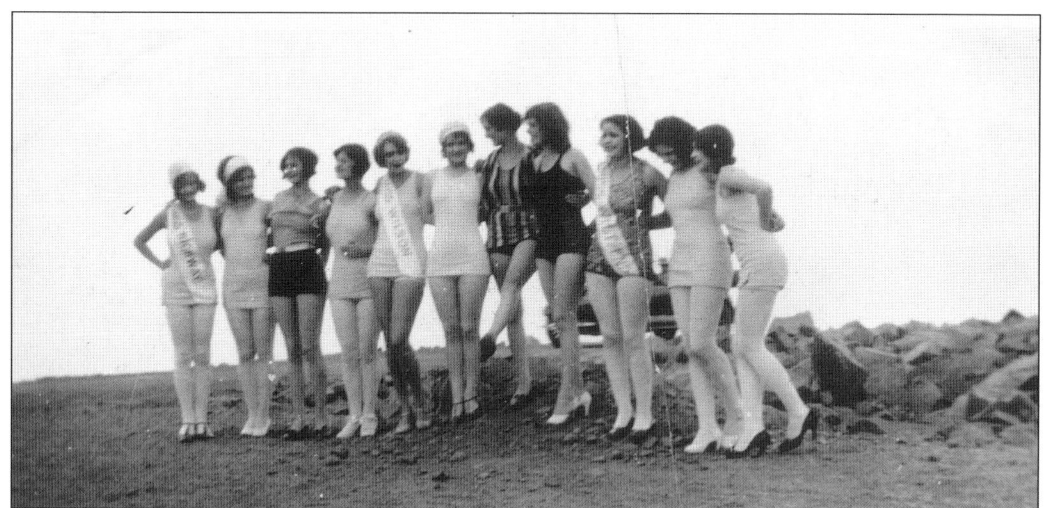

Beautiful Actresses Pose Atop Pike's Peak. (*c.* 1928) The movie industry arrived in Colorado using the natural backdrops such as Ute Pass, Canon City, and Cripple Creek. Believing viewers' attention was limited, directors initially produced films that lasted only a few minutes. As films became more popular, so did their length. Early movies using the region's natural beauty for films such as *Cripple Creek Float* were replaced with famous films like *True Grit*, starring John Wayne. (Courtesy Colorado Springs Pioneer Museum.)

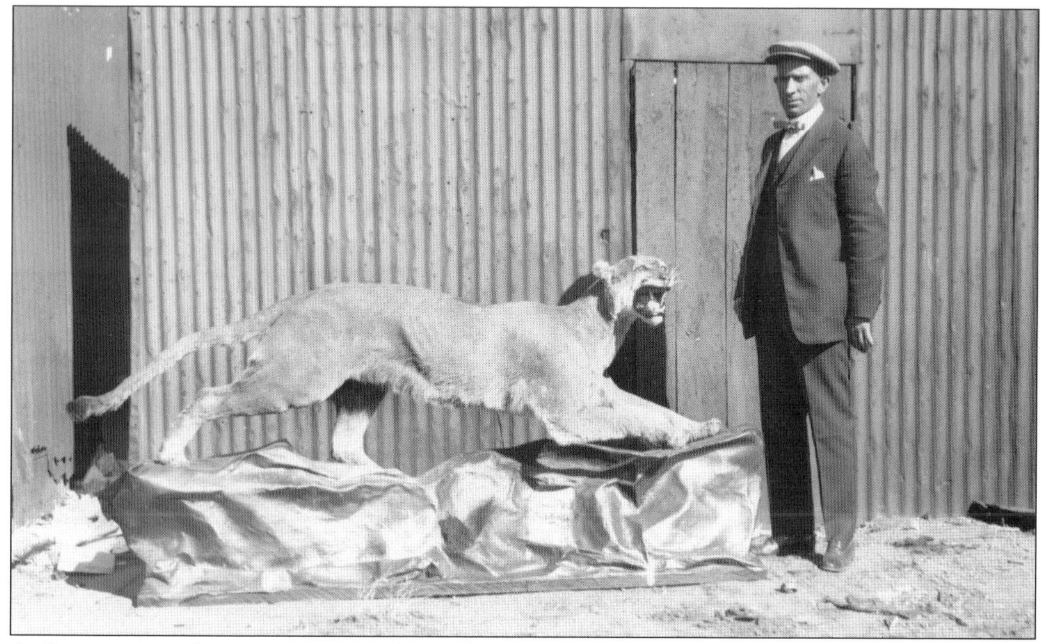

A Bounty of $25.00 on His Head. (*c.* 1920) Ranchers suspected Old Disappearance as the cause of death of many of their livestock. Fred Simpson and his dog Rover tracked Old Disappearance through the snow for over three hours before they caught up with him. They finally treed the mountain lion and he was shot with a 22-caliber rifle. On his death, Old Disappearance weighed 160 pounds, had a paw span of five inches across, was seven feet in length and considered well over fifteen years old. (Courtesy the Palmer Lake Historical Society and Lucretia Vaile Museum.)

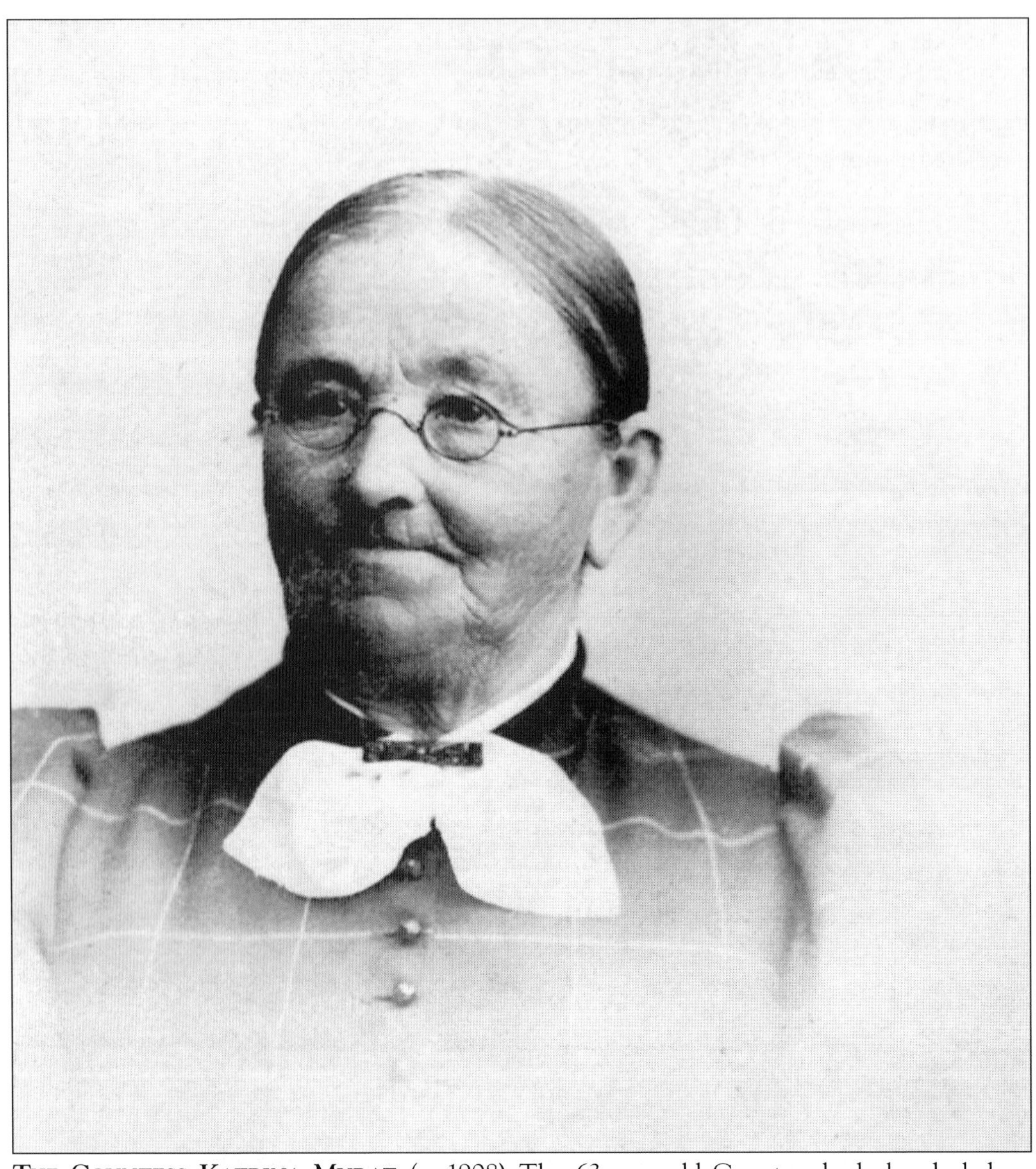

The Countess Katrina Murat (*c.* 1908) The 63 year old Countess had already led an exciting life around the gold camps before she arrived in Palmer Lake and made it her final home. She built a little cottage just below Sundance Mountain and had a 20-foot well dug that she would be kind enough to share with other residents. Lucretia Vaile and her sister often asked Mrs. Murat (as she preferred to be called) for permission to use her well. Lucretia had suspicions, as did most of the residents of Palmer Lake, that the title of Countess was unfounded but said that Mrs. Murat was always, ". . . very nice about letting me get it, and finally won my reluctant conviction that she was really a countess—though I was pretty sure then that countesses were about as rare as fairies in Colorado." (Courtesy the Palmer Lake Historical Society and Lucretia Vaile Museum.)

A Donkey Ride to the Seven Falls. (date unknown) Originally the falls was part of 160 acres that were homesteaded by Nathaniel Colby in 1872. The land was sold several times until Mr. James Hull purchased it with adjacent land. He joined forces with Mr. Hunter, a local man who provided burros to view the falls at 25¢ a ride. For this privilege, he paid Mr. Hull a hefty $500. (Courtesy the Cheyenne Mountain Heritage Center.)

The Millionaires When they Won, The Invalids When they Lost. (*c.* 1902) Founded in 1901, the Colorado Spring's baseball team was given the name Millionaires by Hiram Rogers, who teased the team when they had a losing streak by calling them the Invalids. Although they worked hard, they ended up at the bottom of the league their first year. The following year they were sixth in the Western League of 1902. (Courtesy the Colorado Historical Society.)

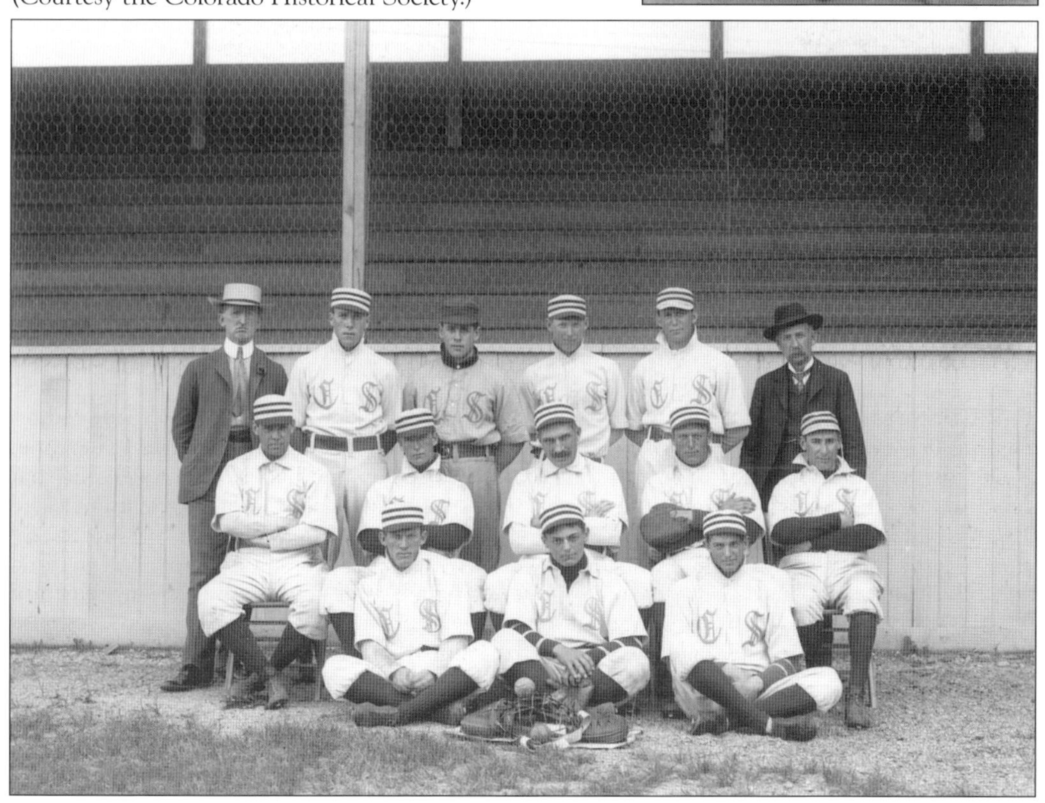

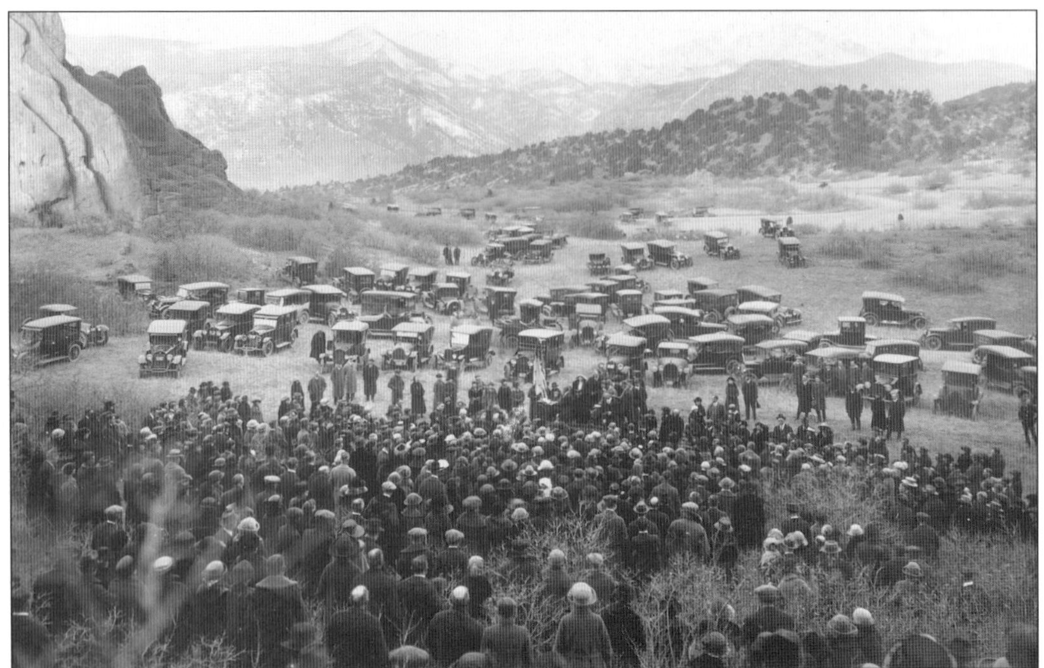

The Easter Sunrise Service at The Garden of the Gods. (*c.* 1923) For the first few years, only two churches were represented at the special Easter services at the Garden of the Gods but later the services became a non-denominational event and all different faiths were invited. The services were also broadcast to millions of people overseas, including the Armed Forces Radio Network, CBS Radio, and the Voice of America. (Courtesy Colorado Springs Pioneer Museum.)

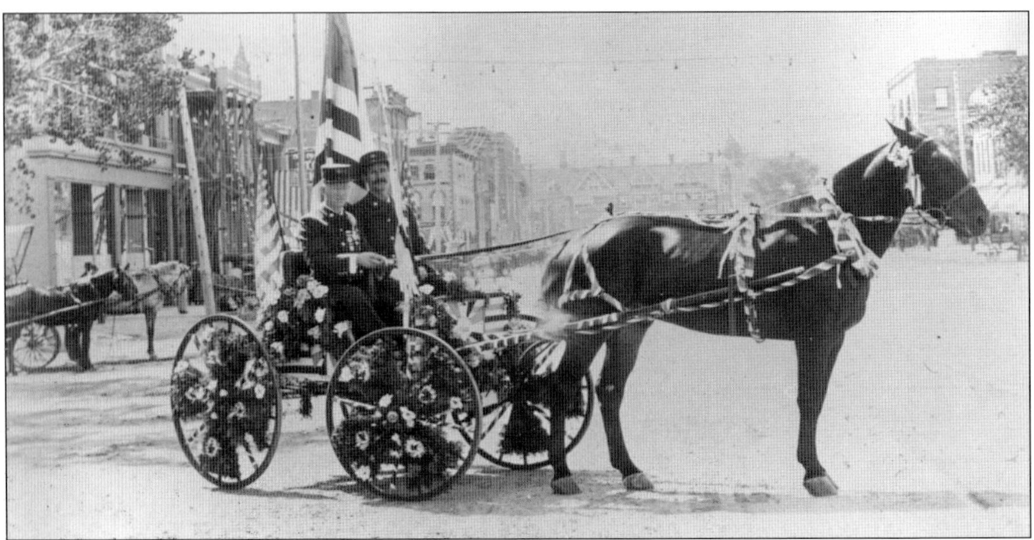

The Annual Flower Parade. (*c.* 1898) From left to right are B.B. McReynolds, acting chief, and Fred Armbruster. The Chief's sulky is highly decorated with flowers for the parade. It is believed that B.B. Reynolds was filling in as chief, for E.E. Baty was away fighting in the Spanish American War. At the far end of the street is the Antlers Hotel that burned to the ground on October 1, 1898. (Courtesy Dr. Lester L. Williams Museum.)

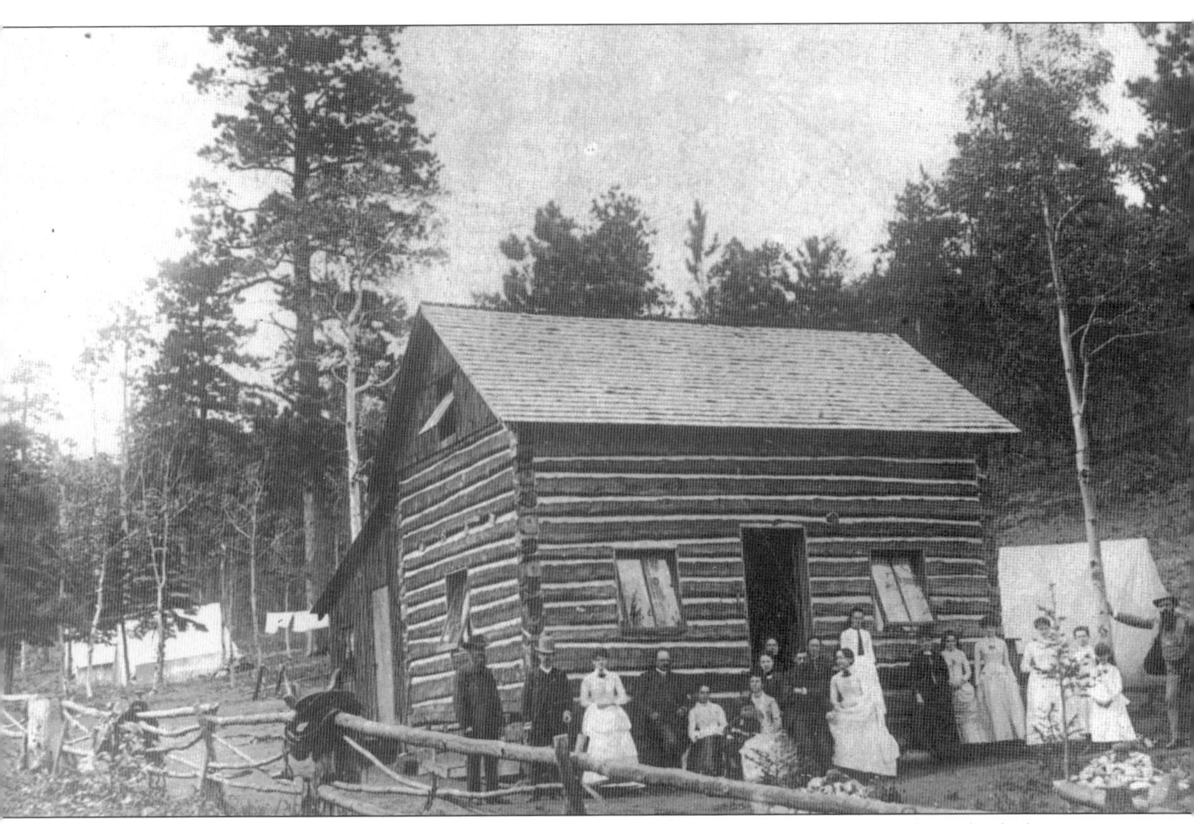

The Crystal Park Hotel. (*c.* 1882–1900) In 1881, a local publication described the area around Crystal Park as " . . . one of these natural gardens in which this country abounds. It lies at an altitude of about 9,000 feet above sea level. . . . [I]t is threaded by three beautiful streams of water uniting to form one, and is by all odds one of the most picturesquely diversified and most lovely mountain glens to be found in the Rocky Mountain Range." Another comment on July 29, 1882, states "the hotel at Crystal Park is now in order for the reception of guests, and all visiting there will be treated in the most hospitable manner. No more charming retreat than Crystal Park could be imagined located as it is half way up the mountain slope with its sparkling streams and extended view of the surrounding countryside. A number of tents have been provided for sleeping apartments and the meals will be provided at the hotel proper. Just at present there are abundance of wild strawberries and raspberries at the park which the guest can gather at will. . . . " (Courtesy Special Collections, Colorado College.)

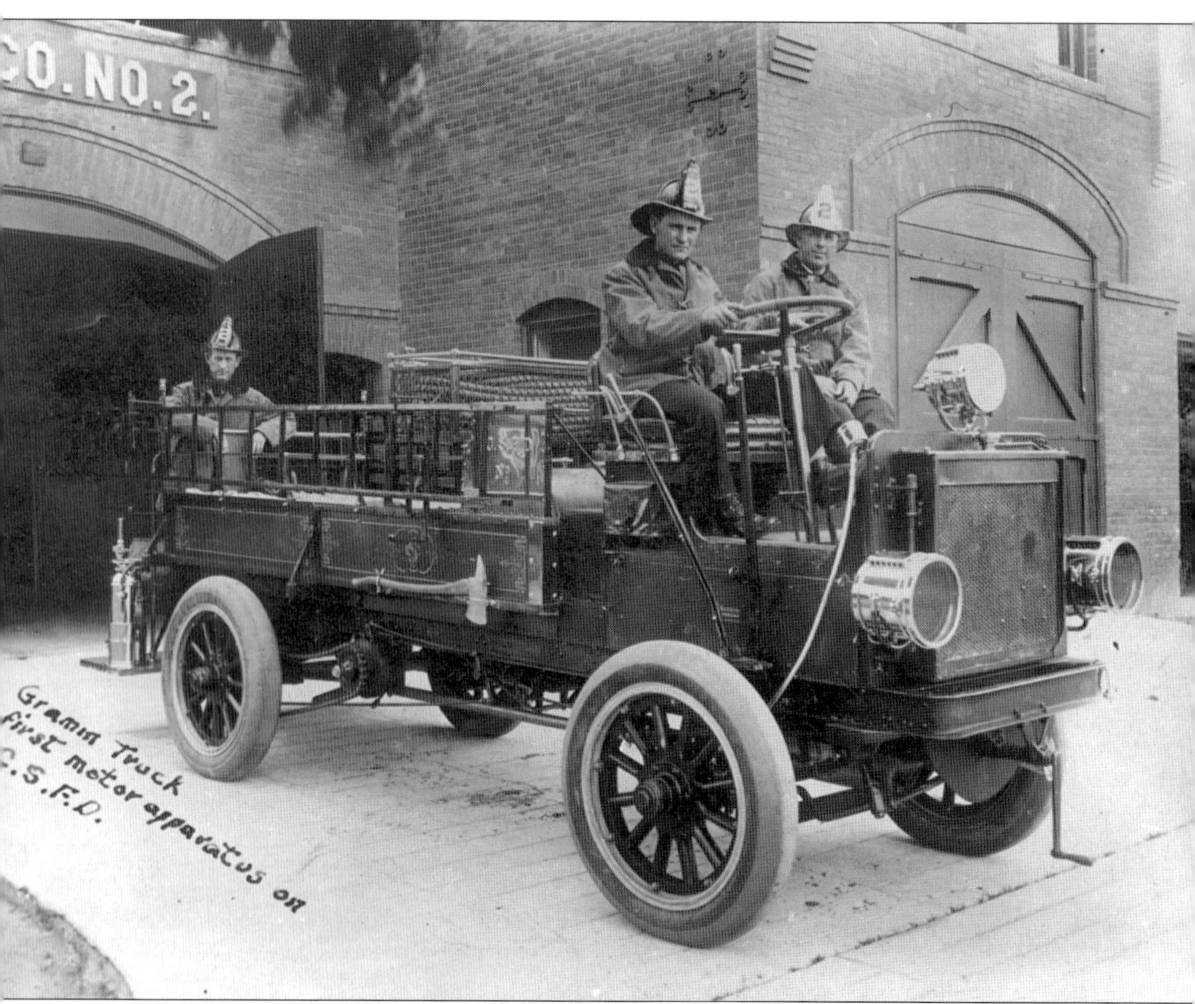

The Gramm Truck—From Horse to Horsepower. (*c.* 1910) In this photo, F.V. Reed is on the rear step, Ray Bradshaw is the driver, and Captain George May sits in the left front seat. The Gramm was the first motorized apparatus used by the C.S.F.D. It cost almost $2,500, was right-hand drive, and had a top speed of 30 miles an hour. Hand cranked, it kicked furiously and even broke the wrist of one firefighter. Tests were conducted with the Gramm, most notably to the Glockner Sanitarium over two miles away. The distance was covered in 4 minutes, 30 seconds. In the past when horses drew the equipment, the team could run at a fast pace for a mile, then walk a few blocks to recoup, and then off again at top speed arriving at the Glockner in about 25 minutes. The uniforms changed too. Ray Turner, of the Dr. Lester Williams Firemen's Museum said, "For a while, in the late 1800s and early 1900s, the bib overall and a Chambray shirt were the most practical and comfortable things to wear." (Courtesy Dr. Lester L. Williams Museum.)

Five

The Cities Take Shape

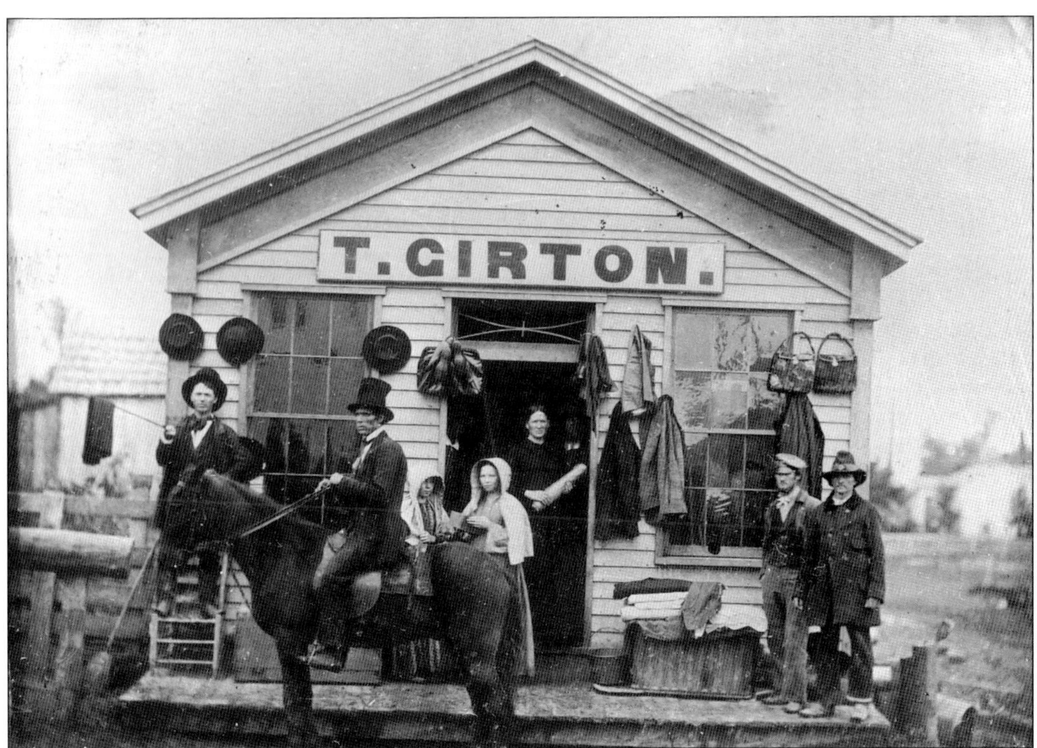

Colorado City Giron General Store. (*c.* 1868) The general store sold just about everything a homesteader or resident needed. In 1886, the Colorado Midland Railroad made Colorado City its headquarters, providing jobs at the terminal and repair yard. When gold was discovered in Cripple Creek in 1891, Colorado City's four gold ore reduction mills went into full production and brought more prosperity to the town. (Courtesy Colorado Springs Pioneer Museum.)

REGULATIONS
OF THE
Colorado Springs Hotel,
COLORADO SPRINGS, COL.

Guests are requested to register their names at the Office on their arrival.

Guests intending to leave in the morning, will please give notice at the Office early the evening before.

All accounts made up and payable weekly.

Price of Board per week, ...	$18.00
Price of Day Board per week, ...	$ 8.00
Price of Board per day, ...	$ 3.50
Dinner, ...	$ 1.00
Supper, Lodging, and Breakfast, ...	$ 2.50

Children occupying seats at the first table, full price.

Other Children, and Servants, half price.

Breakfast from 6:30 to 9:30, A. M. Dinner, 1 to 3, P. M. Tea, 6 to 8 P. M.

Servants are not allowed to take any meals from the Dining Room unless having an order for the same from the Office.

No washing allowed in rooms: Laundry provided for that purpose.

No silver allowed to be taken from the Dining Room without an order.

An extra charge will be made for all Lunches or Meals served in rooms.

A charge will be made for all orders not on Bill of Fare.

It is requested that waiters be not taken away at meal times.

THE DOORS AT BREAKFAST POSITIVELY CLOSED AT 9:30 A. M.

A Fire Proof Safe is provided at the Office for the deposit of all money, jewelry, and other valuables.

All articles taken from the rooms will be at the risk of the owners, as the Proprietor cannot be responsible for articles carelessly left out or mislaid in rooms; they will therefore be cautious in laying out temptations.

Guests will please inform the Proprietor of any inattention on the part of the waiters.

H. A. McINTIRE, Manager.

Colorado Springs, Jan. 1, 1872.

"OUT WEST" PRINTING OFFICES.

COLORADO SPRINGS HOTEL REGULATIONS. (c. January 1, 1872) In the early days, a visitor to Colorado Springs had only one place to eat and perhaps stay: the old Log Cabin (next to the depot). General Palmer saw the need for more accomodations and set about building the Colorado Springs Hotel. Mr. Henry Azle McIntyre managed the hotel and issued the list of regulations to the guests. Henry would later meet Marian Young, a beautiful girl of fourteen standing at the register with her family. It was love at first sight, but since Marian was so young; Henry had to wait many years before he could make her his bride. The regulations state that the guests are required to sign in at the register, advise their intention of leaving the day before and had to pay extra for meals served in the rooms. Full board cost $18.00 per week, day board was $8.00 and dinner cost an extra $1.00. Servants and children were charged at half price and guests were advised not to leave valuable items unattended and "…be cautious in laying out temptations." (Courtesy Rogers Davis.)

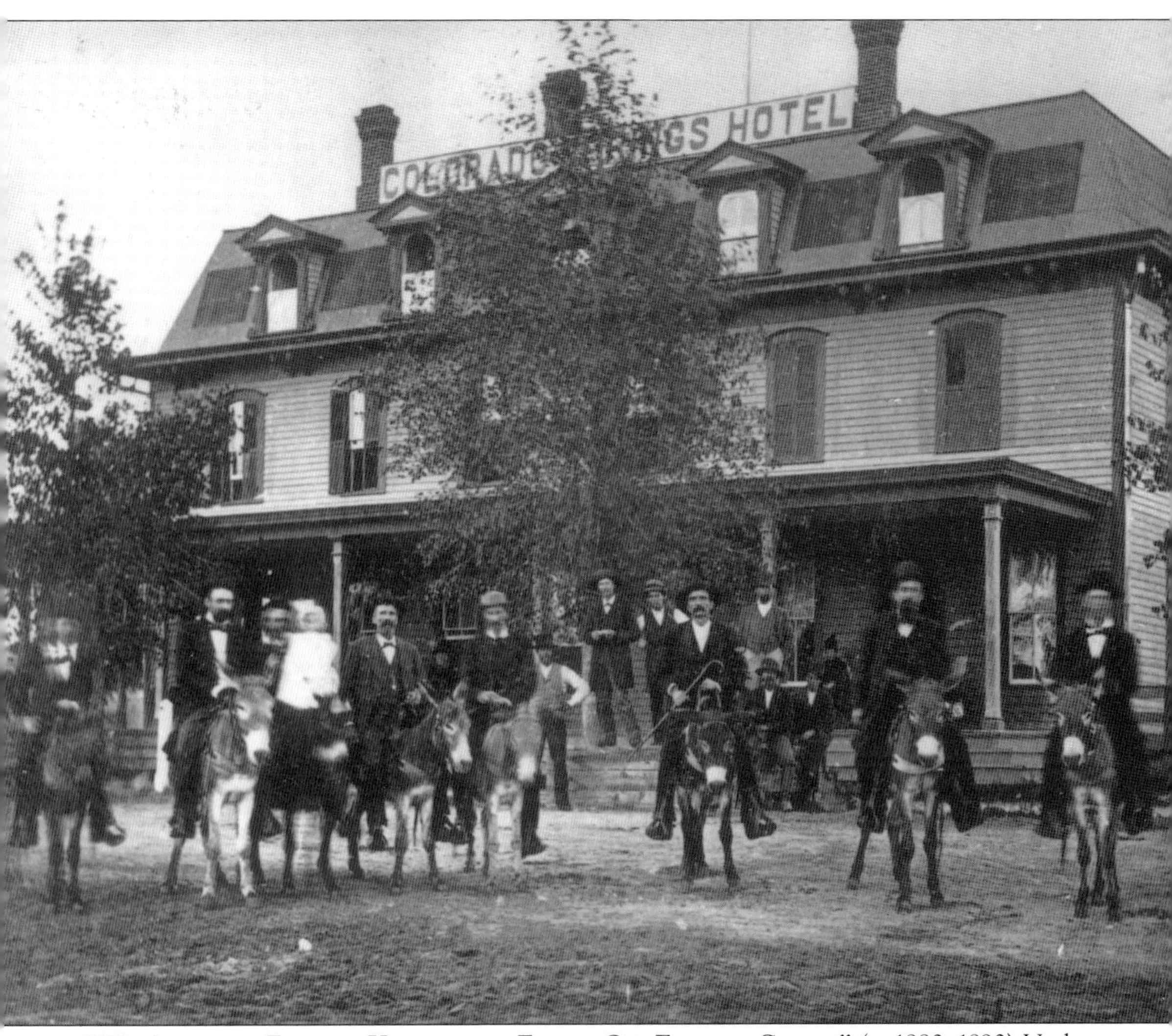

"We Ate with English Knives and Forks, Off English China." (*c.* 1880–1890) Under the direction of General Palmer and Dr. Bell, William Iles arrived from London, having procured all the necessary items required for a fine hotel. Eventually, Henry McIntyre was engaged as manager with the understanding that Iles would become the chef. However, the two men disagreed on the sale of liquor on the premises, and the relationship ended. On January 1, 1872, the hotel was opened with McIntyre as the sole proprietor. Rose Kingsley wrote of the opening, "After two months of delay the Colorado Springs Hotel was opened at 2 p.m. and we went to our first meal there, and ate with English knives and forks, off English china, a first rate dinner." Eight men sit on burros, one holding a little girl as they pose in front of the hotel. The three-story building has a mansard roof with five dormer windows and a covered porch. (Courtesy the Denver Public Library.)

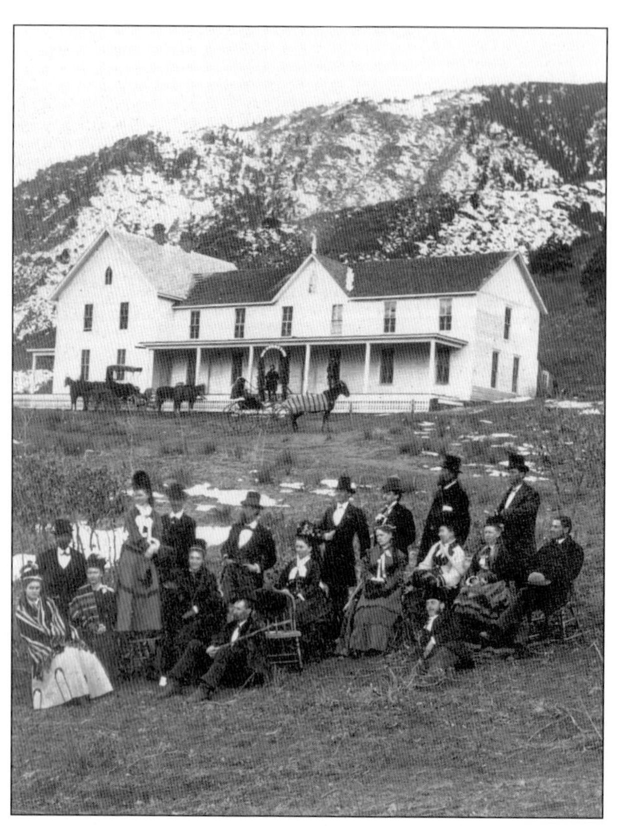

A Distinguished Looking Group. (*c.* 1870–1882) A group poses in front of the first Iron Springs Hotel in Manitou Springs. The men wear hats and some lounge on the ground despite the conditions. One woman wears a muff, and others have blankets over their shoulders. A buggy and a Tally-Ho, a type of horse-drawn coach given its name from a London to Manchester route, are in the rear of the photograph. (Courtesy the Denver Public Library.)

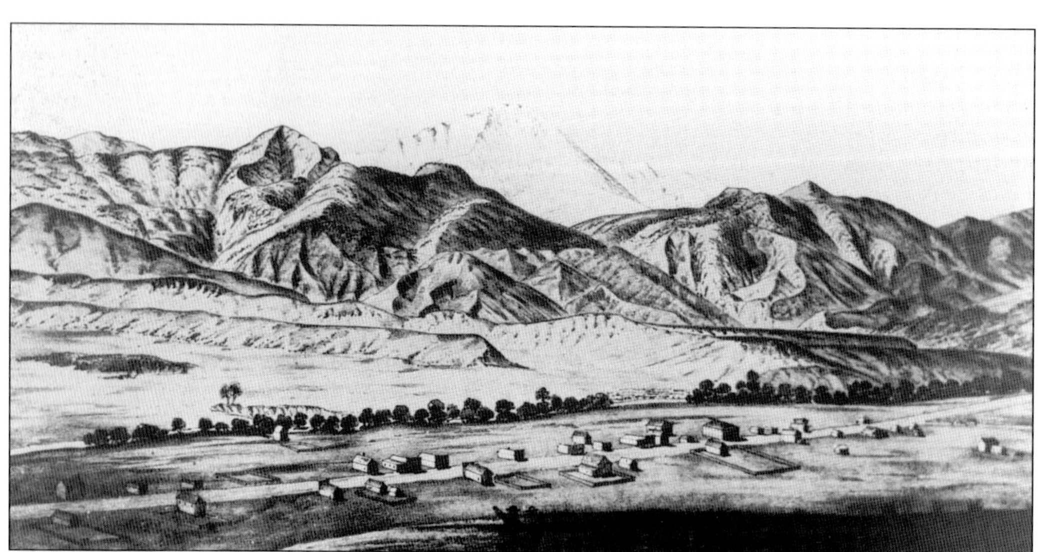

An Early Sketch of Colorado City. (date unknown) It was the first recognized town in the Pikes Peak region. At one point, the town was merely a settlement called El Dorado, but then came a group of enterprising men, S.W. Wagoner, Albert D. Richardson, Lewis N. Tappan, and Henry M. Fosdick, to name a few. Fosdick surveyed and platted the town one mile wide and two miles long. (Courtesy Colorado Springs Pioneer Museum.)

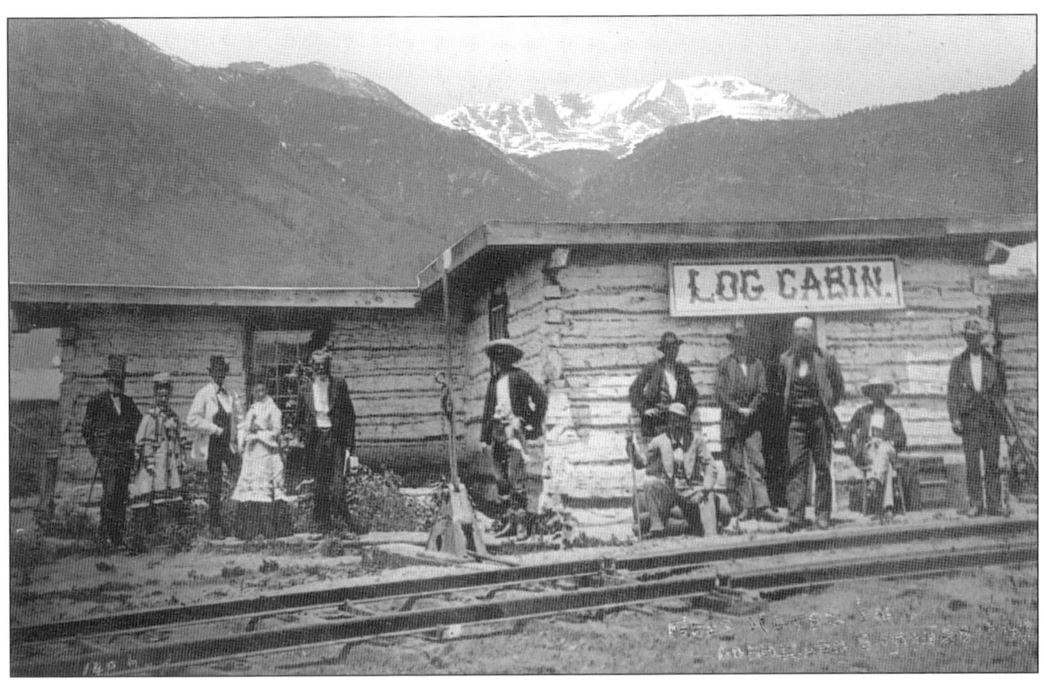

GOVERNOR HUNT BUILT THE LOG CABIN. (*c.* 1871–1875) From left to right are Governor Hunt, Mrs. Elisabeth Hunt McDowell (Hunt's daughter), Mrs. Helen McDowell Malhern, and Major John H. McDowell (Hunt's son-in-law). The cabin became the station restaurant known for its good meals, provided by Mrs. McDowell. On one occasion, a New Englander arrived saying, "Is this the Long Cabin? I've come all the way from Portland, Maine, to get my dinner here." (Courtesy the Denver Public Library.)

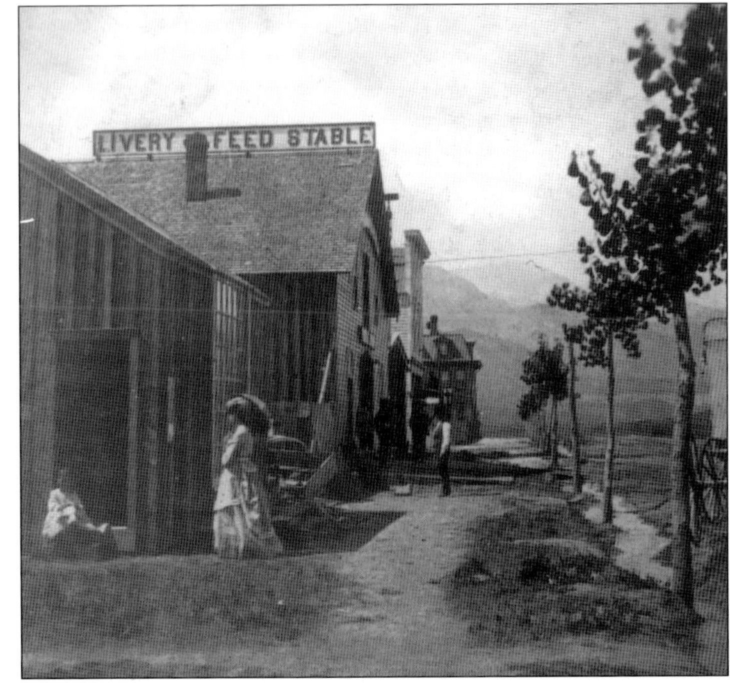

NEW TREES FOR A NEW TOWN. (*c.* 1873) Young trees planted in an irrigation ditch on Pikes Peak Avenue look west from Tejon Street. The well-dressed woman in the photograph is wearing a dress with a peplum and bustle and an elegant hat. She holds a parasol as she speaks with a young girl sitting in a doorway. The bottom of her dress is soiled, perhaps from crossing the irrigation ditch from a buggy seen at the right. Four men stand outside the Livery Feed Stable. (Courtesy the Denver Public Library.)

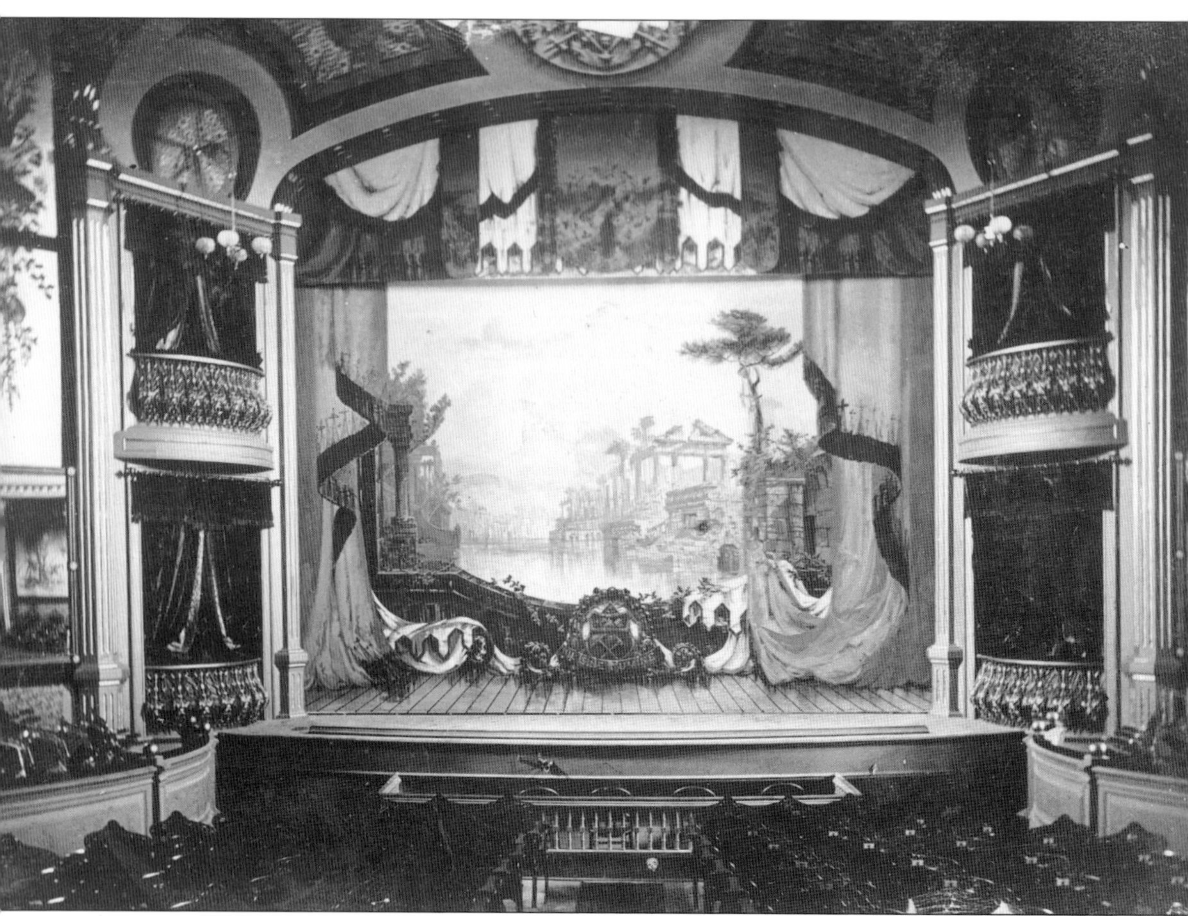

The Elegant Opera House of Colorado Springs. (*c.* 1881) The spectacular Opera House was built in 1880, at a cost of $80,000, and ran approximately 34 productions a year. The programs included all aspects of the arts: musical, ballet, plays, and literary personalities. Lon Chaney, whose family lived on Bijou Street, performed at the Opera House, as well as other notable people such as Oscar Wilde. The controversial novelist and poet appeared in knee britches, and velvet coat, with long hair and shiny buckles on his shoes. He did not appear to be distracted by the low attendance at his lecture on "Interior Decoration" and his presentation was well-received according to reviews. However, since there was a rivalry between the cities of Denver and Colorado Springs, the editor of *The Denver News*, Eugene Field, saw an opportunity to chide the residents of Colorado Springs. He wrote: "It is surprising that Colorado Springs which if nothing is not literary and aesthetic, failed to give Oscar Wilde a good audience." *The Colorado Springs Gazette* responded accordingly. (Courtesy Colorado Springs Pioneer Museum.)

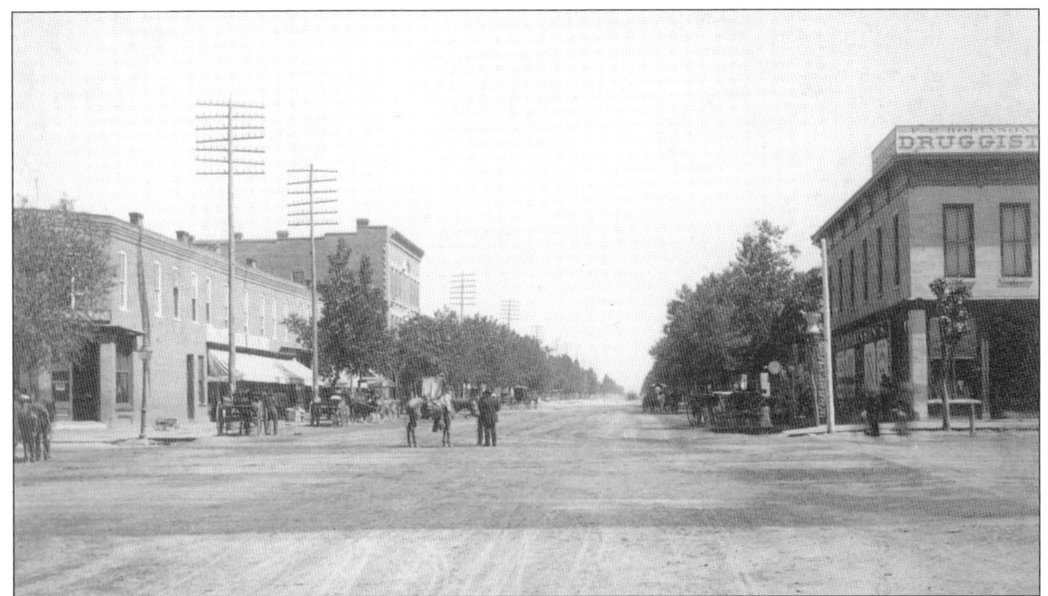

Buggies Line Tejon Street. (*c.* 1882–1890) Two men stand on Tejon Street as buggies, carriages, and horses are tethered outside the buildings, one that reads, "F.E. Robinson Druggist." Palmer decided on the name for Pikes Peak Avenue but it was Cameron, Palmer's foreman, who chose the others such as Huerfano and Cucharras after specific rivers and streams, but he also named some streets after mountain chains like Sierra Madre and Cascade. (Courtesy the Denver Public Library.)

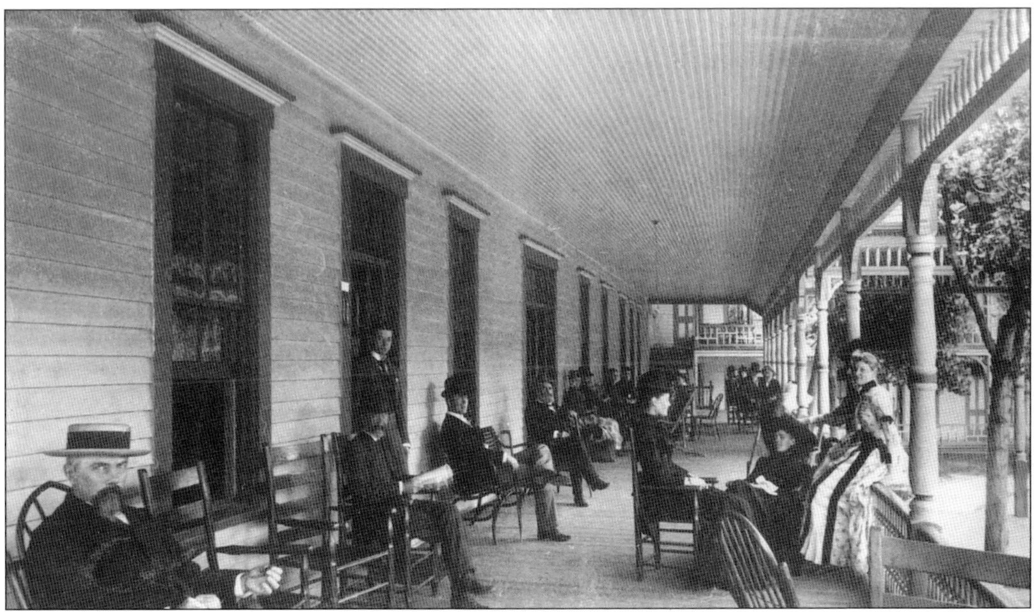

The Cliff House Hotel at Manitou Springs. (*c.* 1889) Catering to 150 guests with good food plus the close locations of four mineral springs made the Cliff House a popular place to visit. Most visitors were wealthy and sophisticated, as can be seen by their clothes. The women wear fine distinguished-looking dresses with one woman (seated) wearing the height of fashion, a "Merry Widow" hat. (Courtesy the Denver Public Library.)

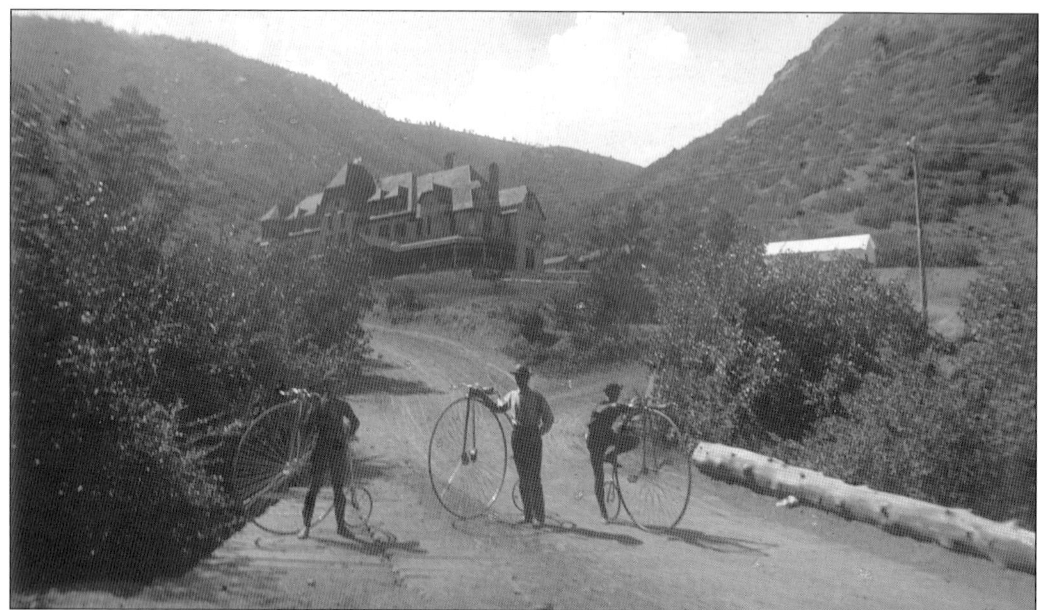

The First Hotel to have Electric Lights and Call Bells. (c. 1890–1900) The elegant Iron Springs Hotel in Manitou boasted of having 65 rooms, all with electric lights and call bells. No cheap rates were available. The two men and a boy in the foreground sport "high-wheeler" bicycles. These bicycles were known in England as Penny Farthings, given the name after the large penny and the much smaller farthing. (Courtesy the Denver Public Library.)

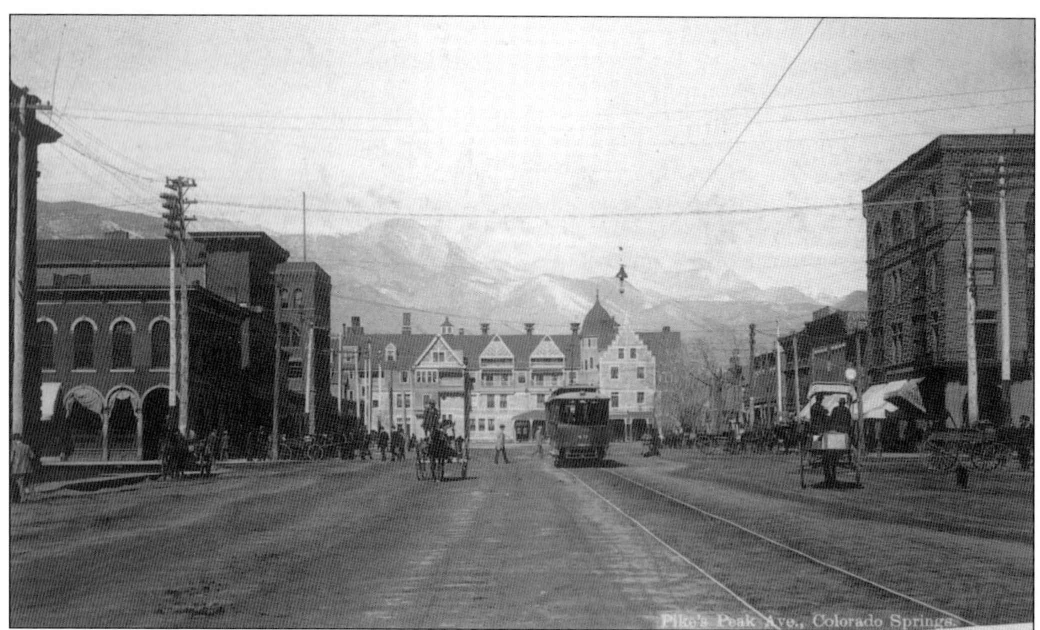

Early Days on Pikes Peak Avenue. (c. 1890–1898) A great view of Pikes Peak Avenue with the Antlers Hotel that burned to the ground on October 1, 1898. The fire originated at the Denver and Rio Grande freight station and spread quickly to the Antlers after a box of dynamite exploded. A streetcar numbered 40 sits in the center of the street and is surrounded by buggies, horses and pedestrians. (Courtesy the Denver Public Library.)

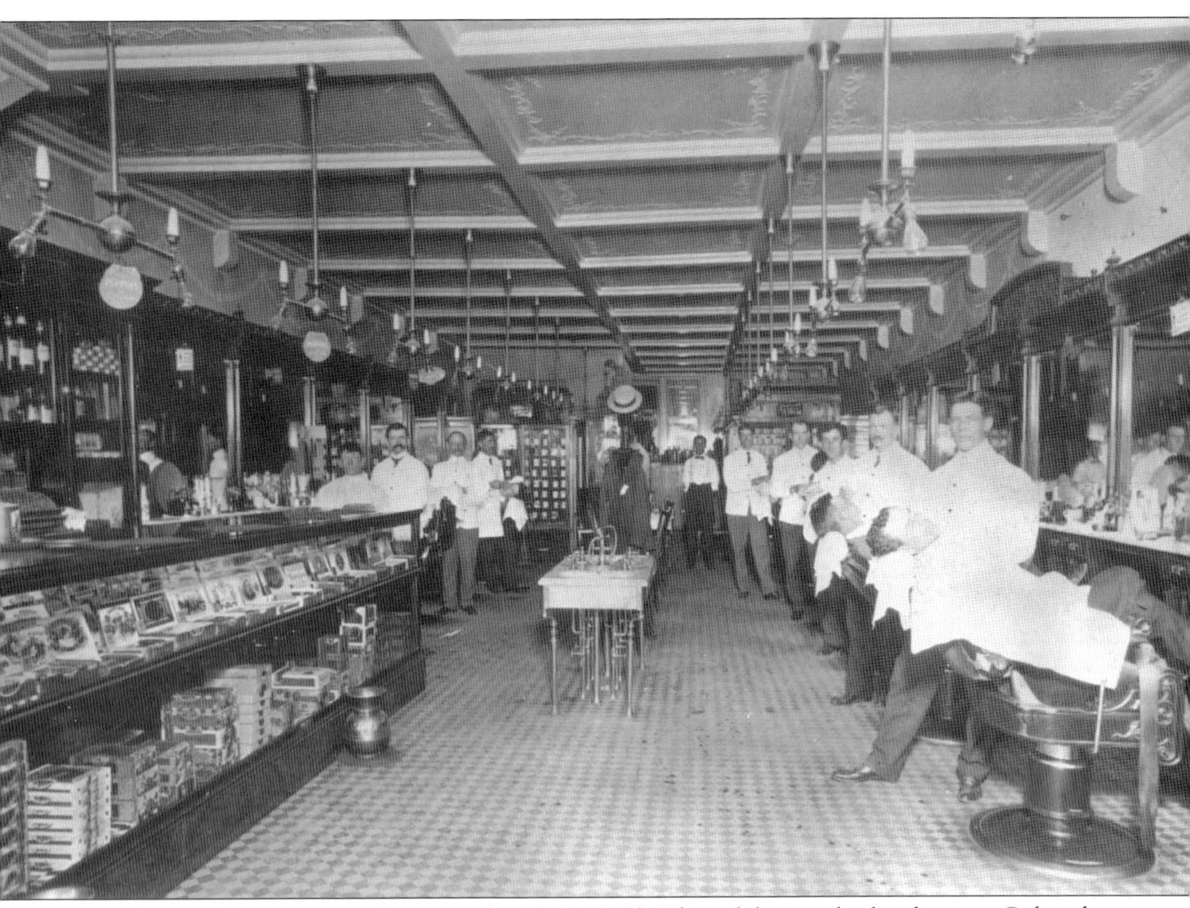

A Haircut, Shave, or Cigars. (*c.* 1890–1900) This elaborate barbershop in Colorado Springs has a decorated ceiling and walls with lights that hang low over the barber's chair. The tiled checkered floor is strewn with hair as the barbers and their customers pose for the photograph. There appear to be bottles of hair lotions or possibly refreshments for sale just behind the cash register. In the center of the shop there are washbasins and a coat rack that holds a straw boater hat and several coats. Spittoons are in front of the display cases, which carry a variety of cigars. Later those cigar box lids would have the beautiful face of Anna Held, the star of the Follies who arrived in Colorado Springs to perform in 1904 with her troupe of 50 chorus girls. In the first telephone directory in 1879–1880, there were four barbershops in Colorado Springs; in 1894 there were twelve. (Courtesy the Denver Public Library.)

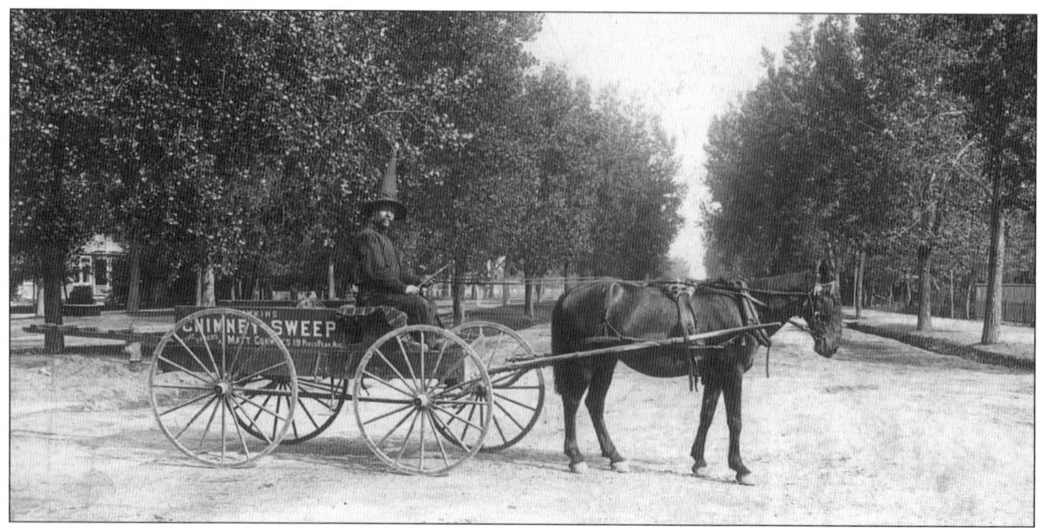

Isaac Hawkins Plying his Trade as a Chimney Sweep. (c. 1890–1900) Wearing a pointed black hat and advertising his trade as a chimney sweep, Isaac's wagon has a sign that reads, "Leave orders at Matt Conway's, 6 S. Tejon Street." In Europe, the chimney sweep is considered a sign of good luck and effigies of them are still given at weddings as a token of long life and good wishes. (Courtesy the Denver Public Library.)

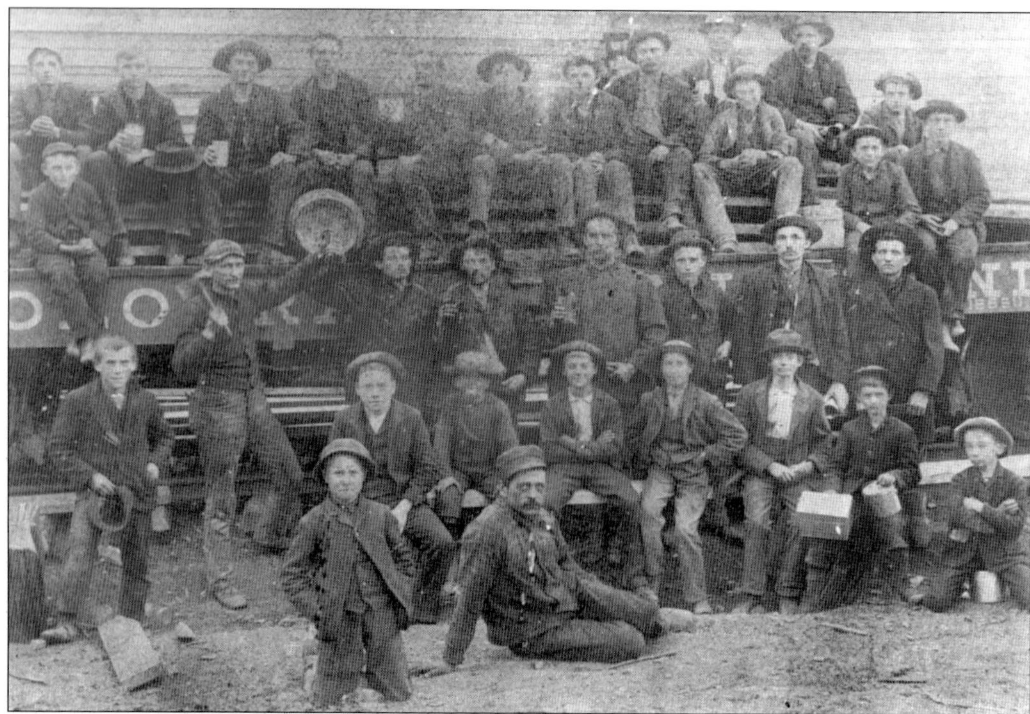

Bohemian Glass, a Specialty at the Old Colorado City Factory. (c. 1890) Over 200 men from Czechoslovakia, each with a helper, produced hundreds of bottles a day at the factory. All bottles were hand blown and made in either brown or green. One of the factory's best customers was the Manitou Mineral Water Company that used the bottles for their ginger "Champaign" that was shipped nationwide. (Courtesy Colorado Springs Pioneer Museum.)

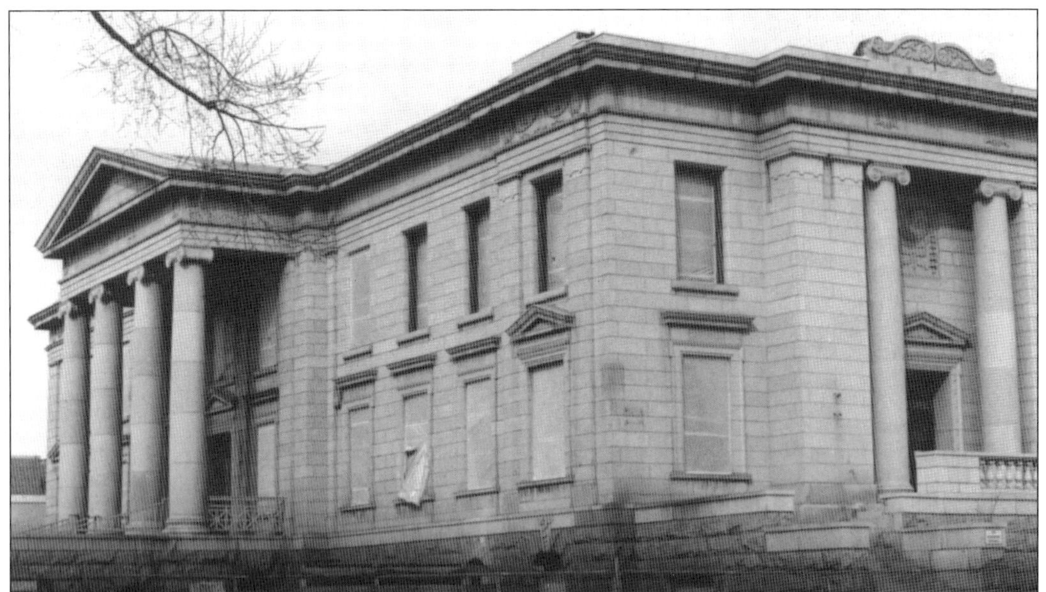

THOMAS MACLAREN, AN ARCHITECT OF THE TIMES. (*c.* 2001) MacLaren was born in Thornhill, Sterling, Scotland, in 1863. He arrived in Colorado Springs hoping the clean, dry climate, plus plenty of good food and rest would cure him of tuberculosis. He was soon well enough to continue his work and went on to design hospitals, churches, schools, and homes in Colorado Springs and other towns before he died in 1928. (Courtesy the Cheyenne Mountain Heritage Center.)

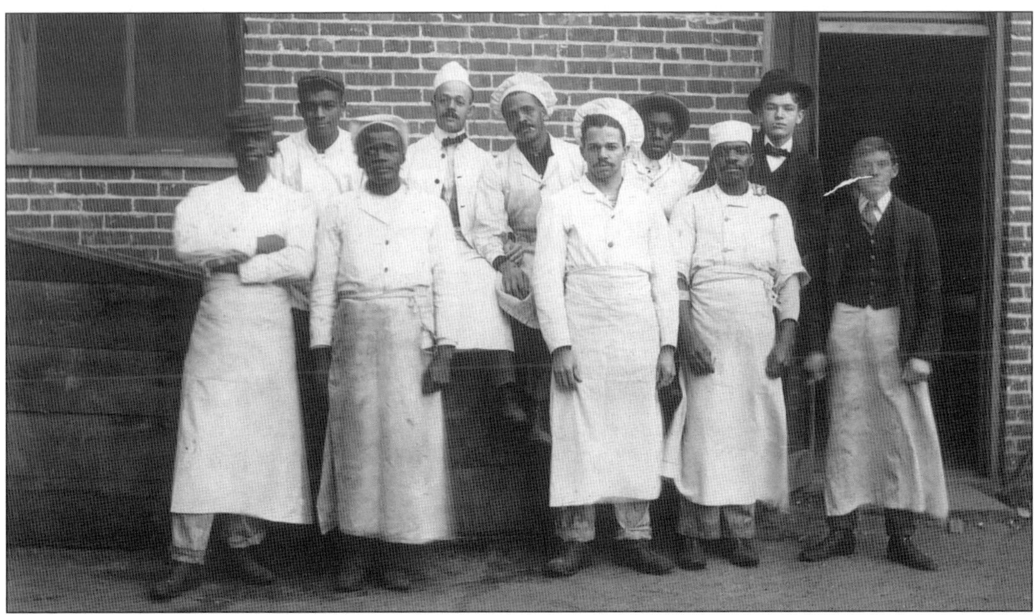

TUCKER'S RESTAURANT KITCHEN CREW. (*c.* 1891–1900) The kitchen crew poses at the rear of Tucker's Restaurant on 110 East Pikes Pike Avenue, Midland Block, Colorado Springs. None of the men are identified. They wear aprons, some of which are spoiled, and a variety of hats from chef to soft-peaked caps. Two men have cigarettes in their mouths and some have cigarettes in their hands. (Courtesy the Denver Public Library.)

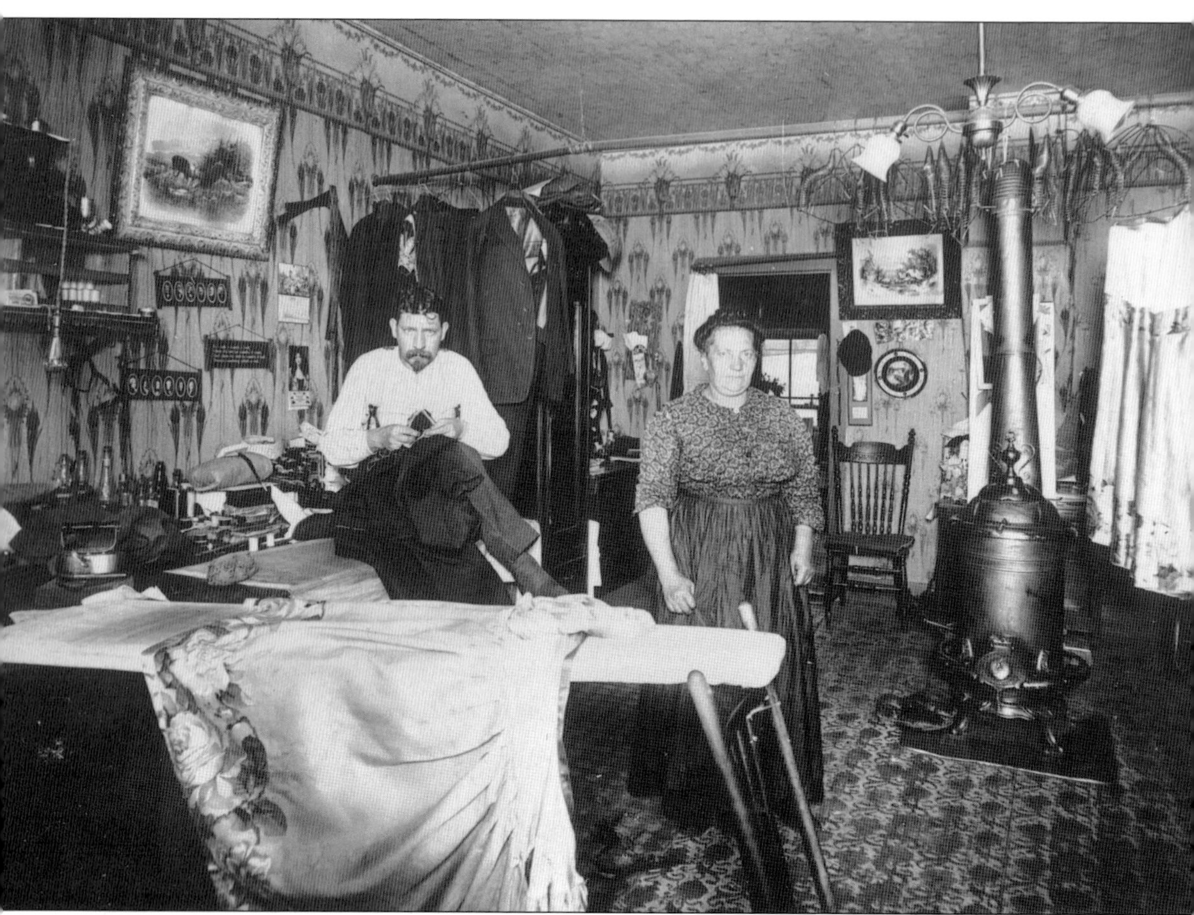

SOME SAY A TAILOR IS WORTH HIS WEIGHT IN GOLD. (c. 1890) Many people treasured their tailors, not only for their confidentiality with regard to their personal measurements, but also for the custom-designed clothes that no other man or woman would be seen wearing. Elizabeth and Frank's shop was known as "Reidel's Tailor Shop" and was located on Colorado Avenue. Mr. Reidel appears to be doing some handwork on a jacket or coat; hand-stitched lapels were considered a sign of a well-heeled man or woman. What looks like a "ham" (a stuffed cloth container similar to a ham and used to shape a collar) can be seen on the table next to Mr. Reidel. What appears to be a woman's skirt is stretched across the scorched ironing board. The wire hangers in the rear of the shop appear to be set particularly high, perhaps to accommodate ladies' long dresses. The free-standing stove in the middle of the shop has a cone-shaped decorative top. (Courtesy Colorado Springs Pioneer Museum.)

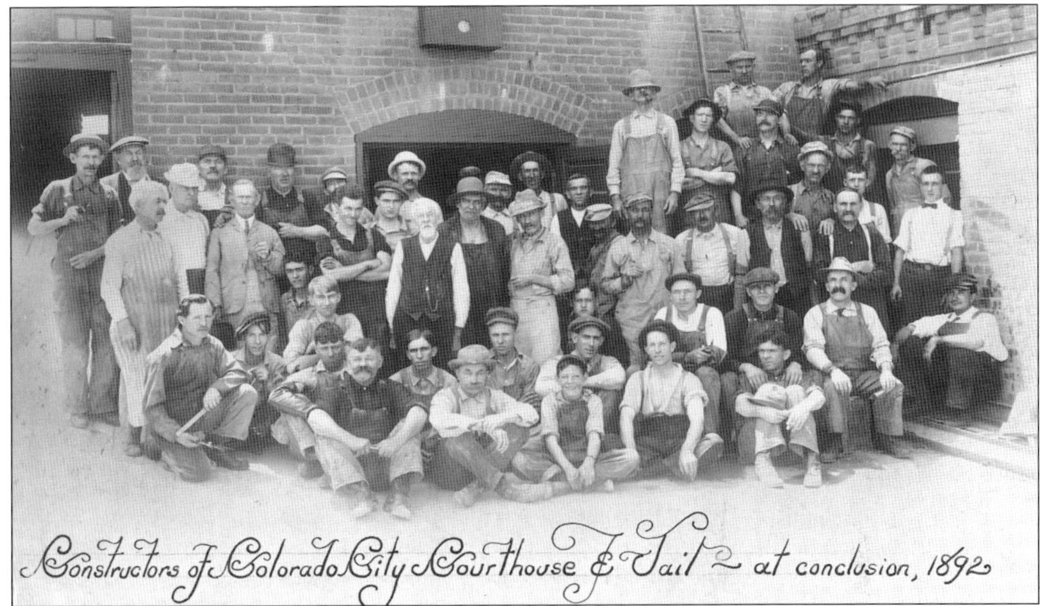

THE COLORADO CITY COURTHOUSE AND JAIL. (*c.* 1892) The workers, not the inmates, pose outside the newly constructed courthouse and jail. Manly Ormes described in his book on Colorado Springs that Colorado City was a rough and lawless place: ". . . there were shootings and killings, and justice stood on no ceremony." Ormes also mentions that the jail had a night guard, but that Sheriff Jackson presumably took charge during daytime hours. (Courtesy Colorado Springs Pioneer Museum.)

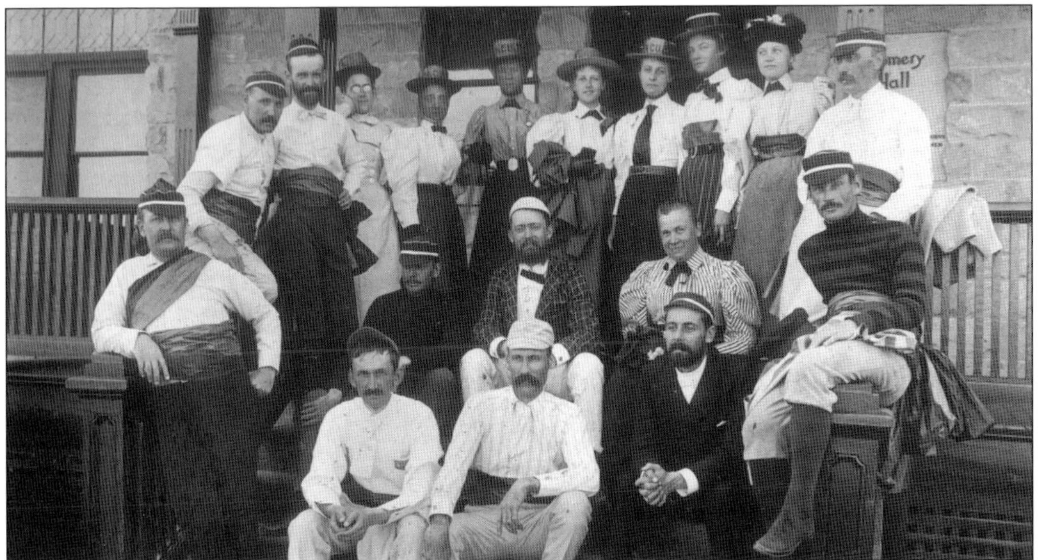

THE COLORADO COLLEGE FACULTY ON THE STEPS OF MONTGOMERY HALL. (*c.* 1896) From the back of photograph: "Back row: Dr. (Florian) Cajori, Dean (Edward S.) Parsons, Misses Stearns, Mary Noble, Foster Dickerman, Sarah Jackson, Nina Lunt, Faith Gregg, Regina Lunt; second row: President (William F.) Slocum, Louis A.W. Ahlers, Mrs. Slocum; front row: Rev. Philip Washburn, Manly D. Ormes, Rev. W.H.R. Boyle, Arthur Stearns." (Courtesy the Denver Public Library.)

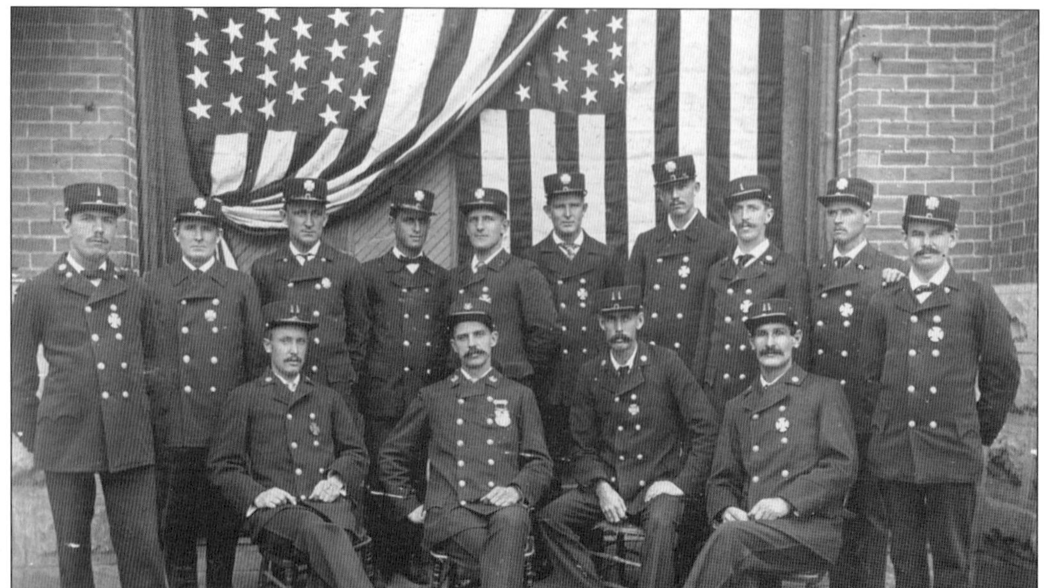

The Colorado Springs Fire Department. (*c.* 1899) Pictured, from left to right, are: (standing) Ben Mayhew, San Cook, Frank Huges, Tom Quinlan, Clyde McReynolds, Carley Reasoner, W.H. McConnell, Walt Griffin, Billy James, and Harvey Gillingham; (sitting) Keith Conacher, Ed Baty (chief), Mike Donahue, and Fred Armbruster. (Courtesy Dr. Lester L. Williams Museum.)

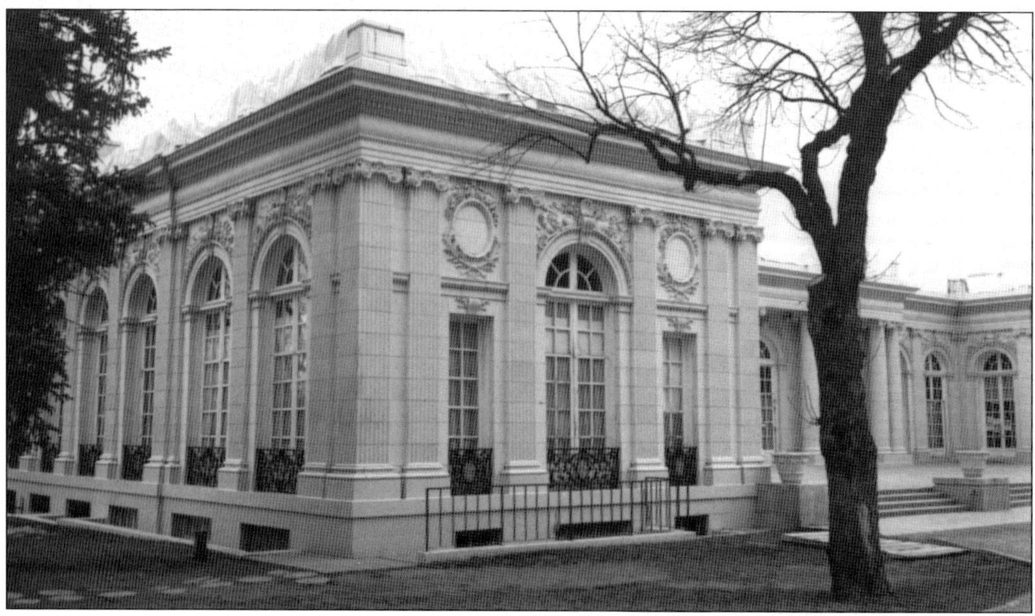

MacLaren Came for his Health—and Stayed. (*c.* 2001) The Trianon building at the Colorado Springs School is just one of MacLaren's designs. A bout of consumption led him to Colorado Springs where his health improved and he went on to design many fine buildings. Over the years, MacLaren's health deteriorated, and on December 4, 1928, after surgery at Glockner Hospital, he died. His friends met at his graveside as one of MacLaren's favorite bagpipe melodies played. (Courtesy the Cheyenne Mountain Heritage Center.)

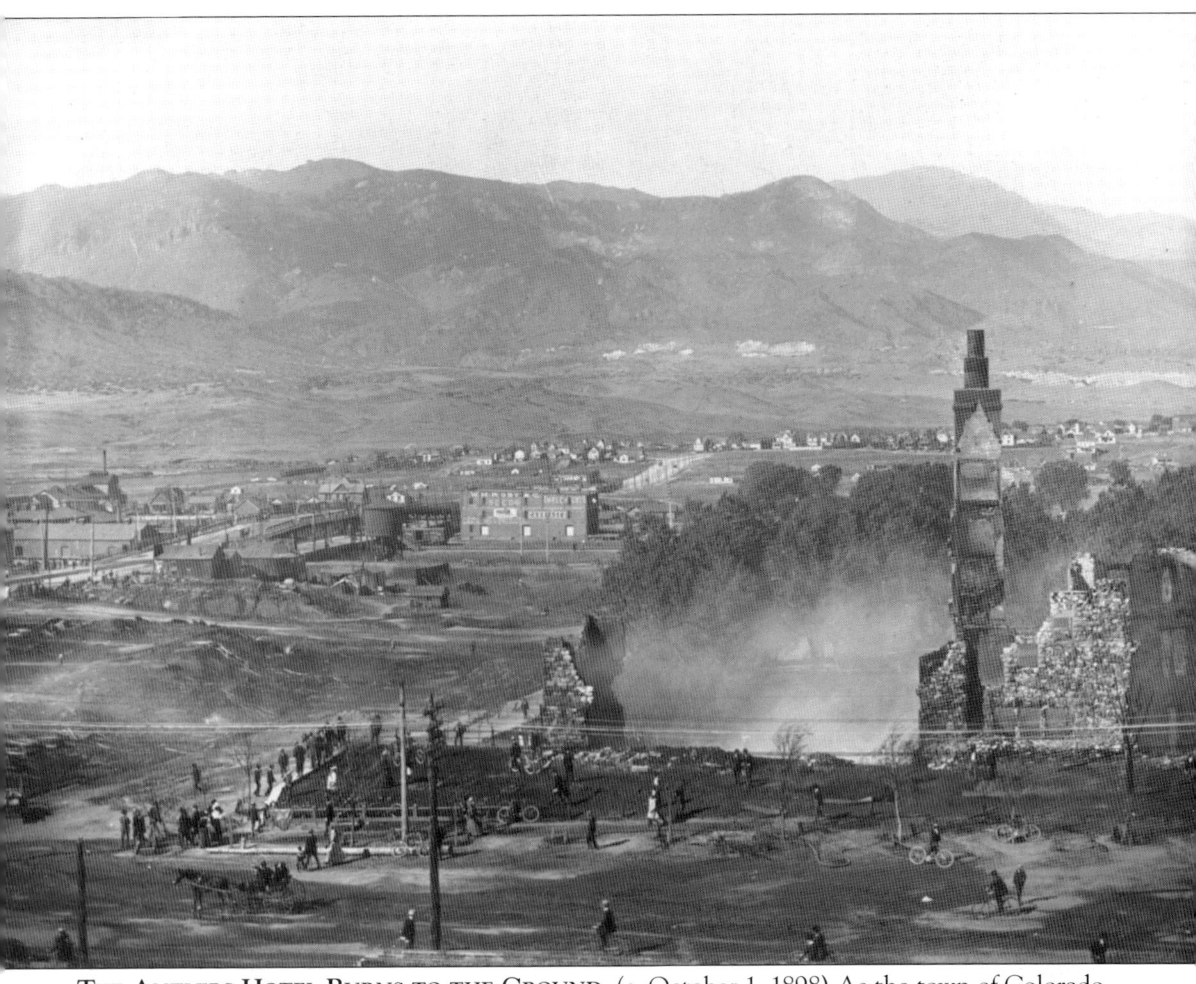

The Antlers Hotel Burns to the Ground. (*c.* October 1, 1898) As the town of Colorado Springs developed, the tourists arrived. The Colorado Springs Hotel could no longer support the high influx of visitors and General Palmer was asked to provide a larger, more impressive hotel. On April 17, 1881, the design was approved and estimated at $100,000, but the final tally was closer to $125,000. Palmer called the hotel The Antlers because at last he had found a home for the many fine sets of antlers in his possession. Lillian Whiting comments in her book of travels that she enjoyed her stay and "one of the definite things of the tourist's stay, was to watch a summer sunset from the western terrace of the Antlers, such an atmosphere of enchantment was there." Unfortunately, the hotel burned to the ground in October 1898. The fire started at the Denver and Rio Grande freight yard and quickly spread to freight cars laden with explosives destined for Cripple Creek. No lives were lost and the furniture was saved, but the hotel was ruined. (Courtesy Dr. Lester L. Williams Museum.)

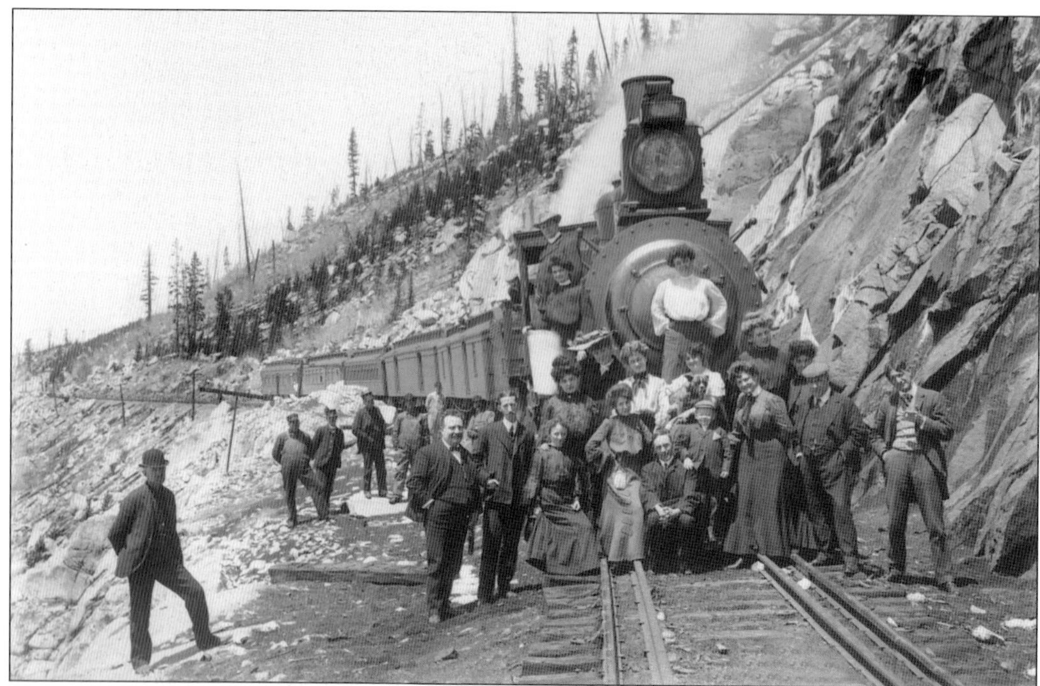

AN ACTRESS AND HER ENTOURAGE COMES TO TOWN. (c. May 10, 1904) Anna Held, said to be a temperamental performer, stands on the train in the center of the photograph with hands on hips. It is reported that Anna said to Ziegfeld, the famous showman, "Your American girls are so beautiful . . . the most beautiful girls in the world. If you could dress them up chic, you'd have a better show than the Folies-Bergére." (Courtesy the Colorado Historical Society.)

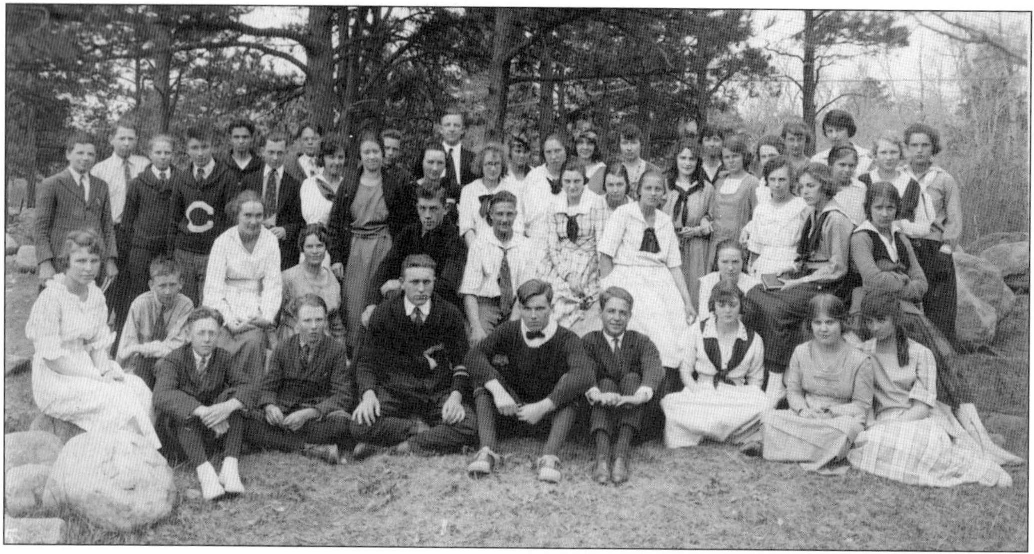

A SQUARE DANCE CALLER. (date unknown) Lloyd Shaw was the principal of the Cheyenne School from 1916–51, but he was also a famous square dance caller. He appeared as a square dance caller in the film *Duel in the Sun* starring Gregory Peck. Richard Marold, of the Cheyenne Mountain Heritage Center, said of Shaw, "He was a good and innovative teacher who encouraged his students to always do their best." (Courtesy the Cheyenne Mountain Heritage Center.)

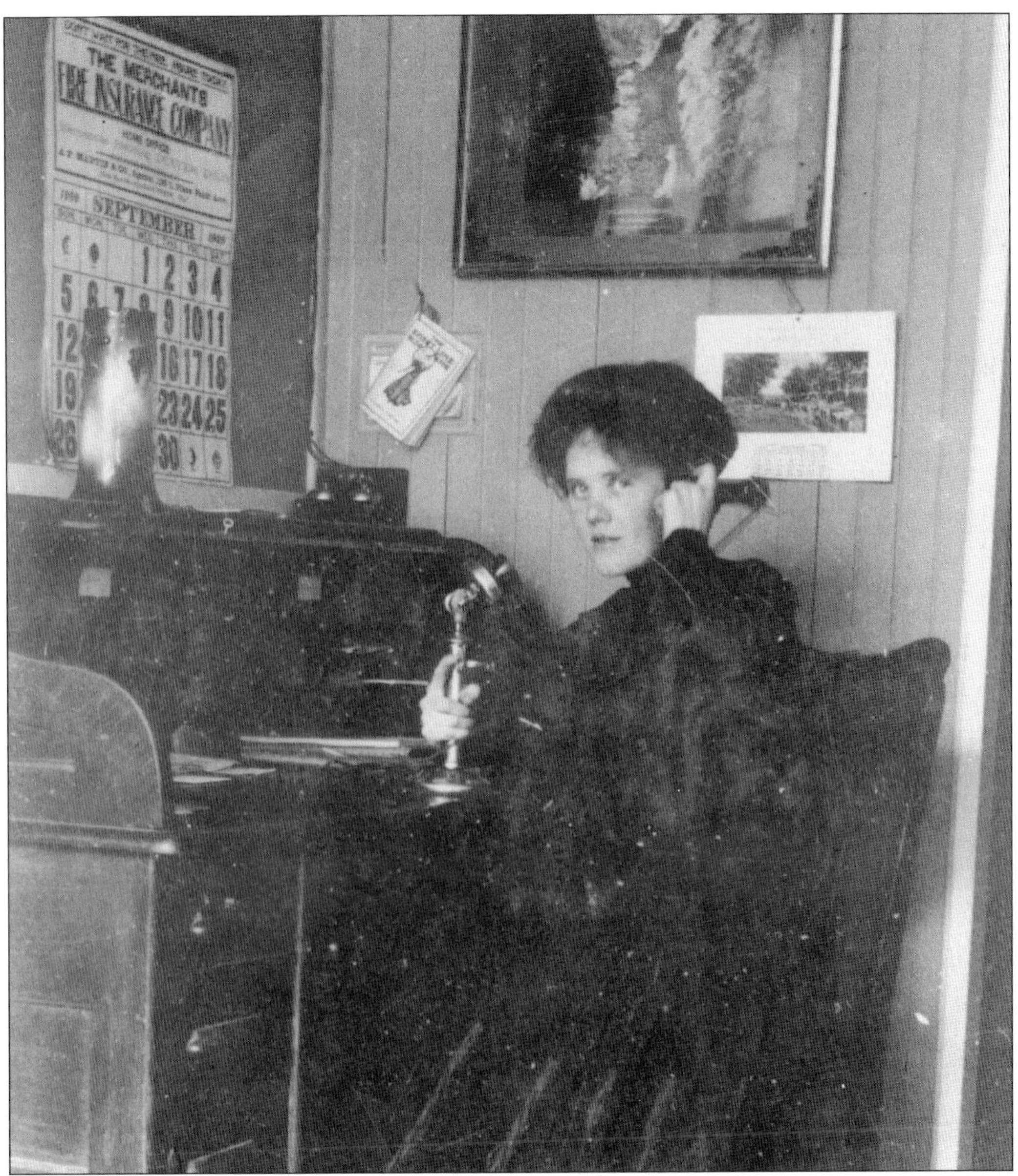

OPERATOR PLEASE! (*c.* 1909) The calendar behind Minnie Kratzer has the date identified as September 1909, and was issued by the Merchants Fire Assurance Company. During the years from 1880–1886, there was much skepticism about the telephone and it was not considered an essential item. However, as the population increased and technology improved, many people began to see the necessity and value the telephone brought to their everyday lives. People would ask each other, "Have you used a telephone yet?" After using the phone for the first time, a woman remarked, "Good gracious, it sounds just like one's conscience." Dr. and Mrs. Bell was one of the first families to take advantage of the telephone system. On frequent trips to Denver, Mrs. Bell would call her daughters and have them recite their prayers into the phone to be sure they were following the correct religious observances. Eventually, the old system was replaced with a new switchboard, costing $15,000, and three 400-wire cables that were installed underground. (Courtesy Pikes Peak Library District.)

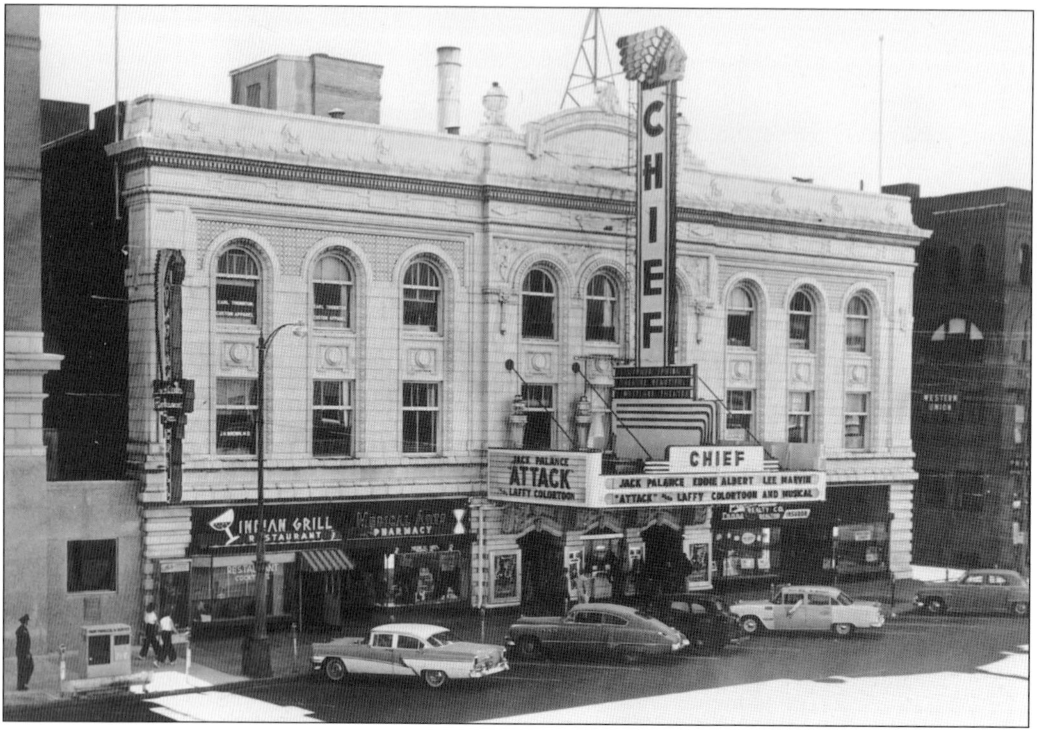

JACK PALANCE STARS AT THE CHIEF THEATRE. (*c.* 1956) The building was originally the Burns Theatre built in 1912. The exterior and interior were beautifully designed with decorative pillars, ornate ceiling, curtained box seats, and a Wurlitzer pipe organ that provided the sound for silent movies. Eventually the name changed to the Chief and movies such as *Attack* starring Jack Palance and *The Four Poster* with Rex Harrison and Lilli Palmer played during the 1950s. (Courtesy Colorado Springs Pioneer Museum.)

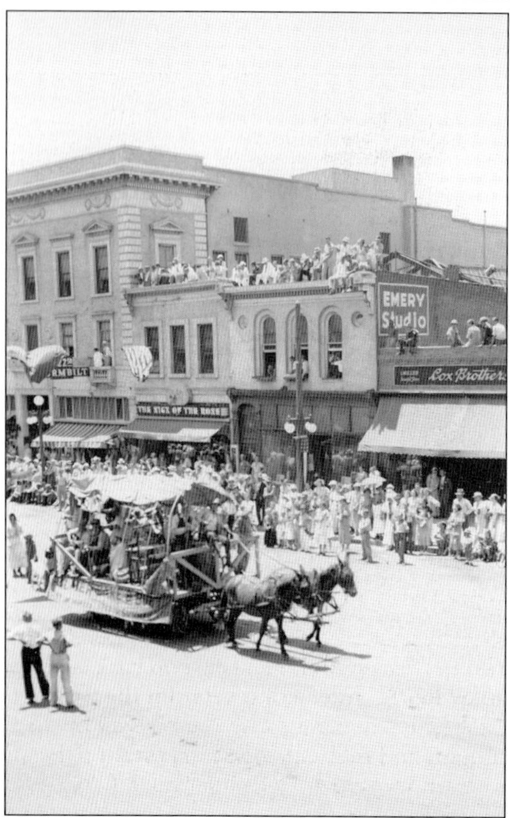

PALMER LAKE JOINS THE PARADE. (*c.* 1936) Palmer Lake sports their decorated entry as it is drawn by two horses in the Pikes Peak or Bust Rodeo Parade. Men, women, and children line the streets as well as watch from atop the buildings as the float walks by the Emery Photographic shop. The parade was the forerunner to the Pikes Peak or Bust Rodeo that began in 1937. (Courtesy the Palmer Lake Historical Society and Lucretia Vaile Museum.)

Six

Mind, Body, and Soul

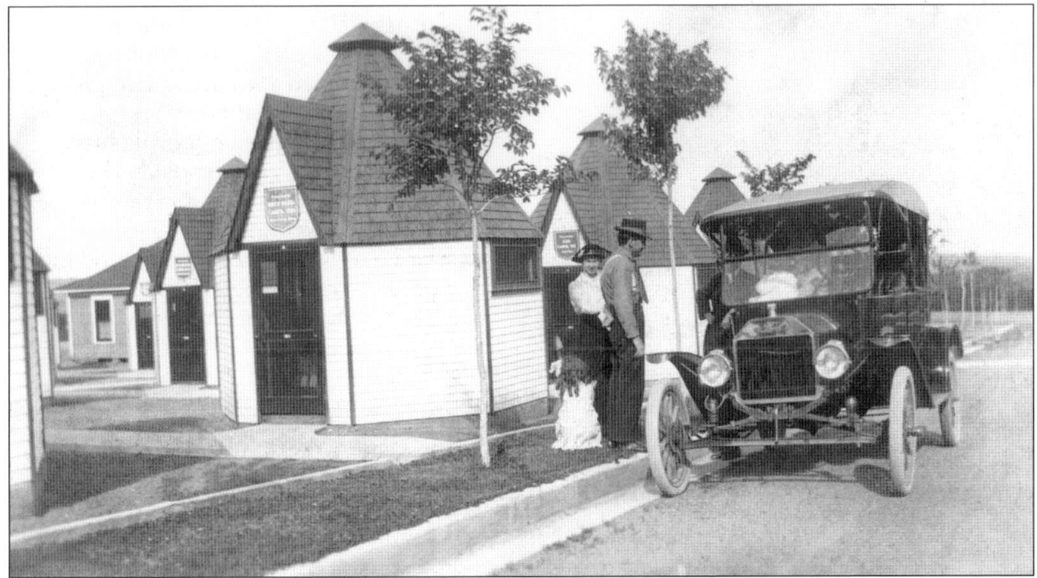

Visitors to Woodmen Sanitarium. (date unknown) The photo is identified on back as "Mr. and Mrs. Robert L. Gragg and Margaret (Mrs. Stanley Reid)." Interaction between the patients as well as with the visitors to the sanitariums was highly encouraged by the physicians who believed that besides a good diet, plenty of rest, sunlight, and fresh air, it was important to keep the patients' morale high. The octagonal "tents" were an invention by Dr. Gardiner. (Courtesy Pikes Peak Library District.)

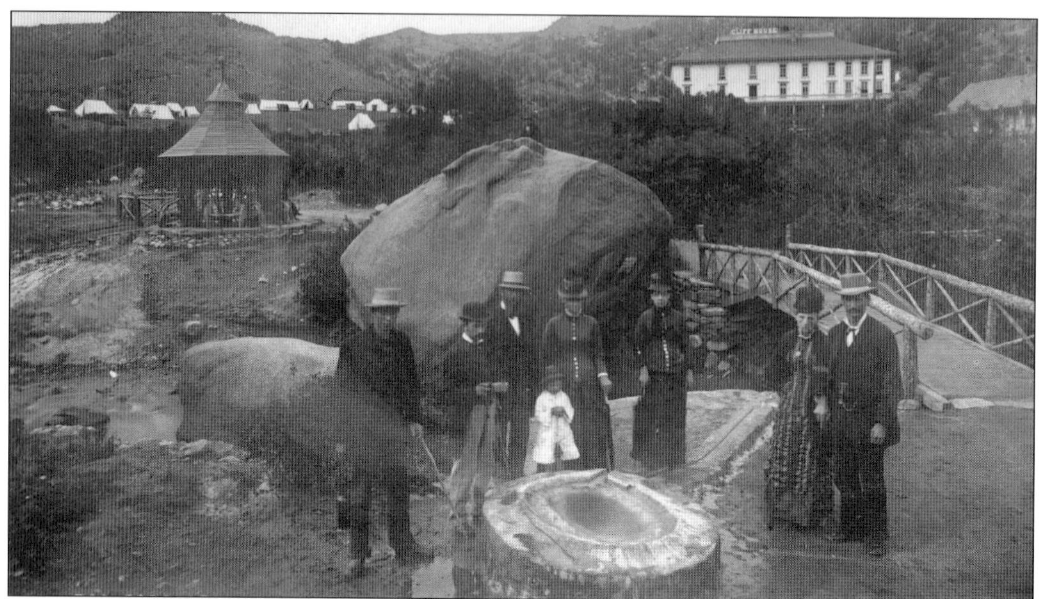

The Healing Powers of the Springs. (*c.* 1878–1880) A man sits atop the boulder that marks the confluence of Fountain and Ruxton Creeks. To the left we can see the conical roof of the Manitou Springs Gazebo, and on the right is Cliff House that boasted of having the capacity to accommodate 150 guests. The man at far left holds a bottle perhaps containing souvenir spring water. (Courtesy the Denver Public Library.)

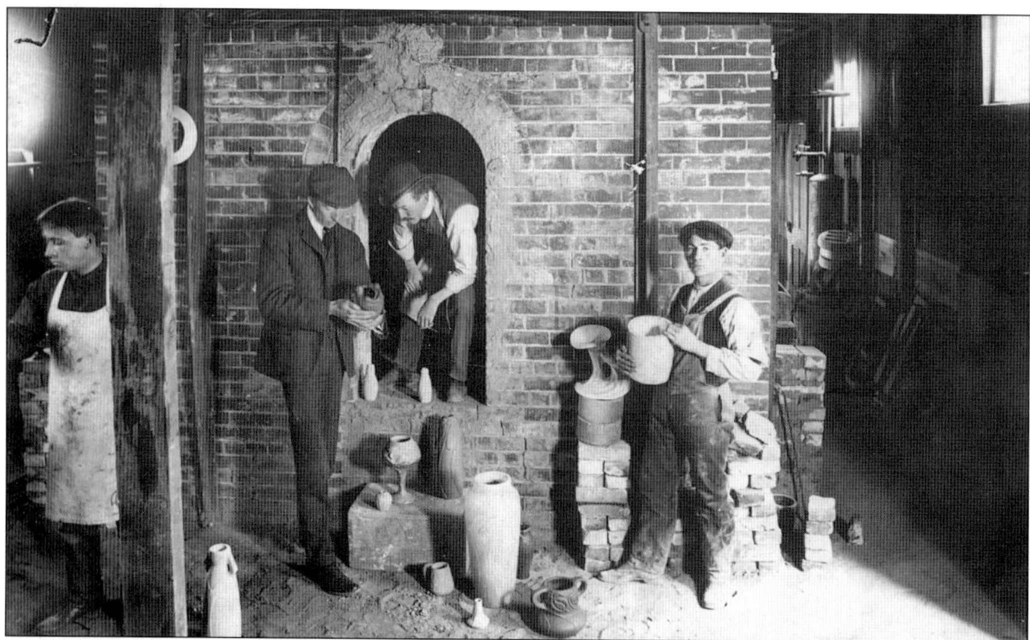

Artus Van Briggle Arrived in Colorado Springs Seeking a Cure. (*c.* 1902) In 1899, at 30 years of age, Artus arrived in Colorado Springs, suffering from an advanced stage of tuberculosis. He soon benefited from the climate, good food, and rest, and was able resume his work. He experimented with different clays, pigments, and glazes and his first kiln produced many of the most spectacular works of pottery ever created. (Courtesy the Denver Public Library.)

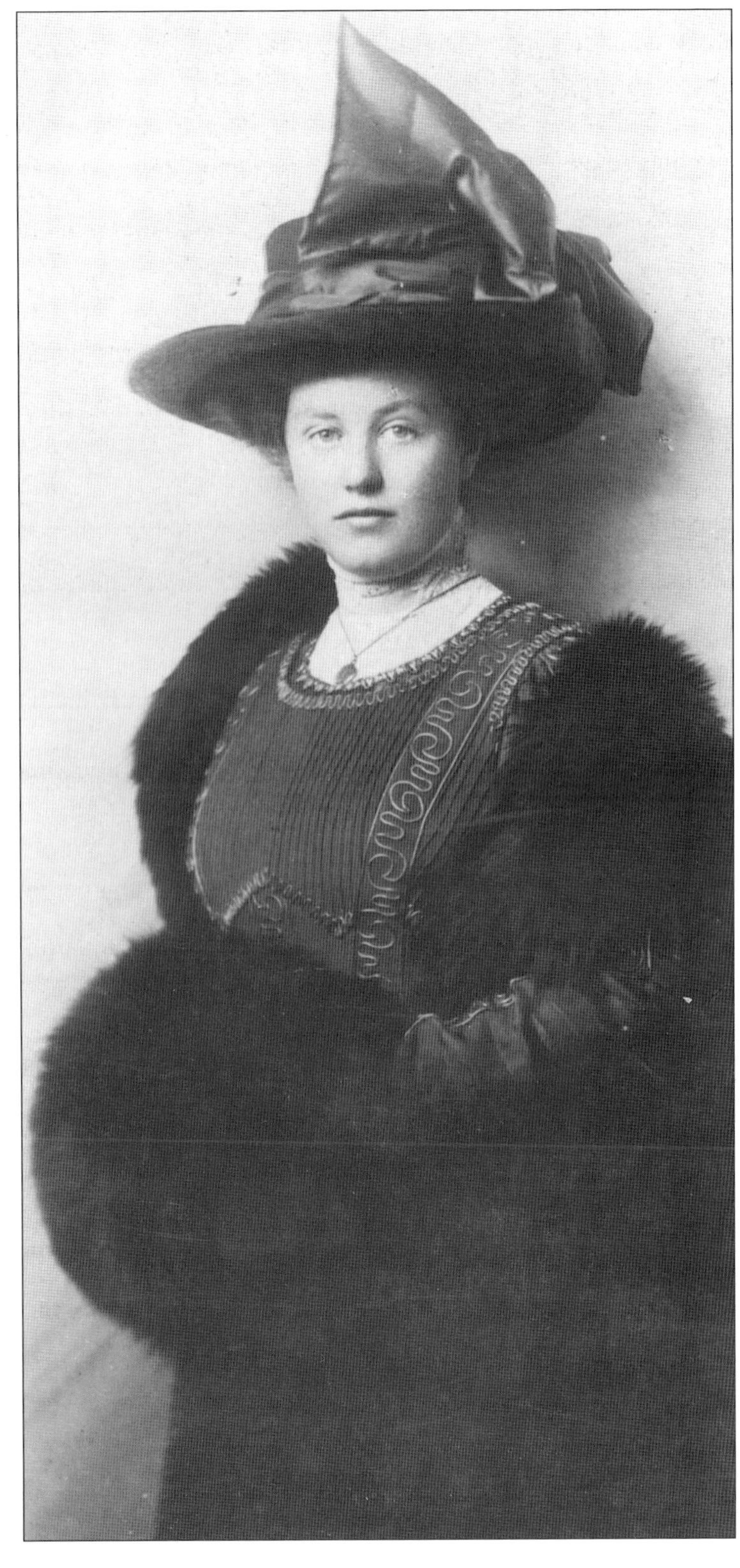

LAURA GILPIN—A WOMAN BEFORE HER TIME. (date unknown) Born in 1891, Laura Gilpin's interest in photography began when she received a Brownie camera for her 12th birthday in 1903, and then a developing tank from her parents at Christmas. When she was 14 she was brought to New York where her mother commissioned photographs taken by Gertrude Kasebier. This visit made an impression on young Laura, who later returned to New York to study at the Clarence H. White School. Her struggles with schoolwork were worsened by a double mastoid infection that sent her home to recuperate in Colorado Springs. After the setback, she continued her love of photography and eventually her work was exhibited nationally and then internationally. Some of her best pieces are photographs of the Pueblo and Navajo Indians, spectacular landscapes, and portraits. Manly Dayton Ormes mentioned in his book that Laura Gilpin was the first to establish her studio at the house of Mr. and Mrs. Spencer Penrose, who began an Art Society at their home on West Dale in October of 1919. (Courtesy Colorado Springs Pioneer Museum.)

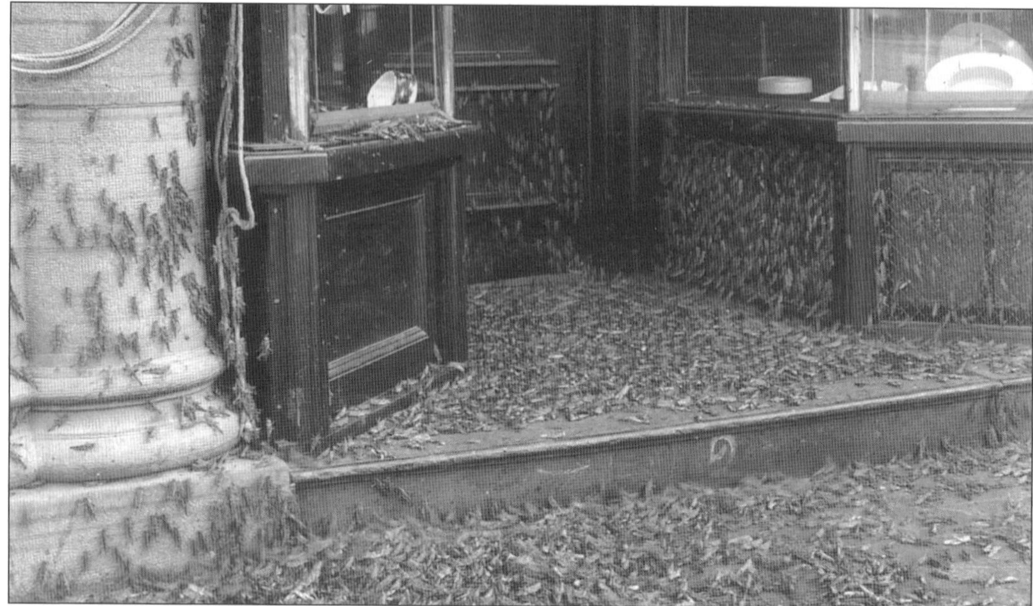

"They Came By the Millions" (c. 1899) The Grasshopper Plague of 1899 was nothing new; the insects came every year, only the number varied. A homesteader remembers: ". . . they would come in the evening about 5:00 or 6:00 and our family would take our tubs with sticks and start making a noise . . . they kind of turned and went around into the sagebrush . . . then, when it got dark, my father and brother would set light to the sagebrush . . . " (Courtesy Pikes Peak Library District.)

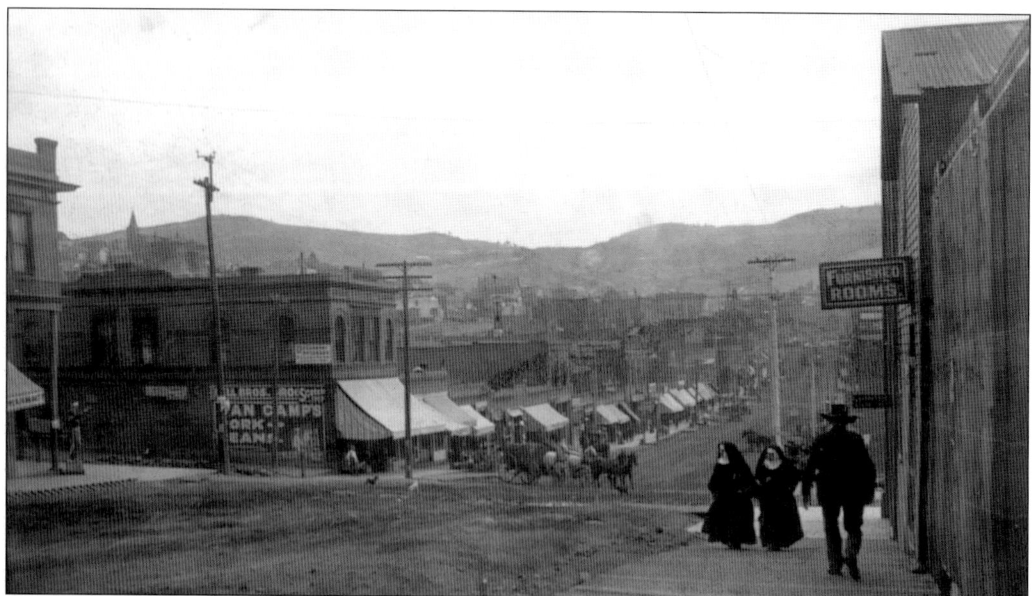

Two Nuns Go About Their Business. (date unknown) During the late 1880s, approximately one third of the residents of Cripple Creek were Irish Catholics who may (or may not) have needed the clergy's presence in the town. The nuns in the photograph appear strangely out of place on the boardwalk of Bennett Street. Two dogs rush down the street toward another that stands its ground next to a buggy and horses. (Courtesy the Colorado Historical Society.)

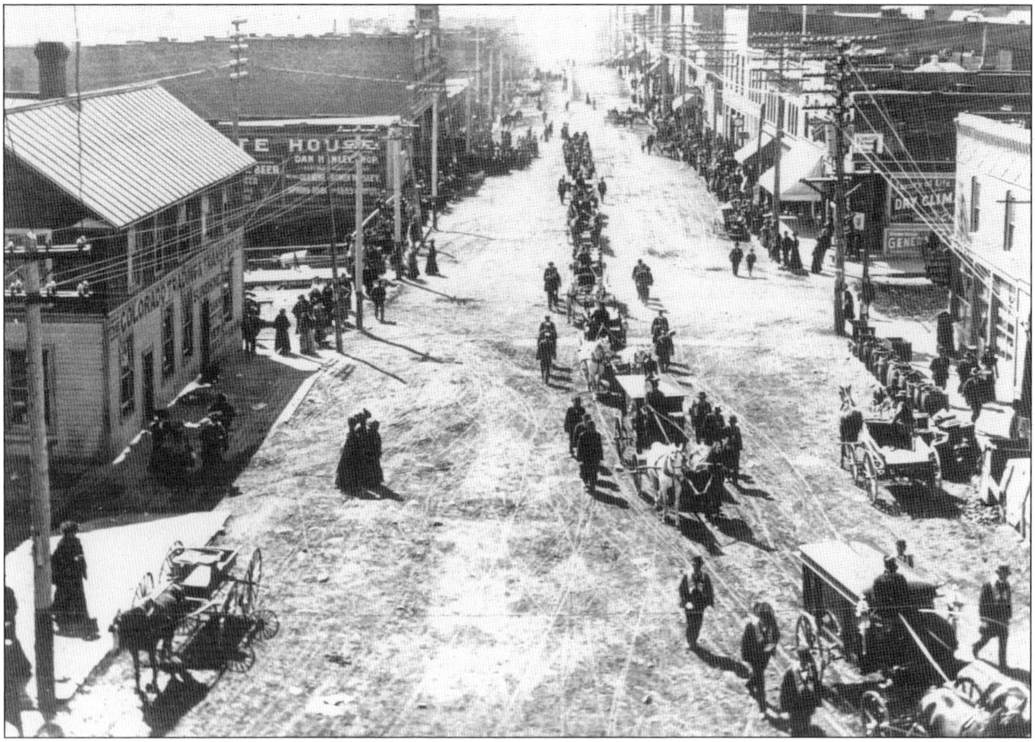

A SAD DAY IN CRIPPLE CREEK. (*c.* 1904) The horse-drawn hearses carry the strike victims' bodies down Bennett Avenue. A war of words in the press between the mine owners and the workers plunged them into a fully-fledged war that ended in death and destruction. Threats and intimidation turned otherwise law-abiding miners onto the streets of Cripple Creek in defense of their rights to be paid $3.00 for an eight-hour shift. (Courtesy Pikes Peak Library District.)

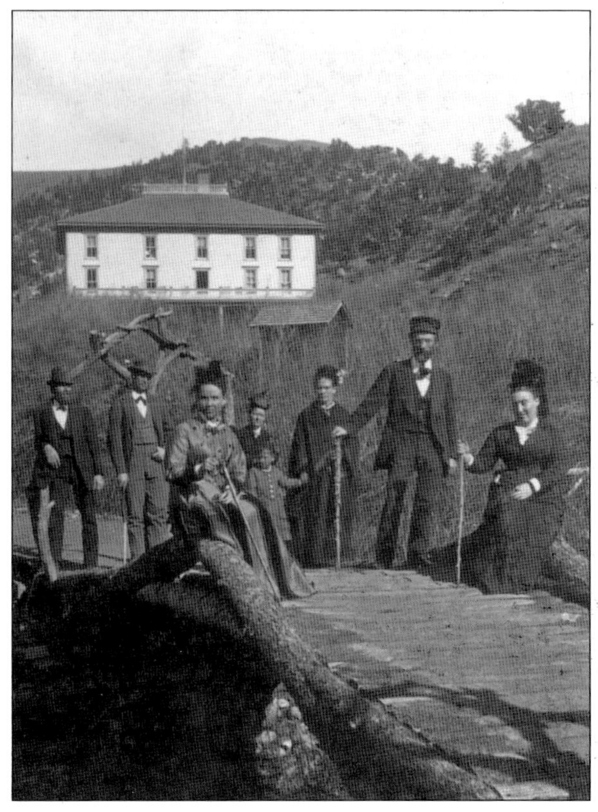

TAKING A HIKE AT MANITOU SPRINGS. (*c.* 1874–1879) A hike was a favorite pastime of tourists who visited Manitou Springs. The individuals have only a walking stick to assist them and are dressed in their normal clothes. The woman in the foreground is wearing a capote hat and wide velvet inserts in her skirt. The woman behind wears a long dark cloak as she holds the hand of a small child. (Courtesy the Denver Public Library.)

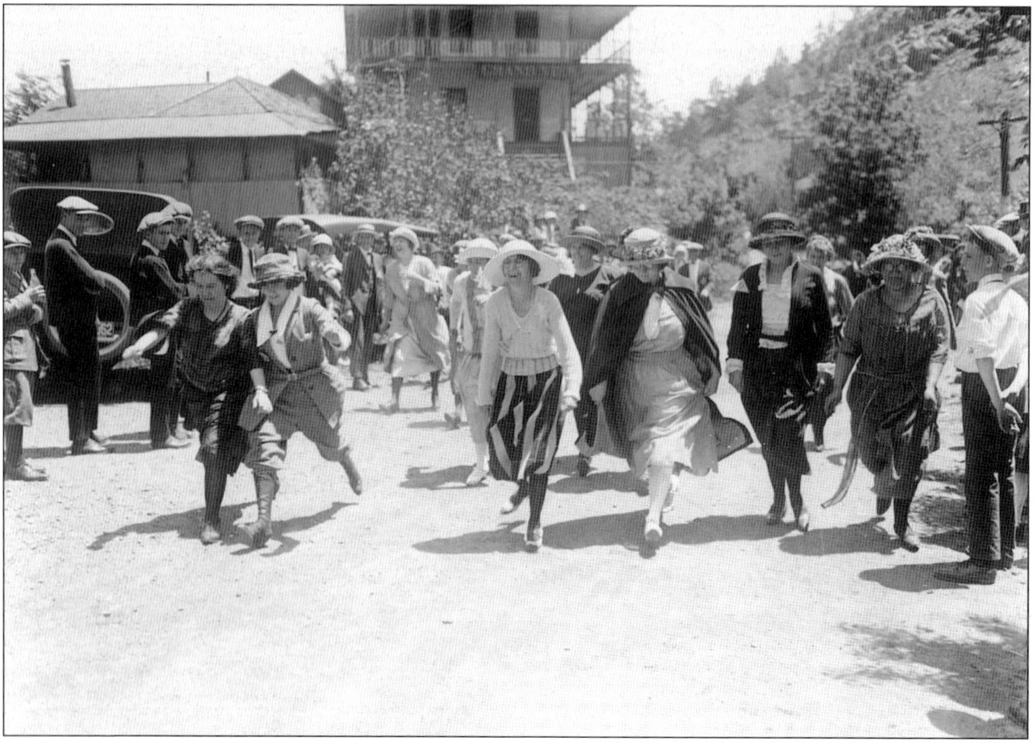

HIGH SPIRITS FROM THE LADIES DURING A RACE. (*c.* 1920–1930) Women take to their heels literally in this race in Manitou Springs, while men stand on the sidelines smiling. The woman second to left appears to be a serious competitor as she wears her trousers tucked into boots, but the woman far left jostles her in an attempt to keep up, or overtake. (Courtesy the Denver Public Library.)

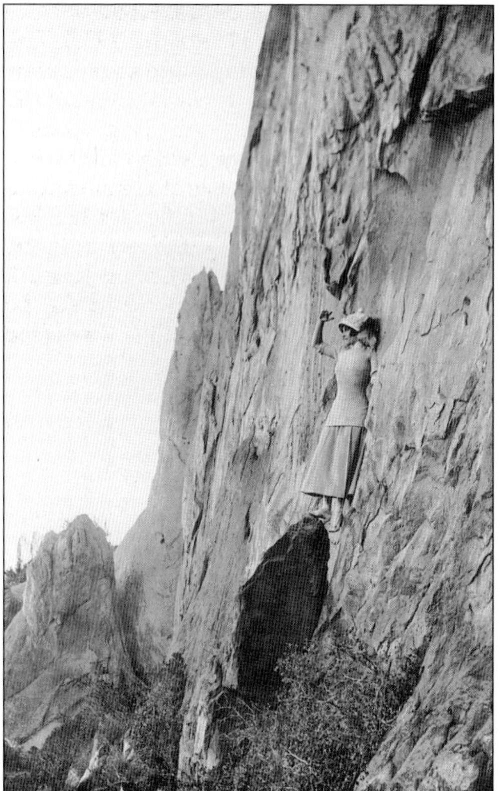

LAND AHOY! (*c.* 1910) A woman stands precariously on a rock at The Garden of the Gods. The garden was a favorite place for courting couples to have a Sunday afternoon picnic. Known for its beautiful and unusual rock formations called the Kissing Camels, Balanced Rock, and the Cathedral Spires, the garden was bequeathed by Charles Perkins to the City of Colorado for all visitors to enjoy free of charge. (Courtesy Colorado Springs Pioneer Museum.)

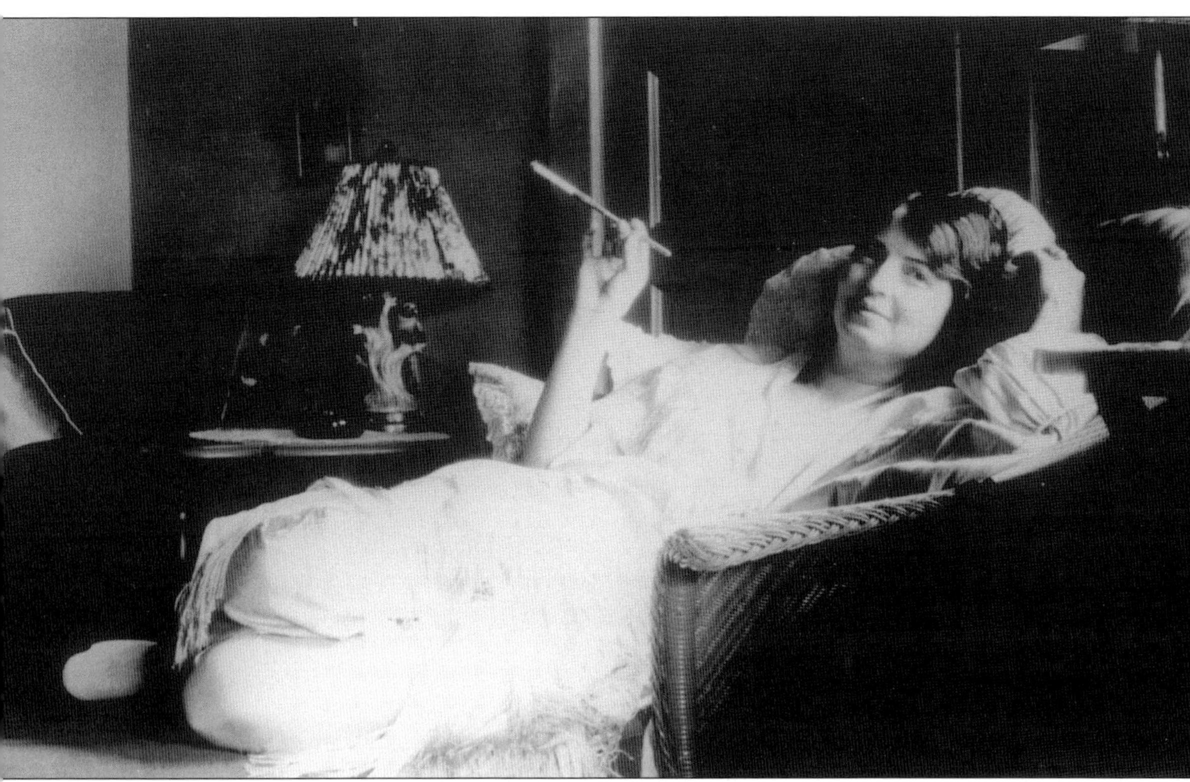

A Woman Reclines at Cragmore Sanitarium, Cigarette in Hand. (*c.* 1920) The unknown woman poses for the camera with cigarette in hand. The Springs were soon known as "Little London" because of the high influx of middle to wealthy Londoners who came to the town seeking a respite from the gloomy, smog-filled air of London. It was not only the clean fresh air of the Rocky Mountains they sought but also healthy food and plenty of rest and relaxation. Dr. Solly, an English physician, proposed an ambitious plan to the Chamber of Commerce in Colorado Springs to provide two sanitariums, one for the wealthy, and another for the less fortunate. General Palmer donated 100 acres of land and contributed $50,000 towards the venture that would be eventually became the Cragmore Sanitarium. It was opened on June 20, 1905, but was short-lived as Dr. Solly died late in 1906, and the sanitarium was closed. At the request of General Palmer, Drs. Gardiner and Hoagland assumed the responsibility of running the sanitarium and it resumed service. (Courtesy Pikes Peak Library District.)

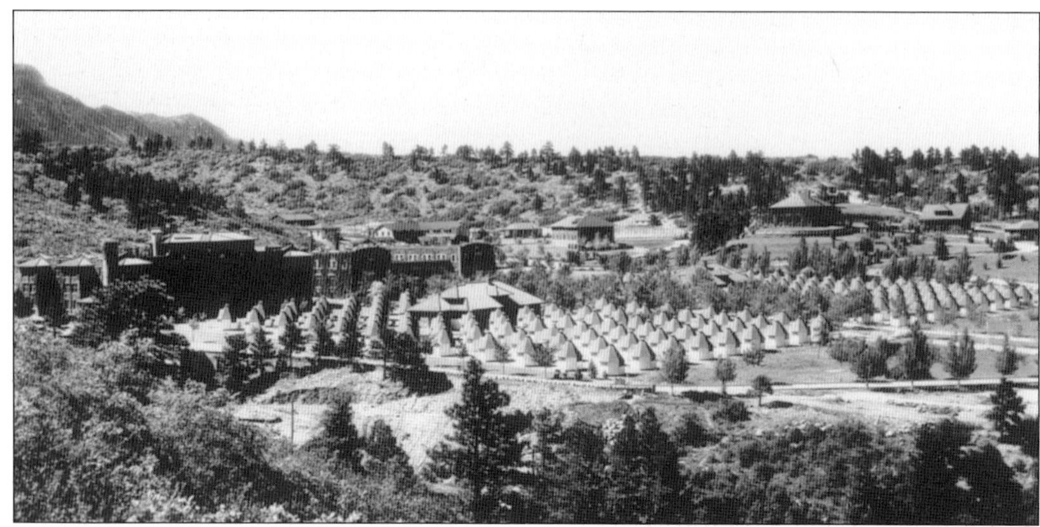

ACCOMMODATION FOR "WEALTHY LUNGERS." (*c.* 1920) It has been known as the White Plague, consumption, and tuberculosis. As word spread of the successful treatment found in Colorado, people came by the thousands and the sanitariums became full. Erecting small, individual, heavy, canvas tents provided emergency accommodation at approximately $7.00 a week, but later small octagonal wooden buildings were built for the patients who stayed an average of three to five months. (Courtesy Pikes Peak Library District.)

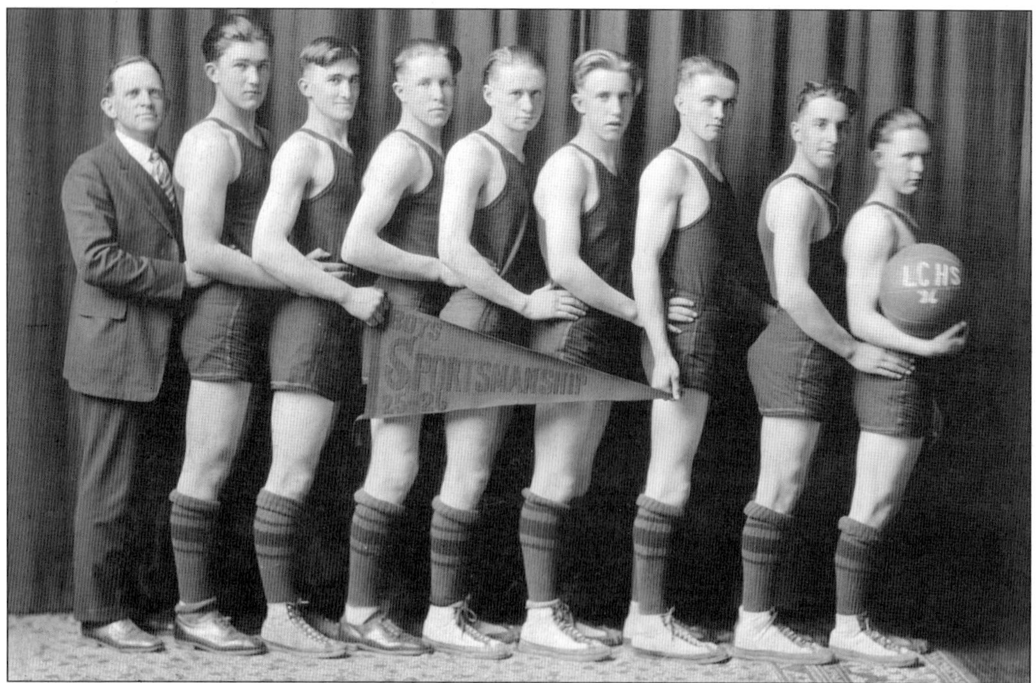

MONUMENT'S BASKETBALL TEAM. (*c.* 1926) Members of the Lewis Consolidated High School basketball team are, from left to right, Mr. N.J. Rice, Frank Barnhart, Russell Hagen, Gregory Dwyer, Byron Medlock, Wilbur Bovard, Bert Gossage, Paul Losey, and John Burnhart. Fifth from left, Byron Medlock would later become mayor of Palmer Lake. (Courtesy the Palmer Lake Historical Society and Lucretia Vaile Museum.)

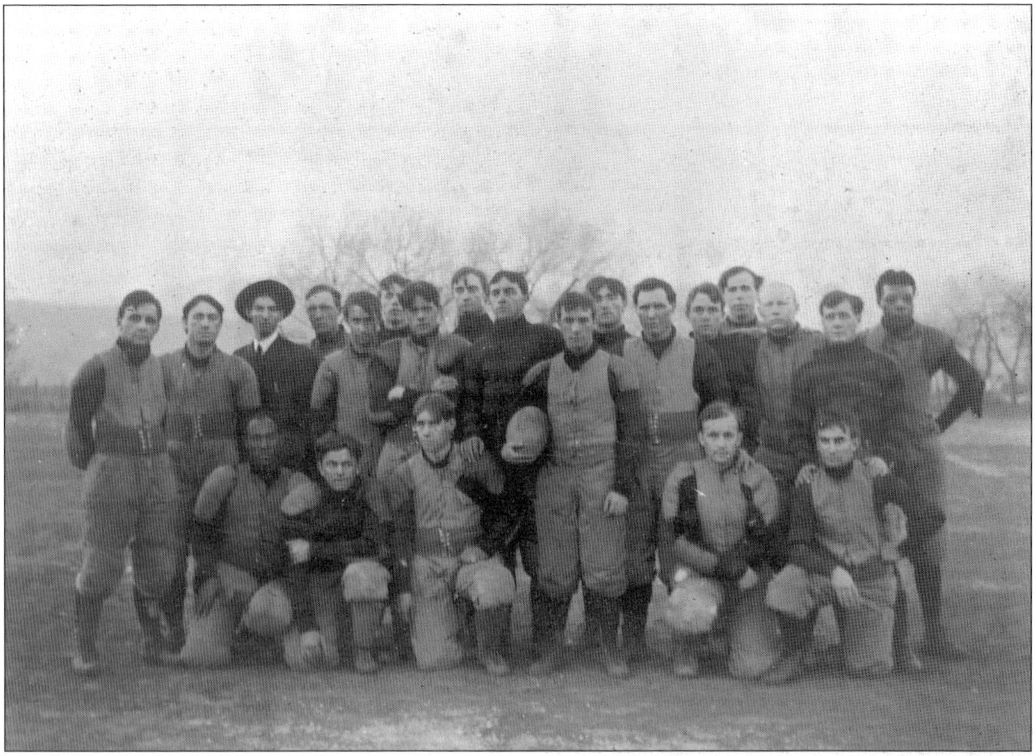

Enough for a Team. (*c.* 1904) This early photograph of the Colorado College football team, the Tigers, shows 21 men, 2 of whom are African Americans—Frederick Roberts kneeling at left, and Jackson, who is standing far right. In 1905, the team arrived in Boulder for a game, but the hotel would not allow Roberts and Jackson accommodation. Instead, the coach collected his team and traveled to Denver where they found suitable rooms. (Courtesy Special Collections, Colorado College.)

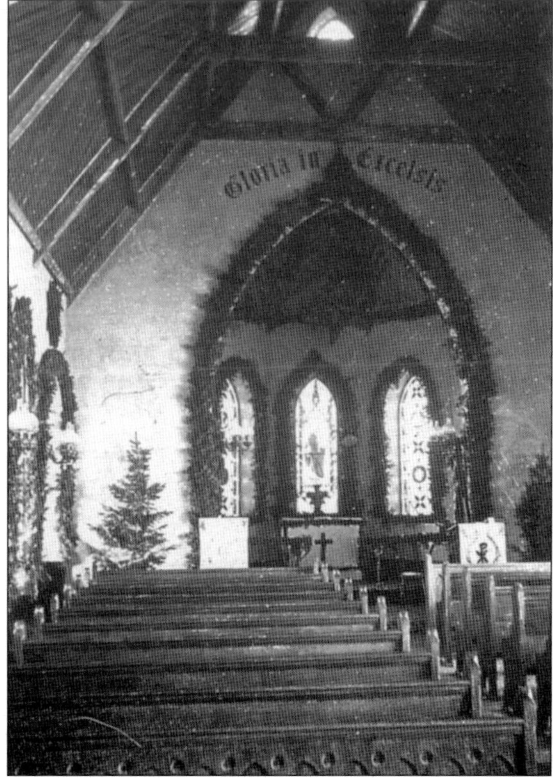

Grace Episcopal Church. (date unknown) General Palmer dedicated a cornerstone to the church and it was laid on the southwest corner in July 1873. In October of the same year, the name was changed from Colorado Springs Episcopal to Grace Church Parish. Two rectors from Grace Church have been made Bishops: Reverends Frank H. Touret and Benjamin Brewster. (Courtesy Special Collections, Colorado College.)

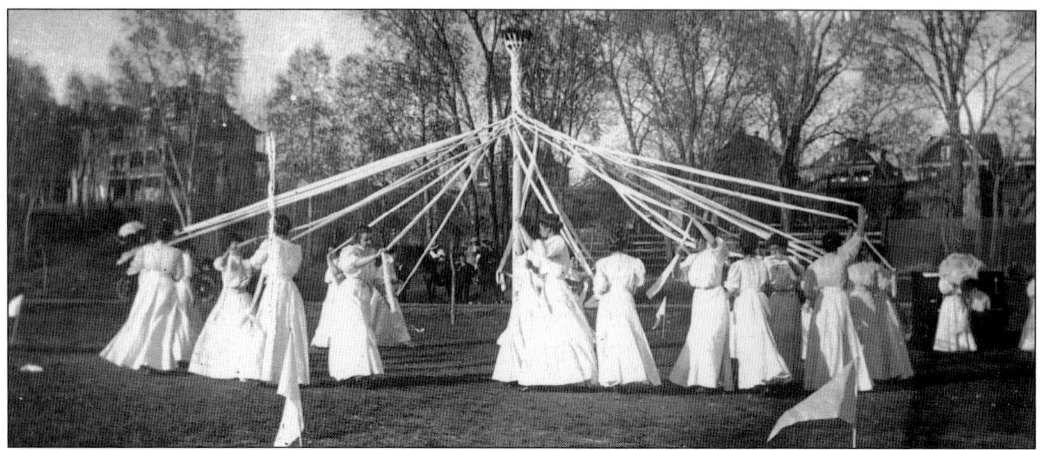

THE COLORADO COLLEGE LADIES DANCE THE MAYPOLE. (*c.* 1908) The May-Pole ceremony appears no different from ancient times when each lady took a ribbon and they swooped over and under each other, and in doing so, made a design on the May-Pole. Traditionally, the dance finished when all the ribbons had been used and the pole completely covered. At the finish, one maiden would be chosen as the May Queen. (Courtesy Special Collections, Colorado College.)

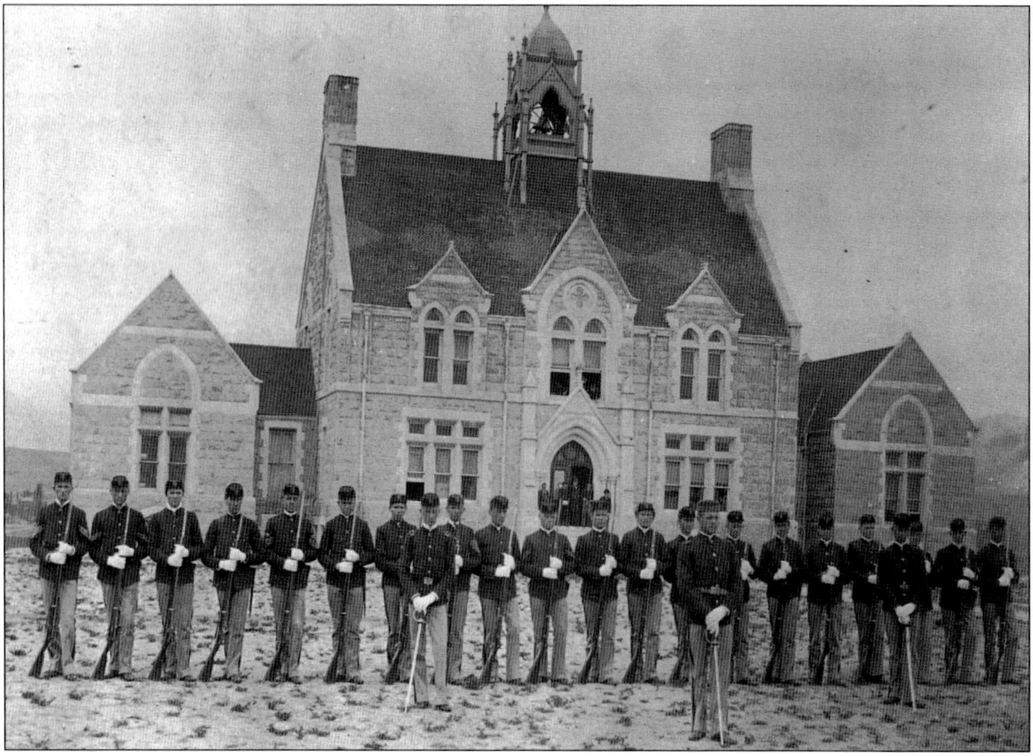

DRILL TEAM IN FRONT OF CUTLER HALL. (*c.* 1891) The Colorado Collegian magazine describes the Colorado College Drill Team as they prepare for the competitive drill. "Capt. Hayley began by giving the familiar orders, and no catch commands until the members had settled down to confidence . . . then increased the commands to ones more difficult . . . they all went down with one exception and that was private W.H. Hartshorn. Thus closed one pleasant drill for the military company. . . . " (Courtesy Special Collections, Colorado College.)

A NEW SCHOOL FOR THE DEAF AND BLIND. (date unknown) Lon Chaney, the famous silent-screen star, born in Colorado Springs on April 1, 1883, was the son of deaf and mute parents. It is believed his observance of his parents' daily lives helped him convey his actions in pantomime. Chaney's grandparents, J.R. and Emma Kennedy, had four hearing-impaired children and believed a school should be provided for their special care. They were instrumental in the appropriation of funds to build the first school for the deaf in Colorado Springs. (Courtesy Special Collections, Colorado College.)

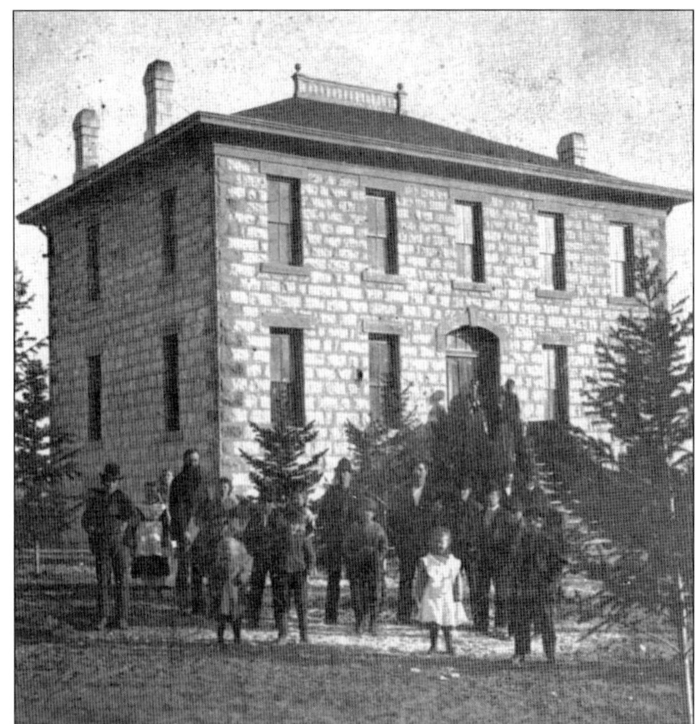

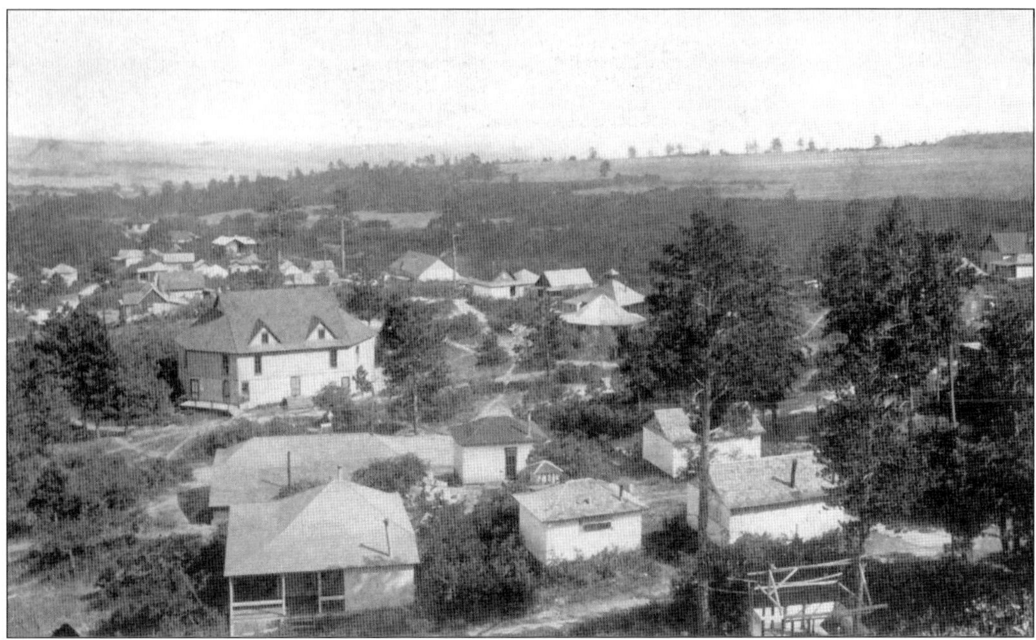

THE ROCKY MOUNTAIN CHAUTAUQUA. (*c.* 1887–1910) Glen Park at Palmer Lake hosted the Rocky Mountain Chautauqua Assembly for the first time in 1887. The origin of the Chautauqua began as a spiritual retreat lasting a few days, but developed into a six-week course including Bible study, botanical and bird study, painting, golf, tennis, and the arts. Accommodation ranged from "House Tents" to "rustic cottages." Room and board cost only $8.50. (Courtesy the Palmer Lake Historical Society and Lucretia Vaile Museum.)

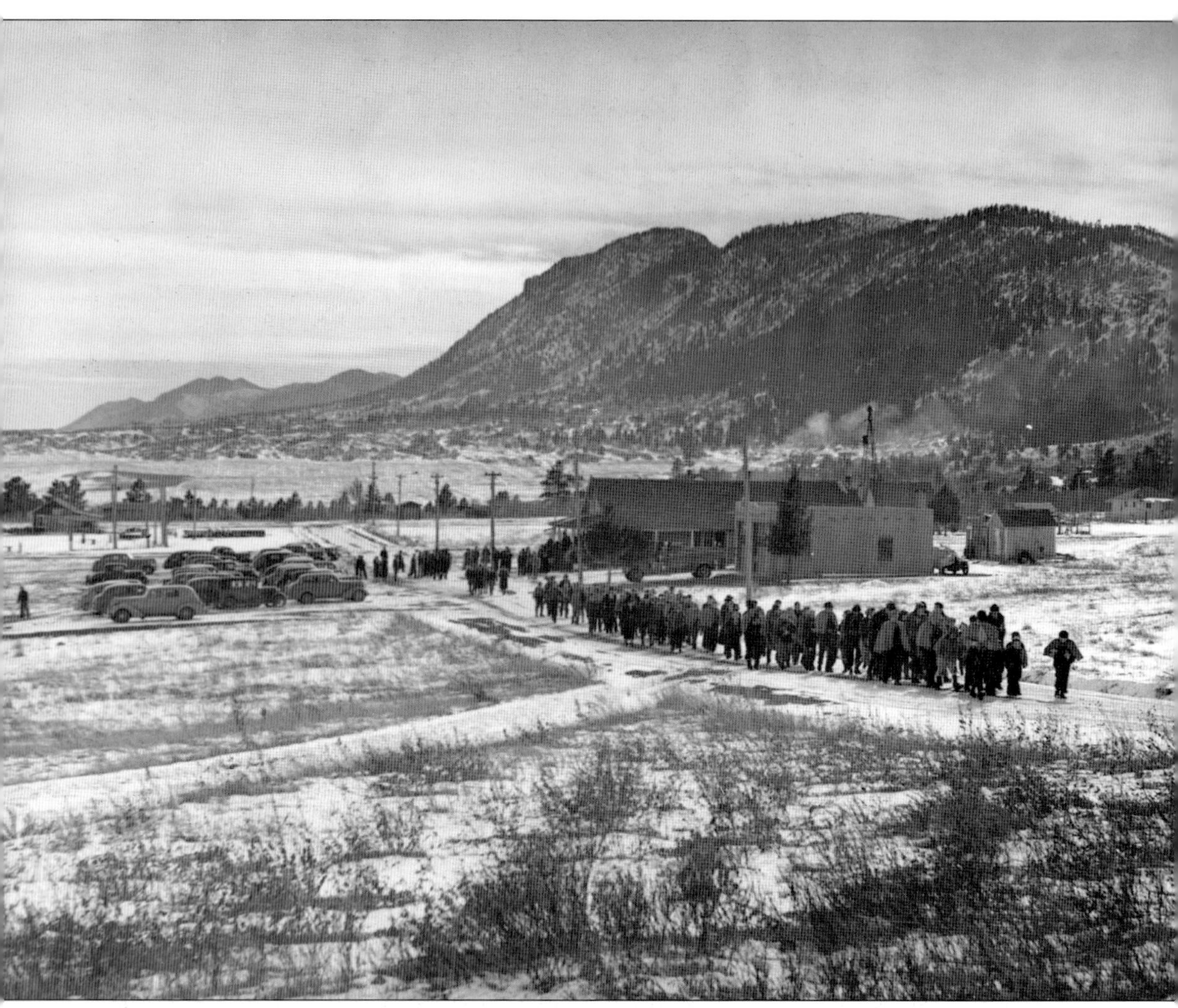

Palmer Lake Yule Log Ceremony. (*c.* 1953) The first celebration of the Yule Log Ceremony began in 1934 and was held in the Charley Orr-Dr. E.M. Spauling home. The custom of choosing and burning a Yule Log on Christmas Eve began around the 12th century and originated in Europe, most likely in Italy where the custom is called a *ceppo*. Traditionally, girls of a family would collect splinters from the burned log and use these as kindling for the following year's celebration. They believed this action protected their home from lightning and would generally bring good luck to the family. In Palmer Lake, the ritual is usually carried out on the Sunday before Christmas but the ceremony is much the same. The hunters, draped in green and red capes, go into the surrounding forest and search for the "Yule Log," previously hidden and marked with a red ribbon. Once the log is found, the hunters pull the lucky finder astride the log back to the Town Hall. The log is cut in half with one piece placed on a blazing fire and the other kept for starting the next year's ceremonial fire. (Courtesy the Palmer Lake Historical Society and Lucretia Vaile Museum.)

Seven

TRANSPORTATION—FROM MULE TO AUTOMOBILE

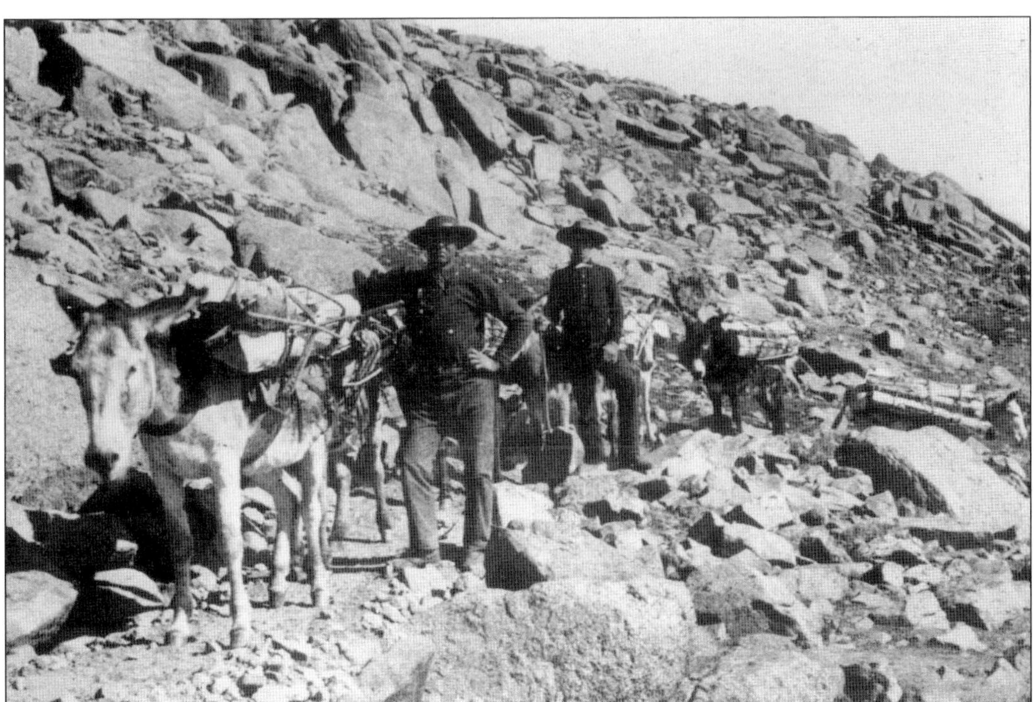

SECONDARY BUSINESSES SPRANG UP AS THE RAILROAD ADVANCED. (*c.* 1885) Hauling wood for the signal stations was only one of many businesses that developed because of the railroad. Two men, identified as John Palsgrove and Frederick Hill Meserve, take a moment to pose for a photograph as they make their precarious journey packing wood to the U.S. Signal Station. (Courtesy Pikes Peak Library District.)

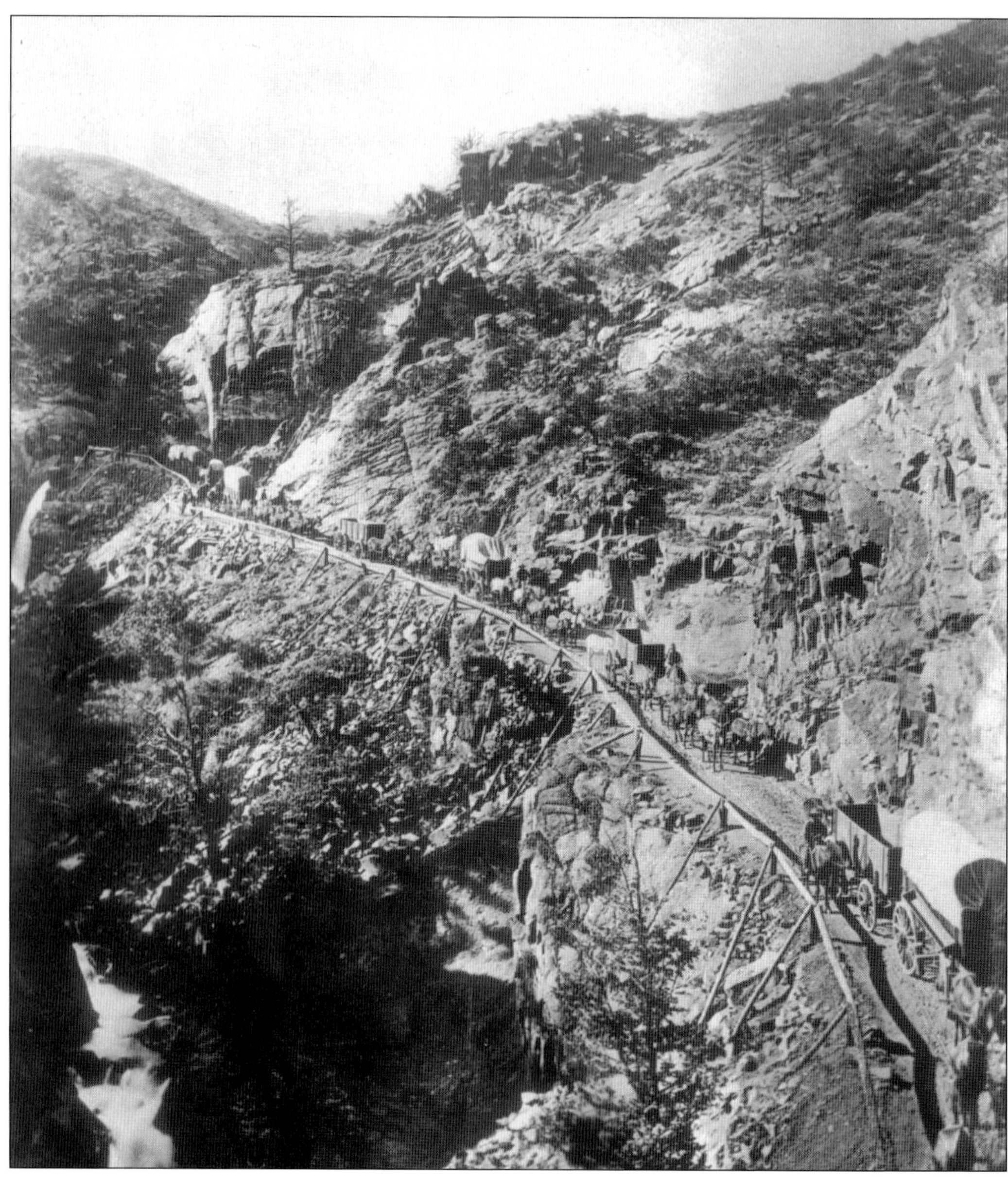

ONE WAY SYSTEM ON UTE PASS. (date unknown) The trail over Ute Pass was so narrow, travelers devised a way of keeping the traffic flowing without causing congestion on the highly traveled route. The remedy was simple: up the mountain during morning hours and down during the afternoon. This provided an orderly method of travel that appeared to be acceptable to most travelers since the road was too narrow for freight wagons to pass. Maintenance of the pass was a particularly dangerous job. Men used felled trees to brace the road and guardrails placed on rocks to insure maximum protection from erosion. The teams of horses wore blinkers to avoid them seeing their precarious situation. In 1912, the Ute Indians were allowed to return from their reservations in Utah and attend a ceremony officially recognizing the Ute Pass Indian Trail. Buckskin Charlie, his braves, and some women from the tribe helped set out the proper location of markings depicting the beginning and end of the trail. (Courtesy the Denver Public Library.)

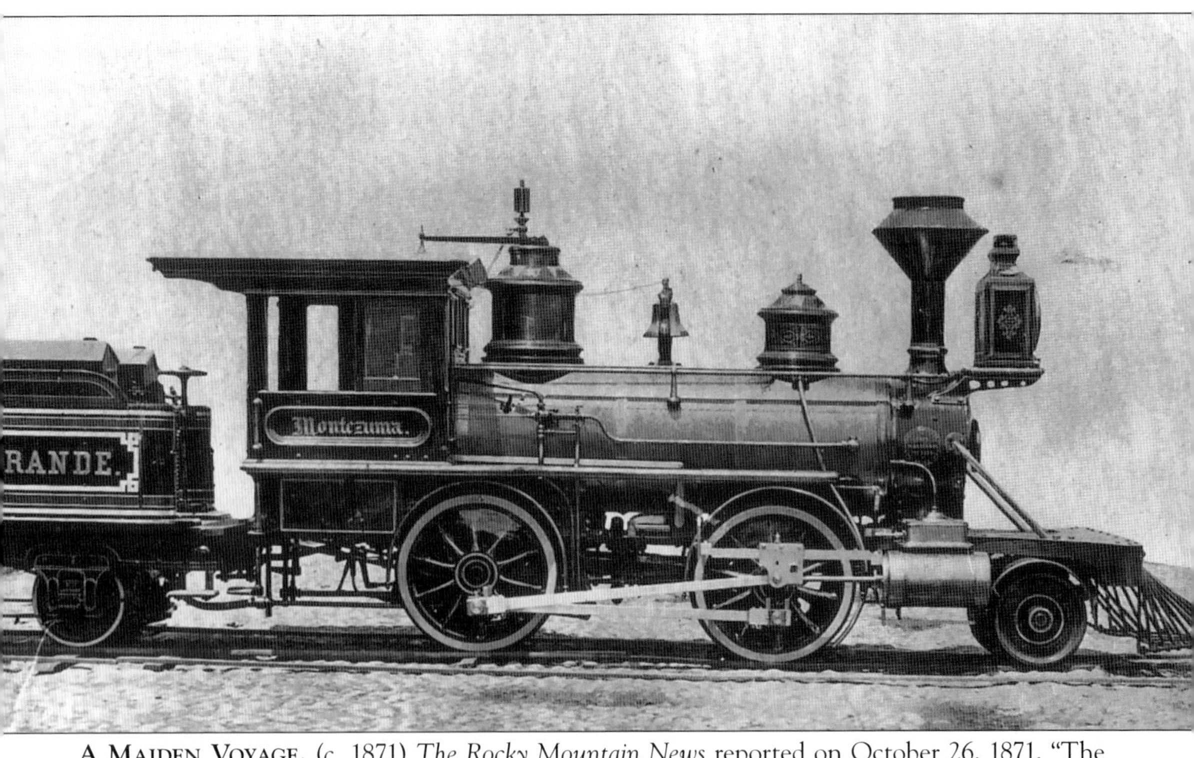

A Maiden Voyage. (*c.* 1871) *The Rocky Mountain News* reported on October 26, 1871, "The train was composed of a baggage and smoking car and two elegant passenger coaches, Denver the name of one and El Paso the other, drawn by the engine Montezuma. The train left Denver at 8:00 this morning. A pleasant run was made to the terminus of the road at Colorado Springs on regular time, all the guests enjoying the magnificent scenery along the line and being highly pleased with the excellent manner in which the road had been constructed . . . arriving at Colorado Springs at 1:00 o'clock, the excursionists were joined by General W.J. Palmer, the distinguished President of the Denver & Rio Grande Railway, and Ex Governor A.C. Hunt, and sat down to a splendid dinner . . . [A]fter dinner, carriages were provided and under lead of General Palmer the party drove over the new town site of Colorado Springs up to the valley of Monument Creek, across to Colorado City, through the Garden of the Gods and up the Fountaine-Qui-Bouille to Villa La Font where the party rested for the night. . . . " (Courtesy Special Collections, Colorado College.)

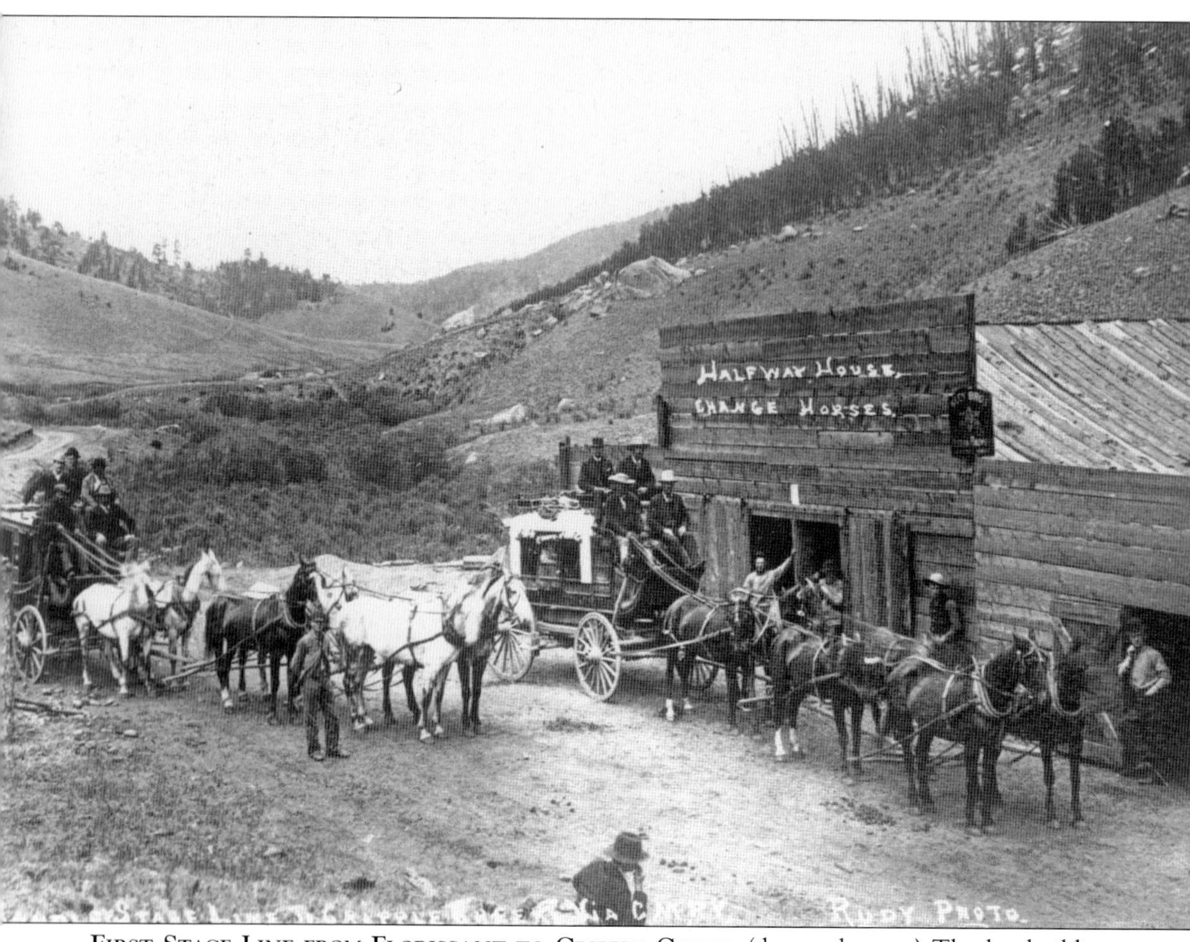

FIRST STAGE LINE FROM FLORISSANT TO CRIPPLE CREEK. (date unknown) The log building has a sign painted on the front stating "Halfway House, Change Horses." Rose Kingsley remarks of watching the stagecoach, "It is a sight I am never tired of watching: the coach with its four splendid bays standing in front of the office . . . the "messenger" stowing his mail-bags safely away; the passengers bundling in for a period of misery of varying length. When all is ready, and not till then, out walks the great man, in yellow coat, and hat securely tied down with a great comforter. He mounts the box, arranges himself leisurely; the messenger in beside him, wrapped in buffalo robes; then the reins are put in his hand, and as he tightens them, away go the horse with a rush that takes one's breath away. The Western stage-driver, on his box, with the "lines," as they call the reins, in his hand, is inferior to one in the Republic. Even the President, when he is on board, must submit to his higher authority." (Courtesy Pikes Peak Library District.)

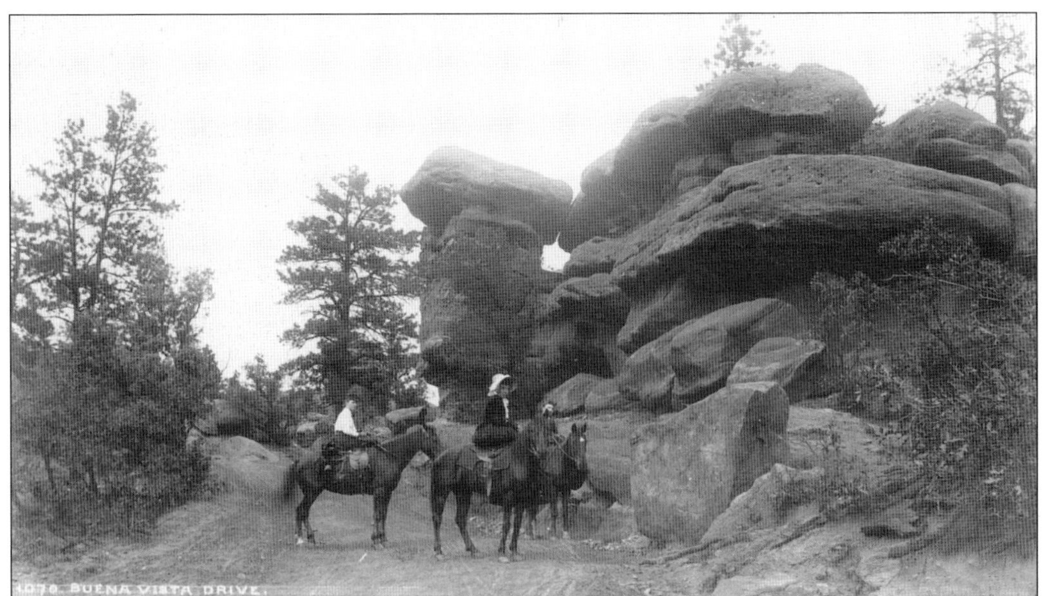

SIDE SADDLE ON BUENA VISTA DRIVE. (*c.* 1882–1900) Three women sit sidesaddle as they explore the Garden of the Gods by horseback. One wears a large sunbonnet, another a cap-like hat, and the third appears not to wear a hat at all. (Courtesy the Denver Public Library.)

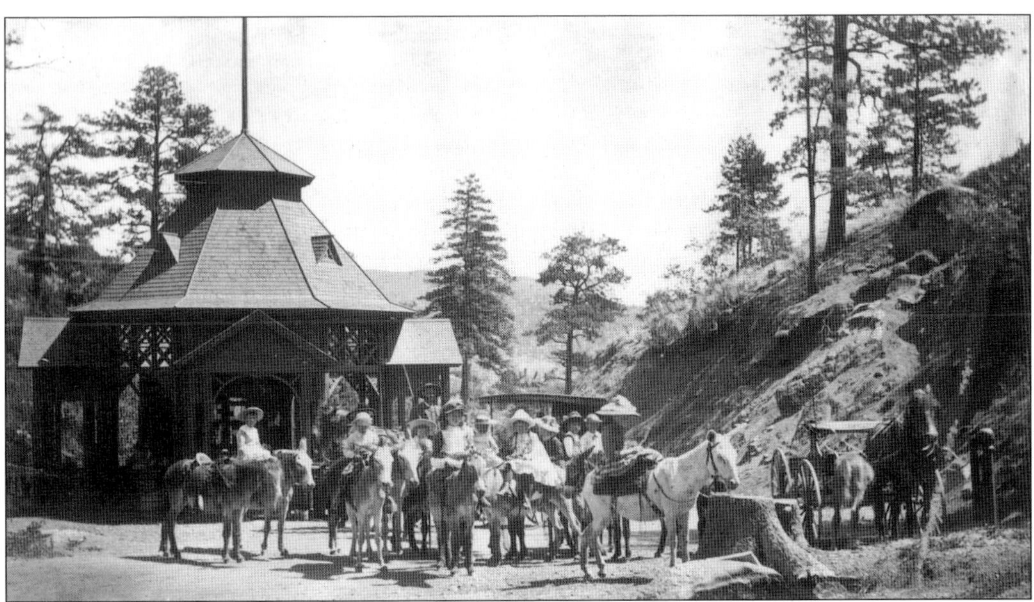

HEAD 'EM UP—MOVE 'EM OUT. (*c.* 1882–1900) Ten boys and girls head for a ride in the hills on their donkeys. They depart from the Ute Iron Spring Chateau in Manitou Springs that is seen in the rear of the photograph. A man in the rear who holds a long stick over his shoulder accompanies them. (Courtesy the Denver Public Library.)

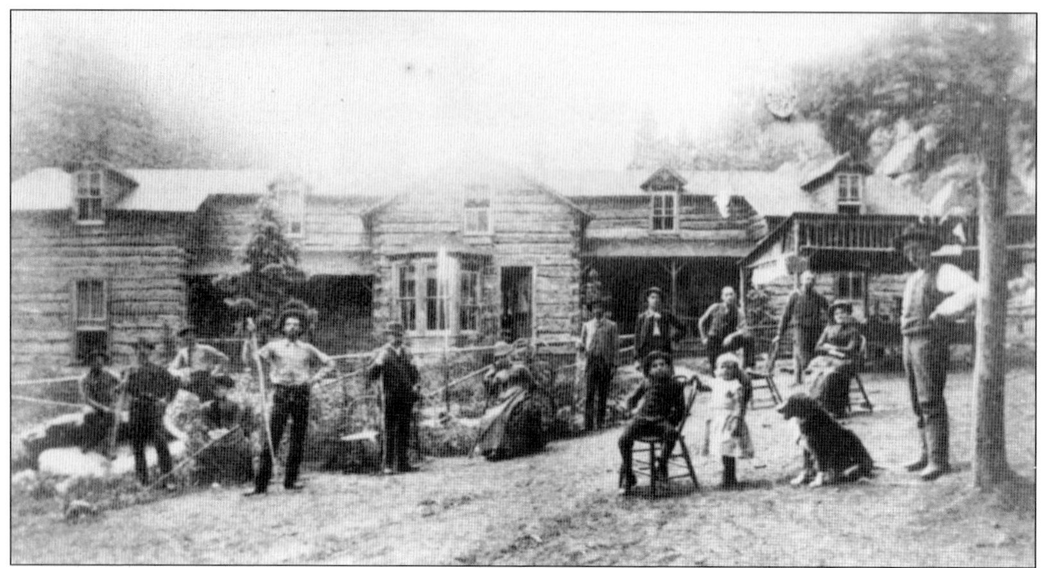

Pikes Peak Halfway House. (*c.* 1888) Despite its name, the house sits approximately one third of the distance from the summit. In 1884, the Palsgrove family owned about 640 acres and built a comfortable home for the family. Mary Palsgrove Hoe later said in her memoirs that when the cog railway came, it spoiled much of the natural beauty of Pikes Peak and the sheep, bears, and mountain lions seemed to disappear. (Courtesy Colorado Springs Pioneer Museum.)

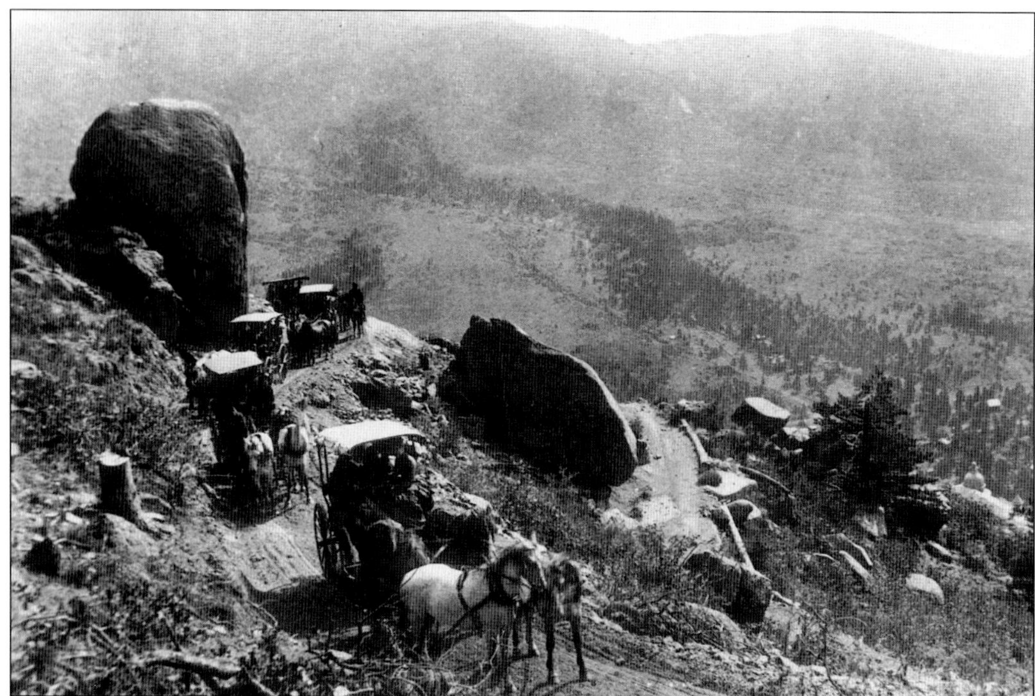

The Carriage Road to Pikes Peak. (*c.* 1890) Five carriages stop to pose for the cameraman as they work their way on the narrow shelf to the top of Pikes Peak. Each carriage has a team of four horses whose owners prescribe blinkers to protect the animals from seeing their precarious route. (Courtesy Colorado Springs Pioneer Museum.)

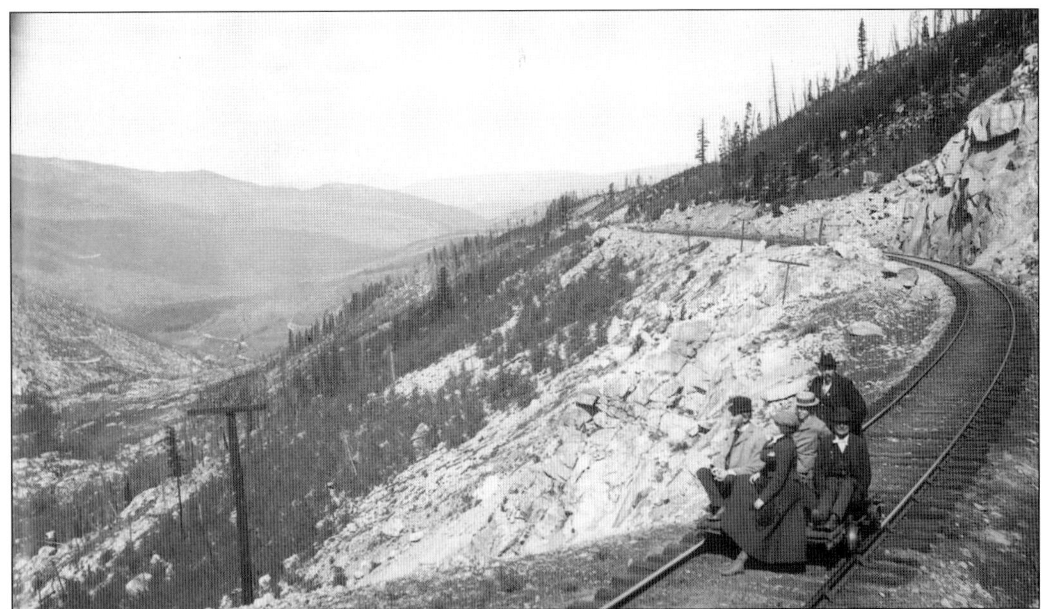

A Spectacular View Across the Valley. (*c.* 1890–1910) The group takes a moment to appreciate a wonderful valley in Teller County from a handcar on the Colorado Springs and Cripple Creek Railway. The day appears to be overcast and perhaps a bit cold, but the little group seem to be dressed in appropriate clothing. (Courtesy the Colorado Historical Society.)

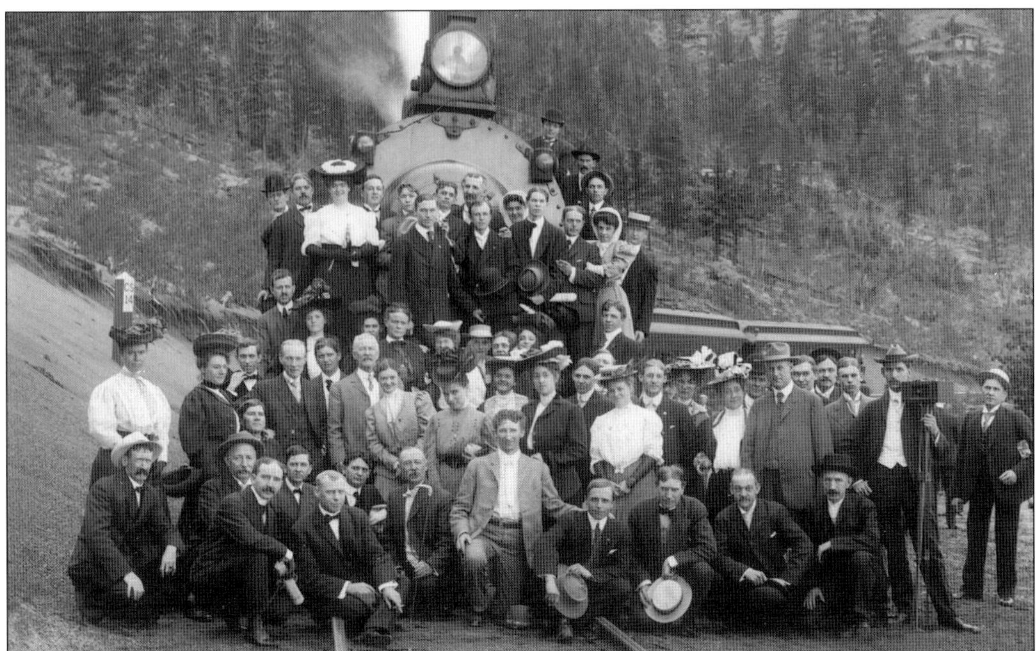

The First Train to Cripple Creek. (*c.* 1890) The first trip to Cripple Creek is celebrated by posing for this photograph en route. Some male passengers are sitting on the tracks and some are standing, but all are wearing fashionable suits, hats, and ties. The ladies too are clothed at the height of fashion in dresses with tight bodices and leg-of-mutton sleeves. Their hats are decorated with flowers, bows, and scarves. (Courtesy the Colorado Historical Society.)

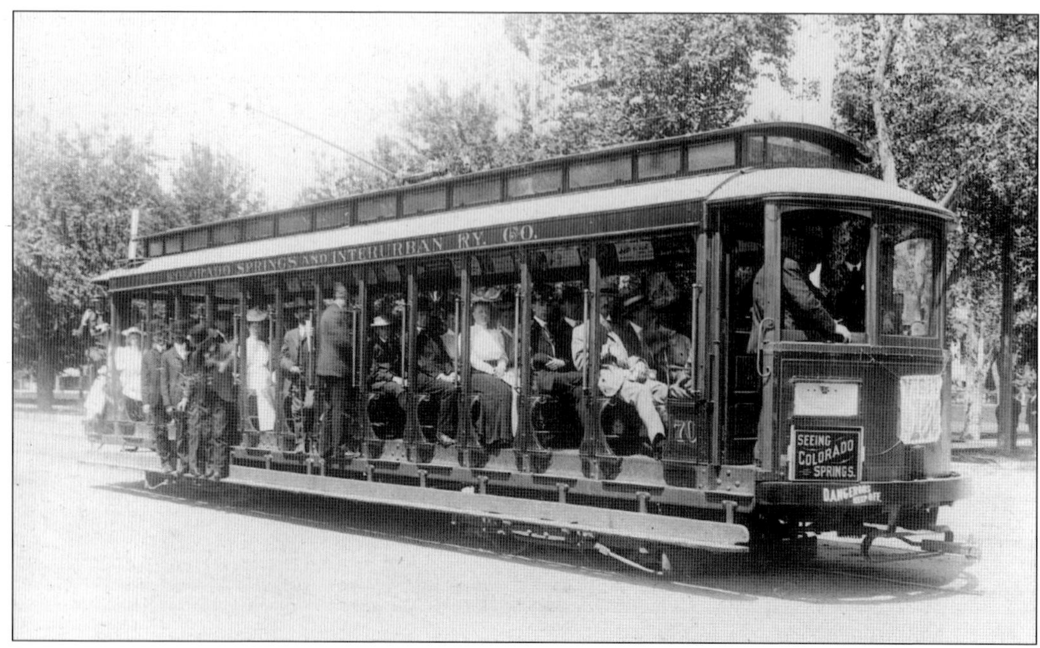

STREETCAR NO. 70 ON THE STREETS OF COLORADO SPRINGS. (*c.* 1890–1910) Filled to overflowing, the well-dressed passengers aboard the streetcar take all the seats available and even cling to the sides of the streetcar. The signs on the streetcar advertise "Seeing Colorado Springs" and "Visit the Zoo." Stratton acquired the Colorado Springs and Interurban Railway Company in 1902 and he restored and improved the whole system, providing a service that surpassed that of much larger communities. (Courtesy the Colorado Historical Society.)

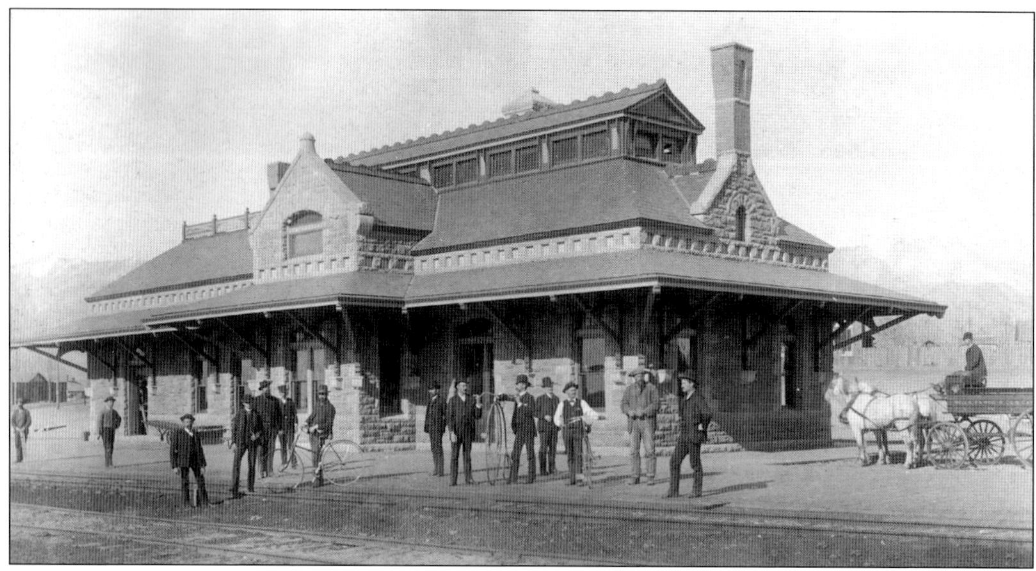

WAITING FOR THE TRAIN IN COLORADO SPRINGS. (*c.* 1892) The men wait, properly attired in their suits and hats, for the arrival of a train in front of the Atchinson, Topeka, Santa Fe & Midland Railway depot in Colorado Springs. Two ride regular bicycles, while one has a "high wheeler." A man is seen sitting atop a horse-drawn wagon with the name Wells Fargo & Co. Express on the side of the wagon. (Courtesy the Colorado Historical Society.)

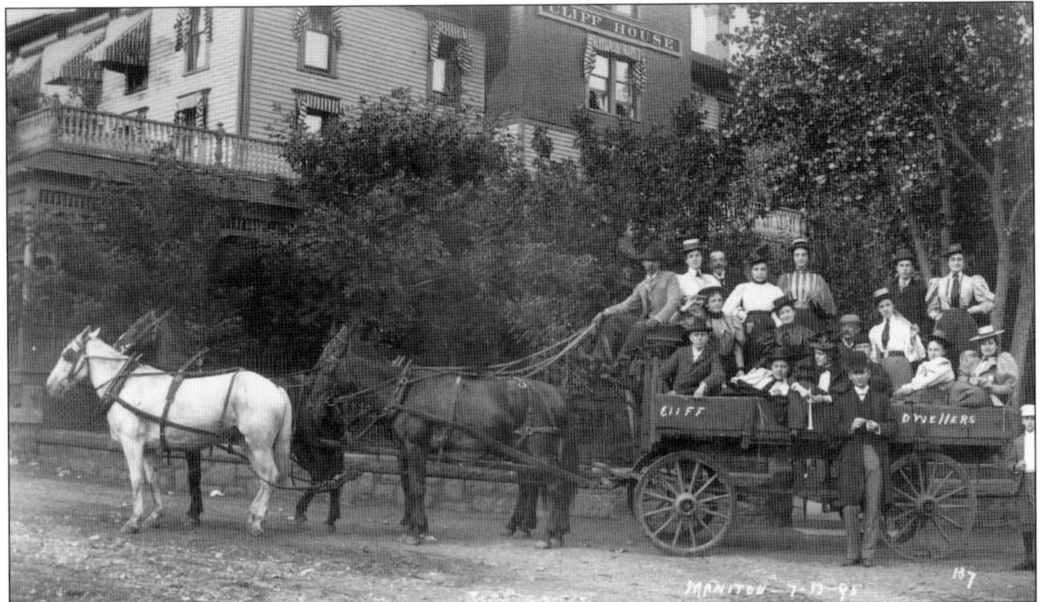

FUN IN MANITOU SPRINGS. (c. July 13, 1895) Sixteen people ready for a day of fun in their open buckboard being pulled by team of four horses, with the lead horses wearing blinkers. The women are elaborately dressed in attractive dresses with leg-of-mutton sleeves, tight bodices, and straw boater hats. A man stands in front of the buggy wearing a long dress coat and bowler hat. (Courtesy the Denver Public Library.)

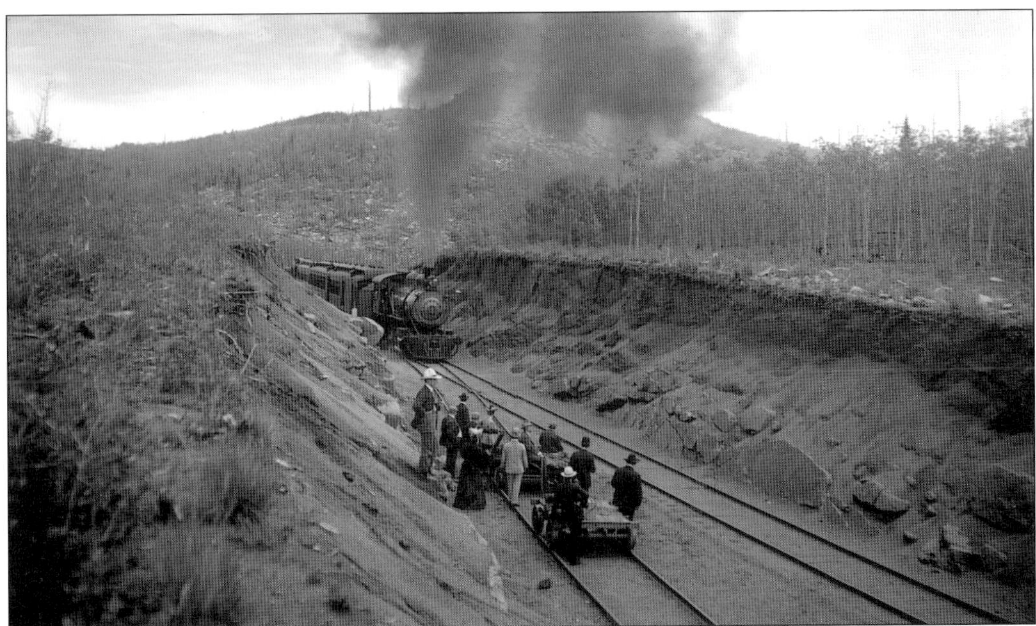

THE CRIPPLE CREEK SHORT LINE TRAIN AT 10,000 FT. (c. 1900–1920) Two parties of travelers await the Cripple Creek train to descend to Colorado Springs. Their luggage sits upon push cars where a few passengers sit waiting for the train to arrive. Most men appear to be fashionably dressed in suits and hats while the women wear bustled dresses with peplums and stylish hats. (Courtesy the Denver Public Library.)

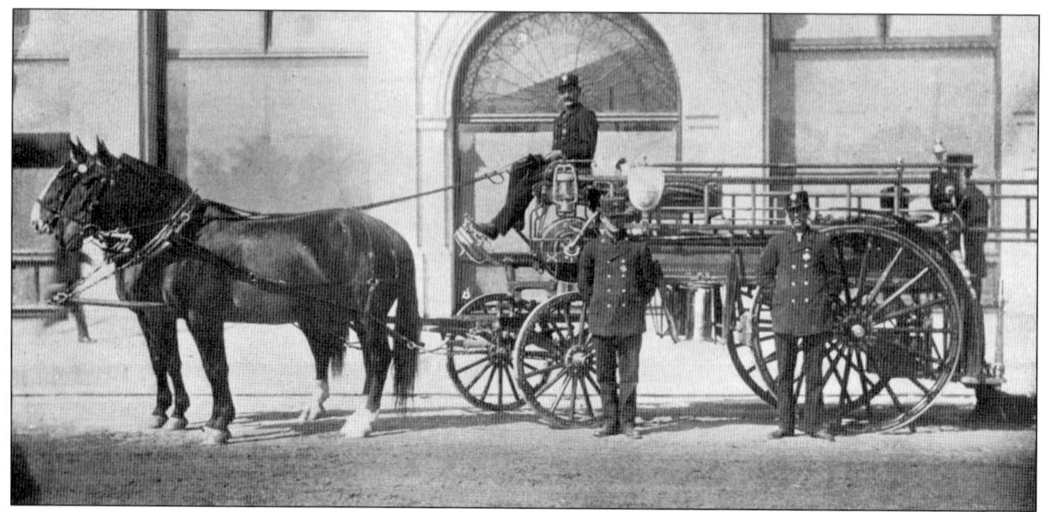

Combination Hose and Chemical Wagon. (*c.* 1902) The driver is Fred Armbruster, and Capt. C.L. Reasoner stands by the front wheel. The other two men are unidentified. Hose Company #1 poses with their team; Sylvan on the left, and Bones on the right. The team was carefully chosen for their strength and disposition. Sylvan was 7 years old and weighed 1400 pounds when he joined the company. There is no record of Bones. (Courtesy Dr. Lester L. Williams Museum.)

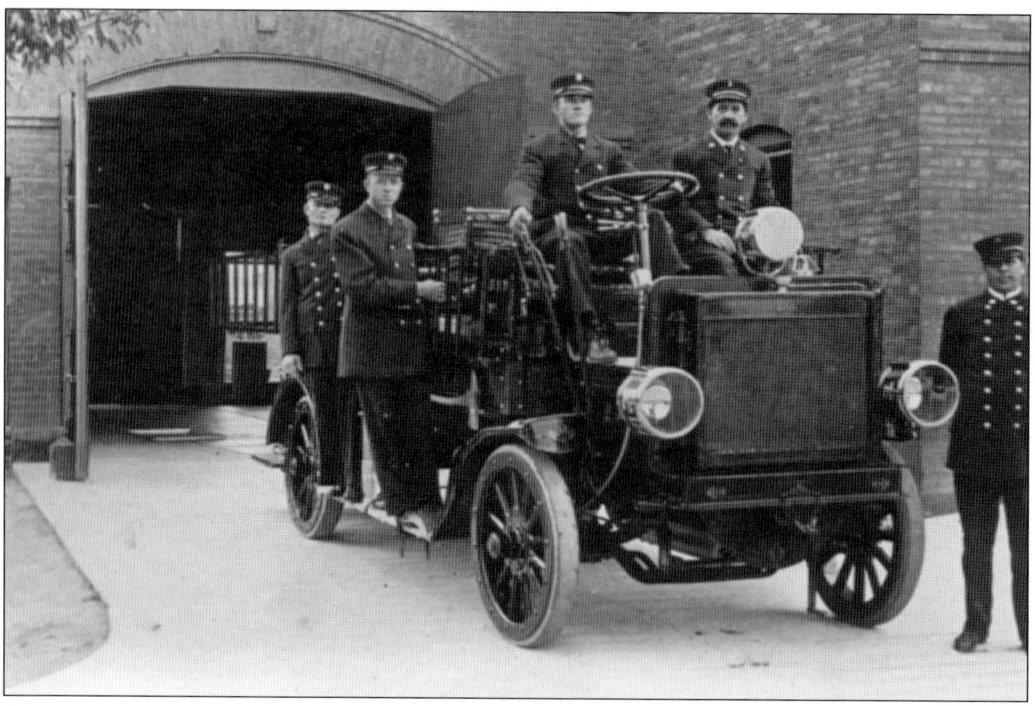

Station #2 Displays its Gramm. (*c.* 1912) From left to right are Bill Shellenberger, Walter McConnell, "Spide" Miller (driver), Lt. C.A. Losey, and Capt. George May. First came the Gramm with a 40-horse power engine, ignition by magnet to a chain drive, with a top speed of 30 miles per hour. It cost $2, 476, and for a couple of years was the pride and joy of the Colorado Springs Fire Department until it was replaced with the Knox. (Courtesy Dr. Lester L. Williams Museum.)

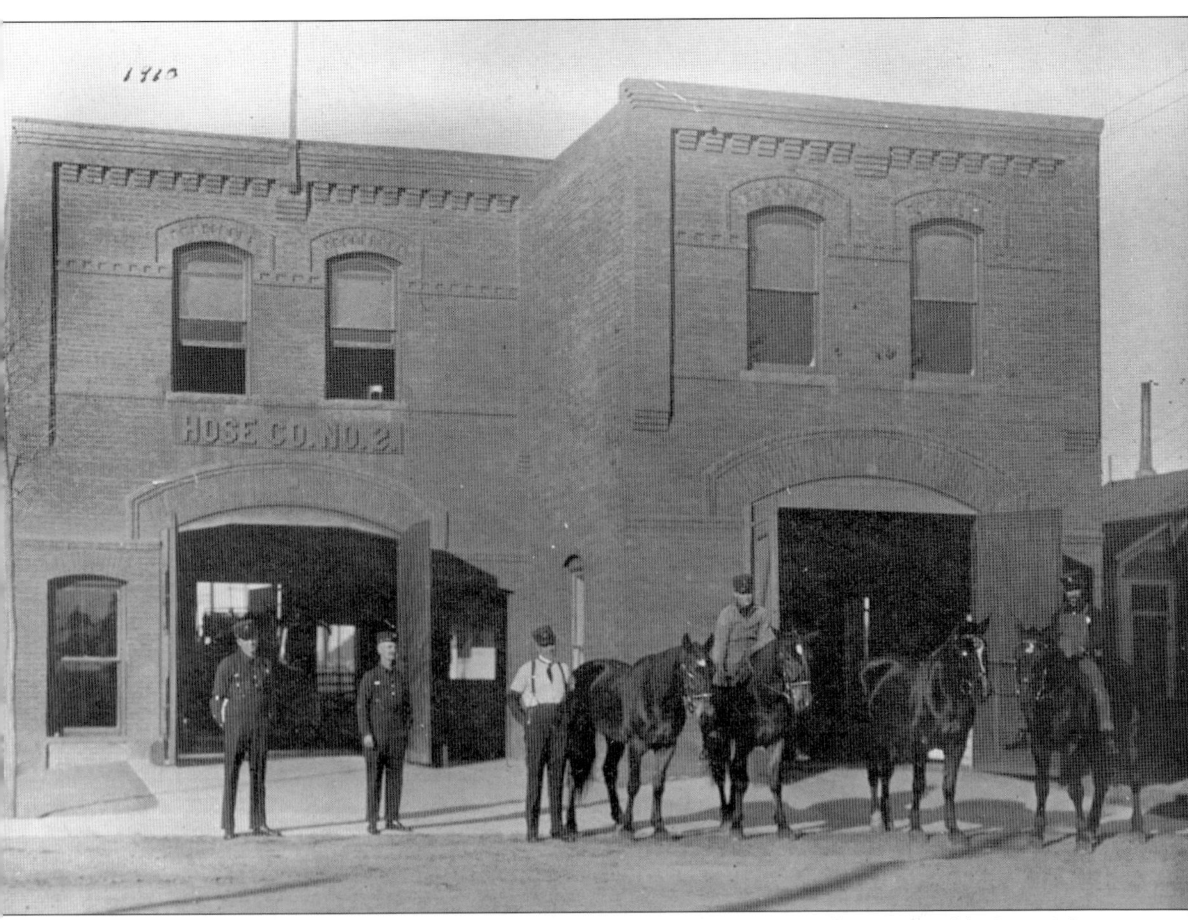

KEEPING THE HORSES FIT. (*c.* 1910) From left to right are McConnell, McDonald, Capt. May, Ray Bradshaw, Hoy, and Miller. The horses from left to right are Gene, Patsy, Barney, and Dan. The horses were exercised regularly but they were never too far from the station. Dr. Lester Williams notes in his book, *Fighting Fire in Colorado Springs,* that many tests were conducted at the station. The horses (and men) were so well trained that a hitching test conducted in 1897 at Fire Station #1 took only two and one fifth minutes. The horses were kept in stalls at the rear of the station with a chain that kept them in position. When the station gong sounded an alarm, the electromagnet that kept the chain in place was released, allowing the chain to drop; the horses then ran forward, side-stepped into place, and waited to be hitched. A heavy rig requiring a three-horse team meant that the third horse would wait until the first two were properly harnessed before it too ran forward to be hitched. (Courtesy Dr. Lester L. Williams Museum.)

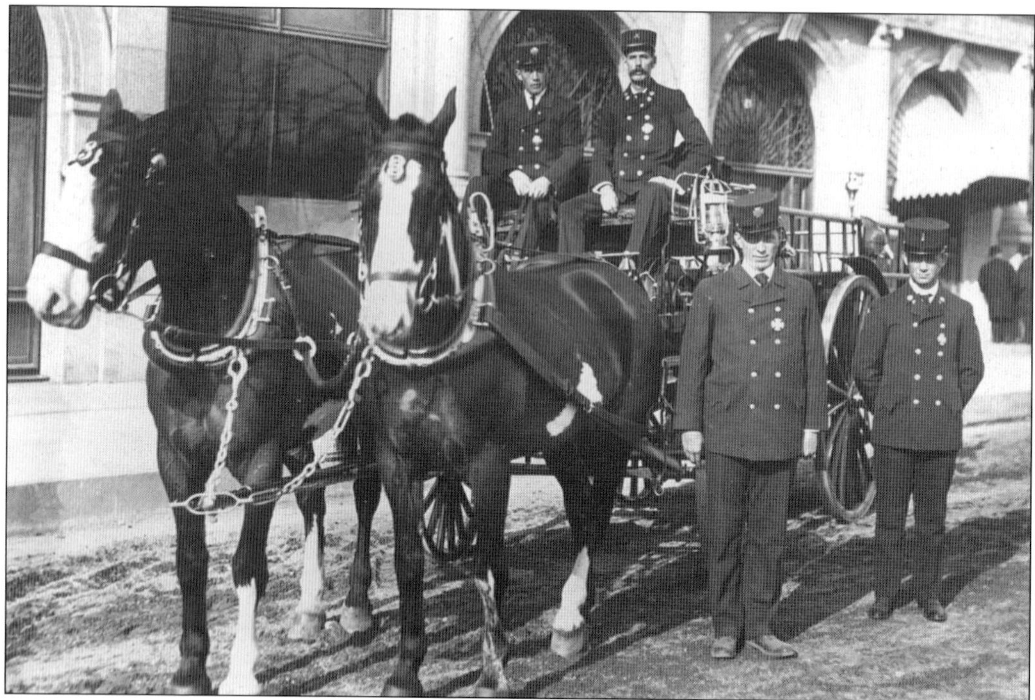

WINNERS OF THE WEST TEST. (date unknown) From left to right are Arthur G. Elstun, M.C. Donahue, H.P. Dennis, and unknown. An important tournament event was the West Test, where 11 men ran 500 feet, pulling a two-wheel hose reel weighing not less than 500 pounds, laden with 250 feet of hose. Colorado Springs Fire Department #3 won the West Test and covered the distance of 500 feet in 33 seconds. (Courtesy Dr. Lester L. Williams Museum.)

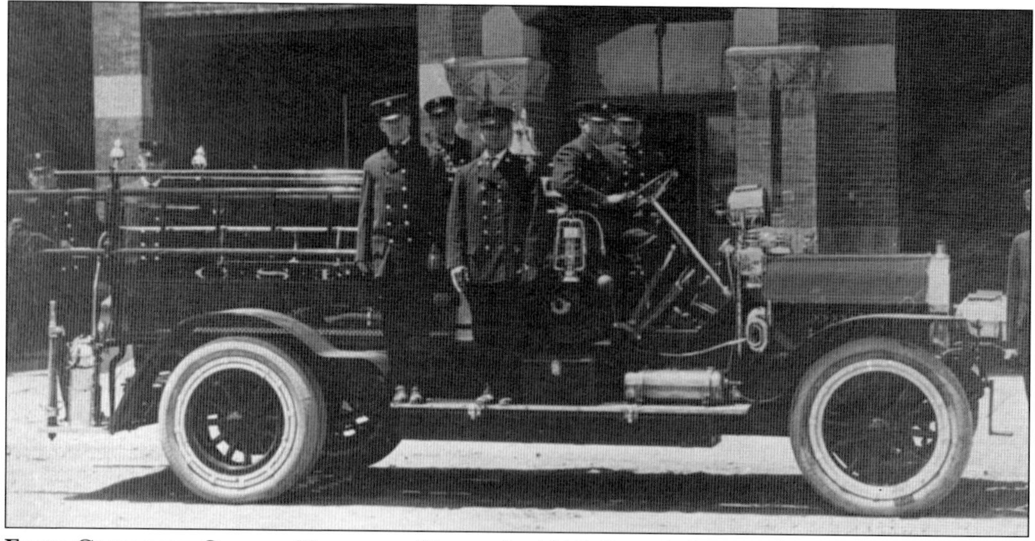

FIRST CAME THE GRAMM THEN THE KNOX. (c. 1912) From left to Right are S.C. Cook, A.W. Palmer, S.E. Johnson, John Aubuchon, Lt. W.T. Lorraine, Fred Temple, Capt. C.H. Dailey, and Asst. Chief Mike Donahue. The Gramm was the first motorized fire truck at Fire Company #1 and was in service from 1910 until April 25, 1912, when the Knox replaced it. (Courtesy Dr. Lester L. Williams Museum.)

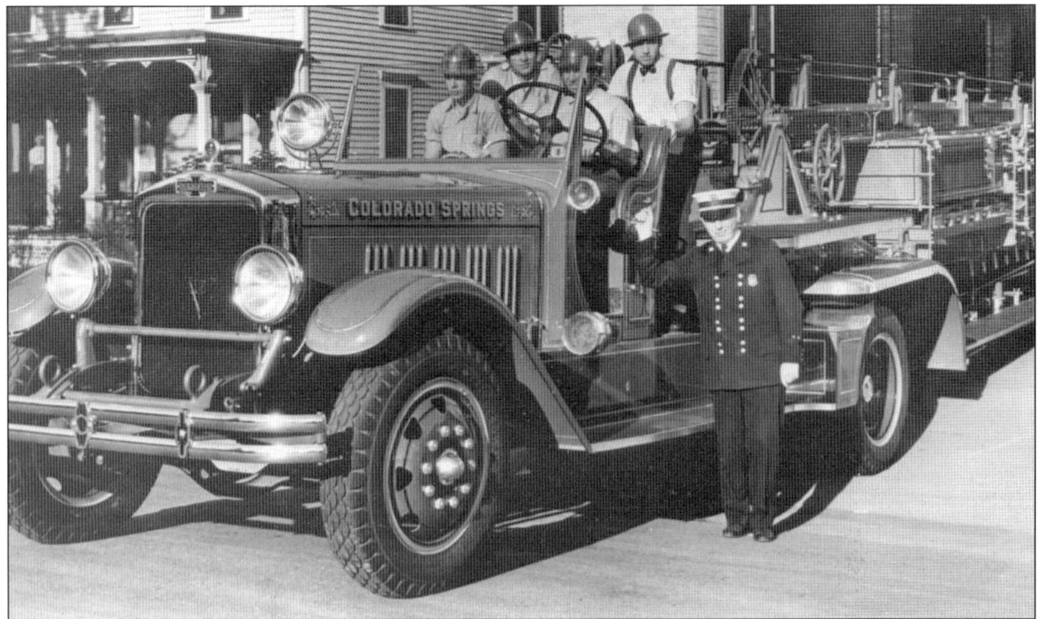

SEVENTY-FIVE FOOTER TO THE RESCUE. (*c.* 1935) The new addition to Fire Station #1 arrived on August 15, 1935, under the direction of W.W. "Billy" Hale, the delivery engineer. It was an American LaFrance 75-foot serial ladder capable of a top speed of 65 miles per hour. The men are seen wearing brown Bakelite helmets, remnants of World War I that were procured in 1932. One man sports a bow tie. (Courtesy Dr. Lester L. Williams Museum.)

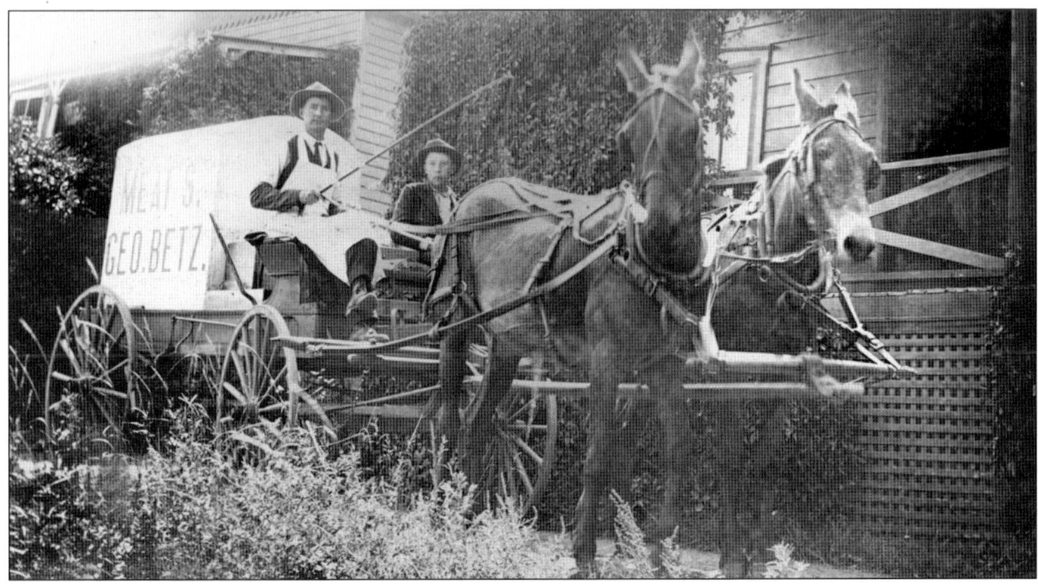

BETZ MEAT WAGON OF MONUMENT. (*c.* 1913) From left to right are Mr. Turner and Mark Schubarth stopping for a moment as they pose for the photograph in front of a cottage called the Pines that was owned by the McDonough family. The Betz meat wagon traveled to Palmer Lake and other neighboring towns, selling meat products by a horse-drawn wagon, but the Betz family was quite well-to-do, and purchased the first chain drive delivery truck in Monument. (Courtesy the Palmer Lake Historical Society and Lucretia Vaile Museum.)

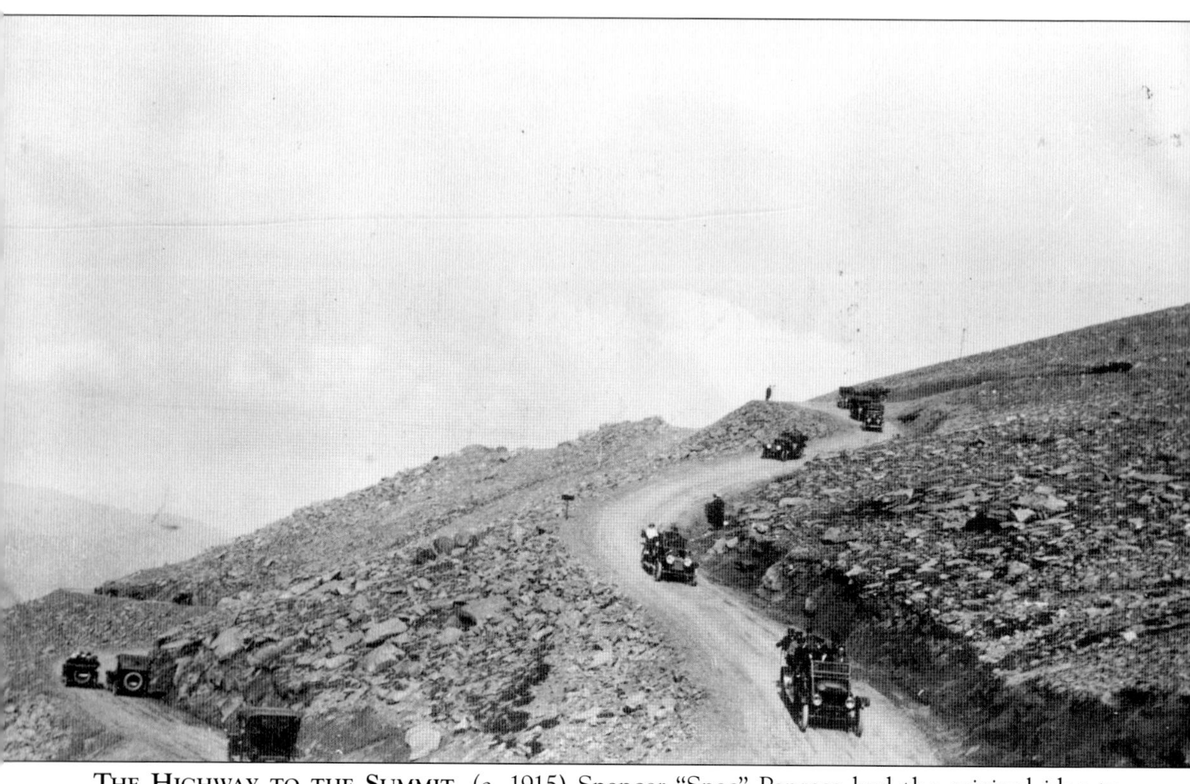

THE HIGHWAY TO THE SUMMIT. (*c.* 1915) Spencer "Spec" Penrose had the original idea to build a highway on Pikes Peak and promoted the concept to two friends, Charlie MacNeill and Bert Carlton, both of whom had made money in mining. A permit was given to build the road and charge a toll for the following 20 years. The road began in the summer and fall of 1915 and eventually cost $250,000. It was a mere 20 feet in width and began at 7,414 feet above sea level and climbed another 6,746 feet as it zig-zagged towards the Signal Station. At 10,000 feet the workmen had to stop and take frequent rests to avoid nosebleeds. The cost of the road was considerably higher than expected, and Spec went back to the investors, who refused to help with the additional cost. He alone incurred the cost of the last mile to the summit at $21,454. The new road was a success as it brought many more tourists to the area and also hosted the first Pikes Peak Hill Climb on a section of the road in 1916. (Courtesy Colorado Springs Pioneer Museum.)

Eight

The Men and Women Who Served

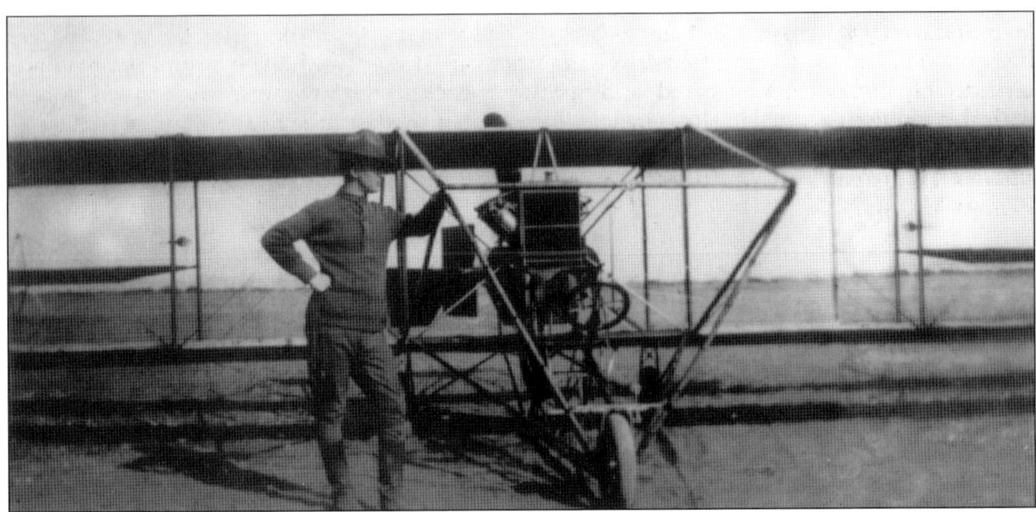

The Curtis Biplane. (c. 1914) Dr. Adna G. Wilde (then 1st lieutenant, U.S. Army Med. Corps), stands in front of a Curtis Biplane, one of the first aircraft ever used in combat. Test pilot Eugene Burton Ely was the first man to successfully take off and land a plane on a ship. He flew a Curtis Biplane from San Francisco to the cruiser Pennsylvania where it snagged the ropes and sandbags on its underside and came to a complete standstill. (Courtesy Adna Wilde.)

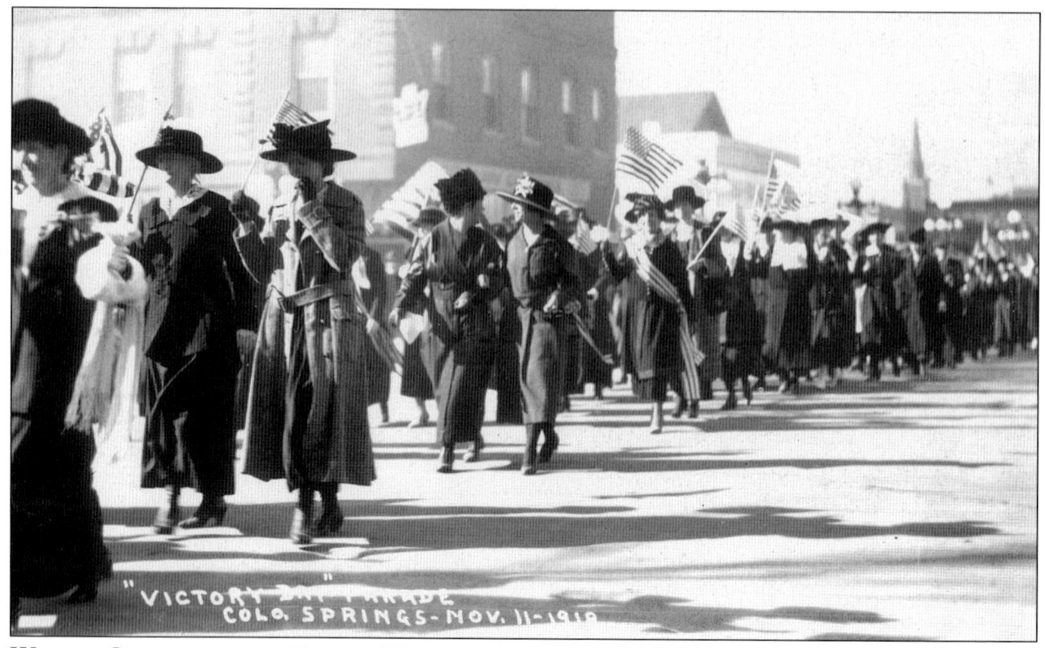

WOMEN CELEBRATE THE END OF WORLD WAR I. (*c.* November 11, 1918) Happiness shows on the faces of these women in the Victory Parade as one woman in the procession turns to look at those behind her. During the war, the railroads employed approximately 100,000 women, whose duties included not only the cleaning and maintenance of the railroad cars, but also the service of the cars and repair of the tracks. (Courtesy Pikes Peak Library District.)

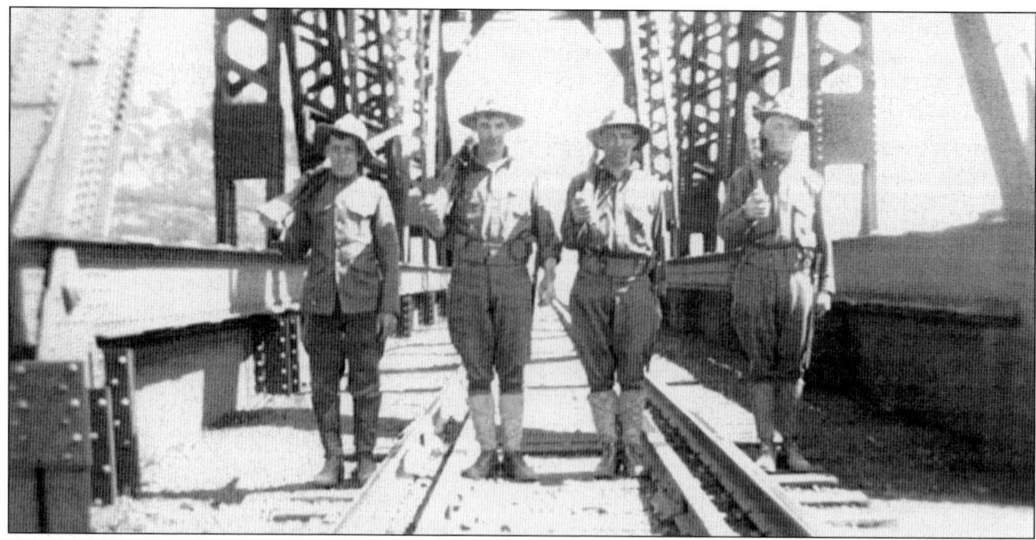

ENGLAND'S ALLIES. (*c.* 1914–18) Four unknown men dressed in World War I uniform stand to attention as they guard a railroad bridge in Palmer Lake. *The Gazette* reported on November 24, 1918, ". . . each month of the nation's participation in the struggle passed by, there were hundreds more until fully 3,000 sons and daughters from the Pikes Peak region donned the khaki . . . forty-five men and two woman have made the supreme sacrifice. . . . Miss Clara Orgren was one of the company of Red Cross nurses . . . who died in London. . . . " (Courtesy the Palmer Lake Historical Society and Lucretia Vaile Museum.)

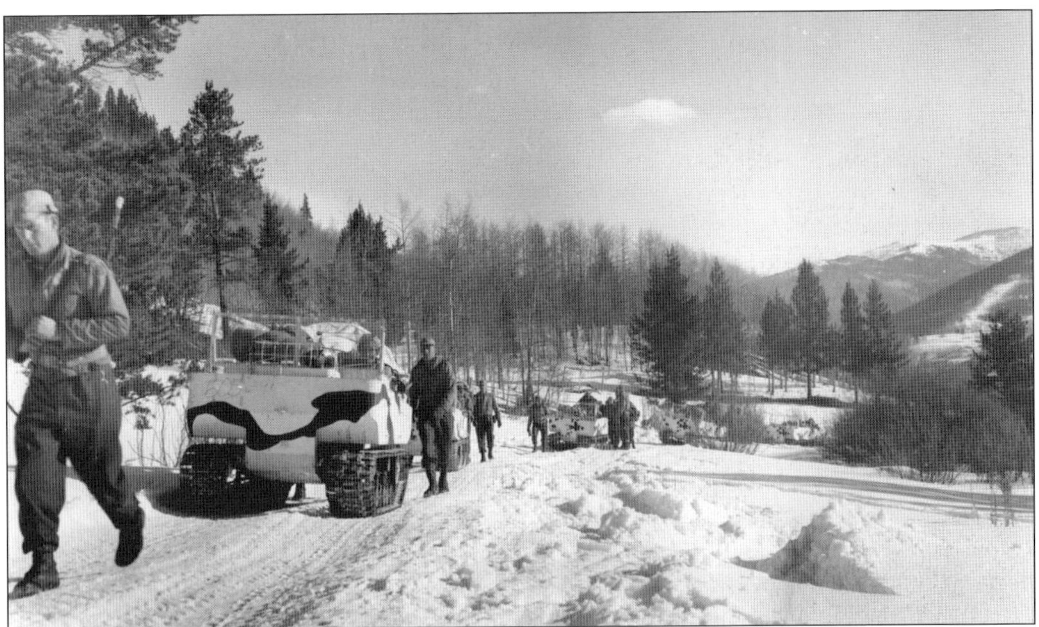

Special Equipment for Mountain Warfare. (*c.* 1945) After the initial handling and stability troubles, Studebaker redesigned the Weasel with the engine placed at the front instead of the back, plus other improvements which made the final version, the M29, perfect as an all-terrain vehicle. (Courtesy Dick Over.)

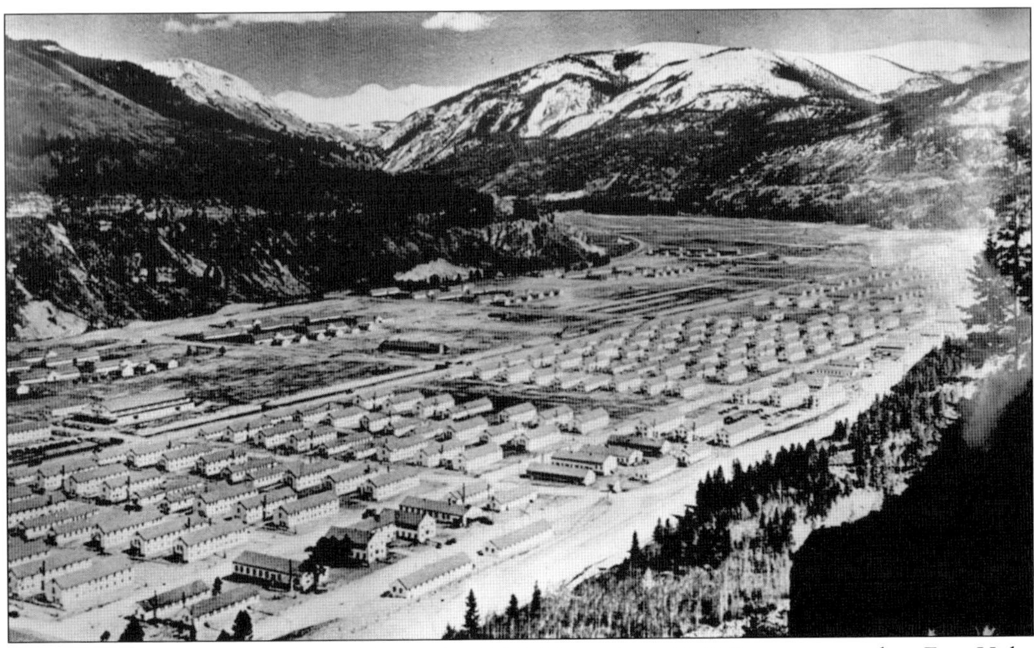

The Men Trained at Camp Hale. (*c.* 1943) More than 12,000 men trained at Fort Hale. They came from every walk of life and were trained to survive under extraordinary conditions to bivouac at night in sub-zero temperatures or build an igloo, climb mountains, and ski and snowshoe across difficult terrain while carrying a rifle and backpack weighing over 90 lbs. (Courtesy Dick Over.)

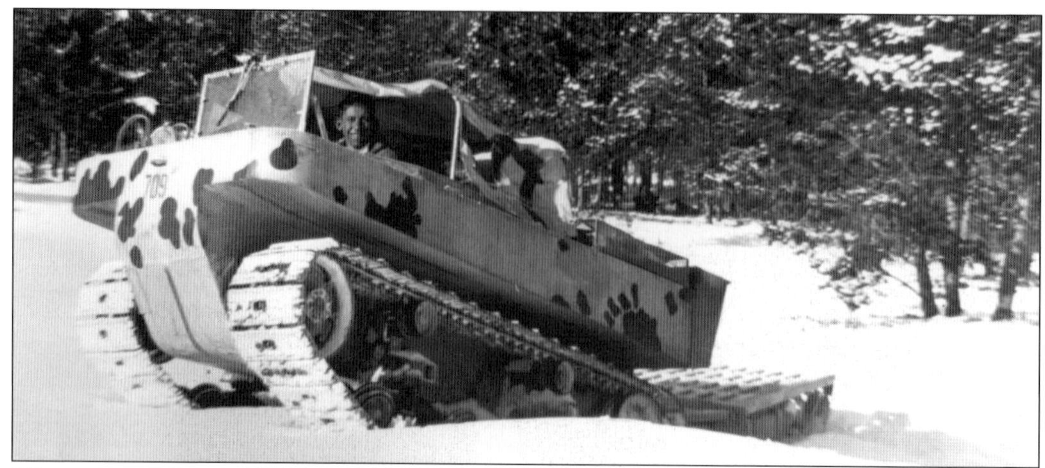

WEASELS ON THE MOVE. (c. 1944) The 10th Mountain's assignment created a need for different equipment to fight in a mountain environment. Studebaker was chosen to manufacture a snow vehicle and received the contract in May of 1942. The first prototype (designated M28) used a Champion 6 cylinder engine and was called the Weasel. It was considered problematic because it often threw its tracks and its handling was somewhat questionable. (Courtesy Dick Over.)

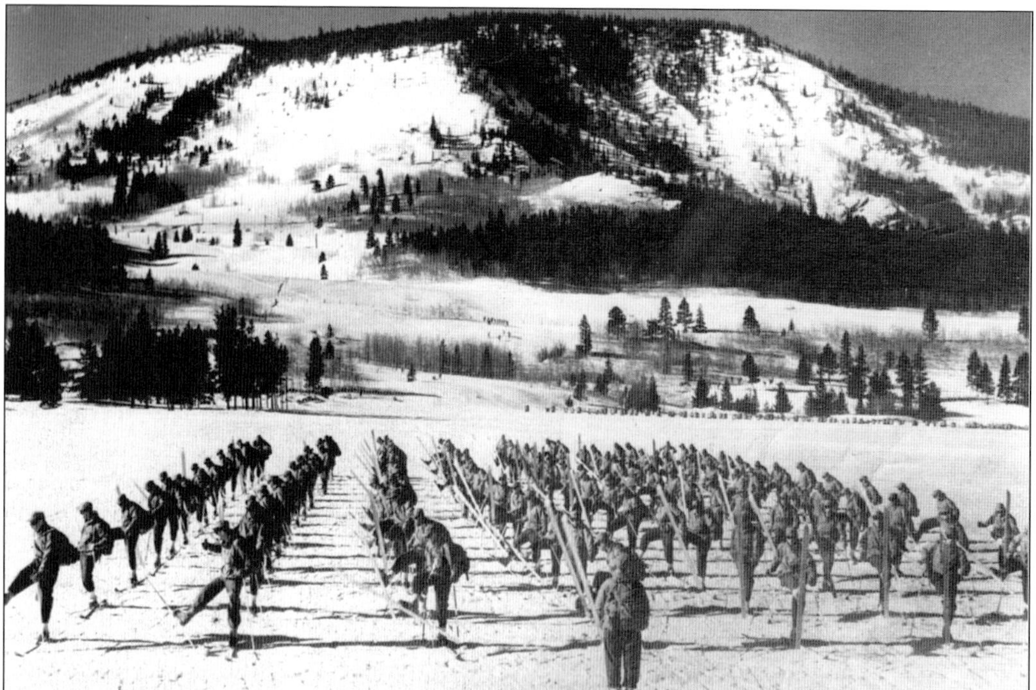

ONLY THE BEST MEN. (c. 1943) Three letters of recommendation proving a man's skills in either skiing, rock climbing, trapping, or timbermen were needed before they could apply for the elite position in the 10th Mountain Division. Once admitted, they were highly trained in mountain warfare and how to survive in sub-zero temperatures. Most men had never left their states before, let alone their country, but were now expected to fight a war in the Apennine Mountains of Italy. (Courtesy Dick Over.)

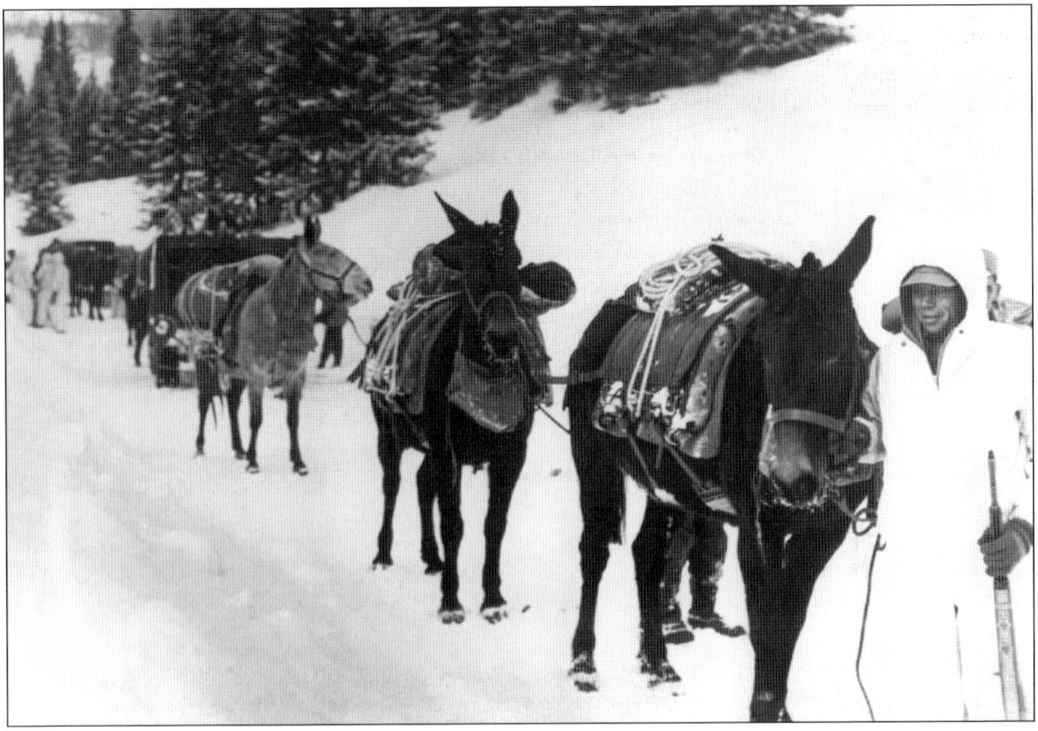

Mountain Soldiers. (*c.* 1944) The quartermaster with seven mules is carrying a dismantled Howitzer. The men wear white camouflage uniforms that were reversible with khaki. Originally, wolverine fur was used around the hood as it provided warmth and repelled the moisture, but as those skins became scarce, rabbit fur was used with a less desirable affect. (Courtesy Dick Over.)

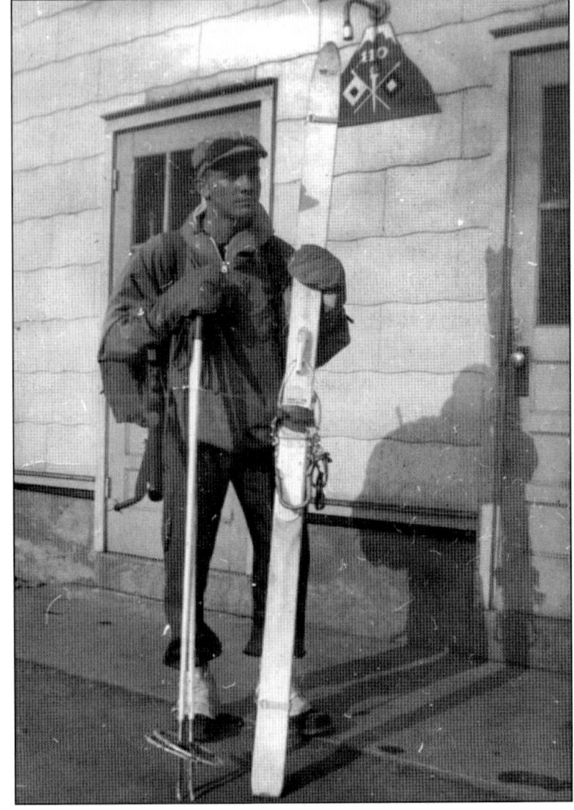

Training for Duty in the Italian Alps. (*c.* 1943) Richard Over stands with 7-foot skis in hand as part of the newly formed 10th Mountain Ski Division. Over was assigned to the Signal Corps whose emblem is displayed above the door. His responsibilities included communications and cryptography with duties of decoding messages. Over 12,000 men were trained at Camp Hale in mountain warfare and how to survive in brutal conditions. (Courtesy Dick Over.)

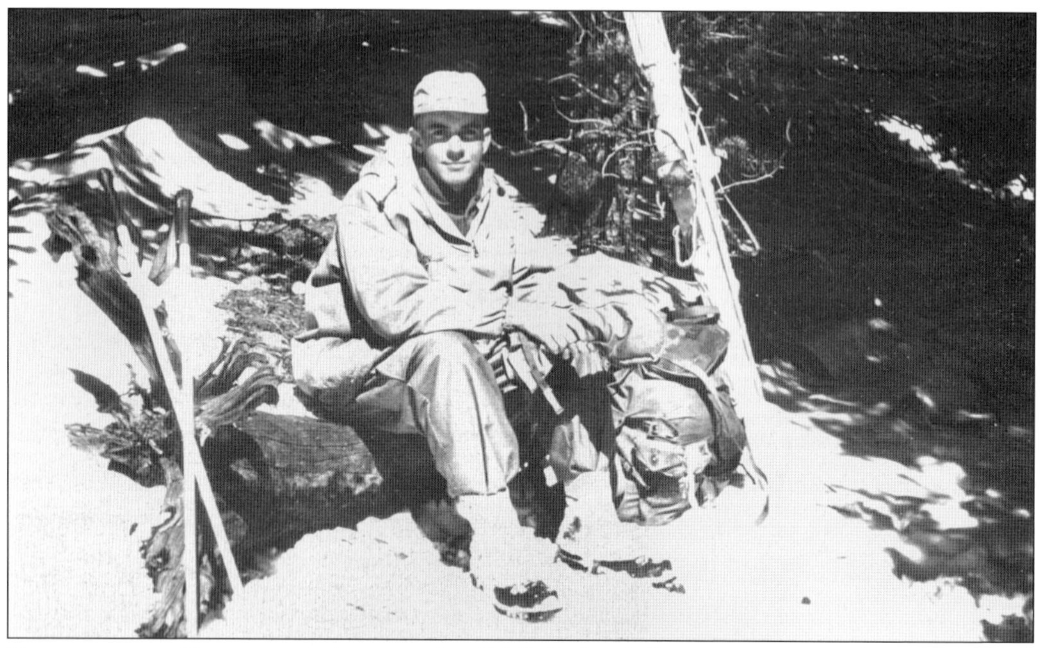

Trained and Ready for Action. (c. 1944) Richard Over poses for a photograph with his backpack, skiis, and poles. As part of the Signal Corps, Over had to wear a battery—for communications—across his chest. Most men had never left their state before, let alone their country, yet they now faced a war in a foreign land. (Courtesy Dick Over.)

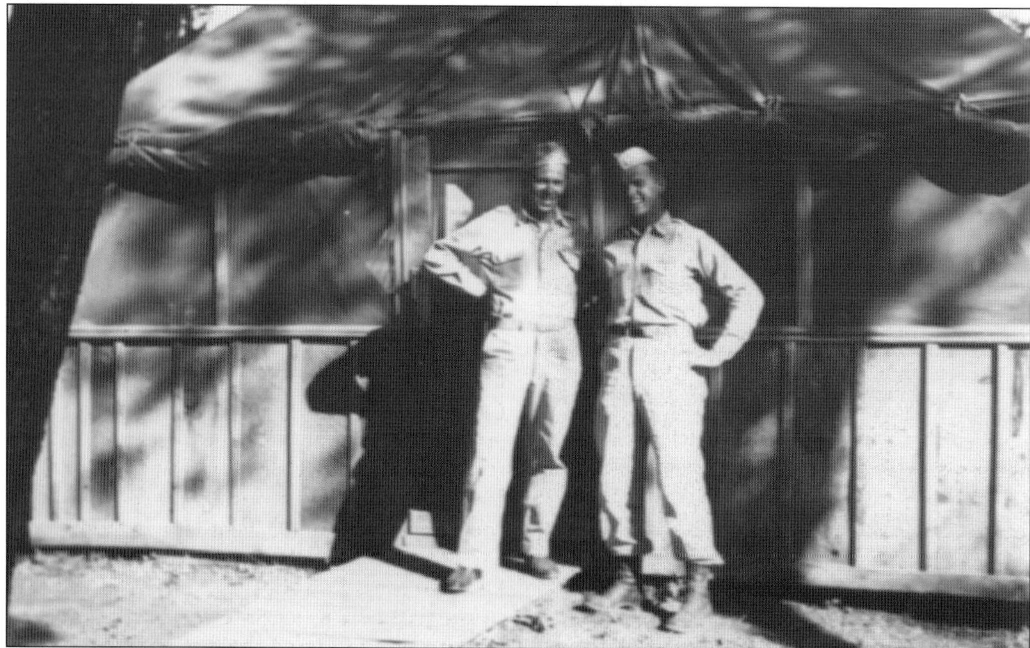

Happy Memories in Italy. (c. 1945) Celebrating the end of the war, Adna G. Wilde and Victor Eklund enjoy sightseeing in Pisa. Wilde remembers, "We were so happy the war was over, we took time to do some sightseeing, some men went to Venice but I had been there before and didn't want to go. We were all so relieved the war was over. . . . " (Courtesy Adna Wilde.)

INJURED IN ACTION. (*c.* 1944) Adna Wilde's last base was at Camp Swift in Texas before his departure to Naples, Italy, on December 23, 1944, as an Infantry platoon leader in the ski troops. Although wounded in action, he returned to the same unit three weeks later. "I thought a soldier had thrown a stone to get my attention, that's what we did rather than call out. I didn't realize I'd been hit until about four hours later when I felt the blood, then I knew." (Courtesy Adna Wilde.)

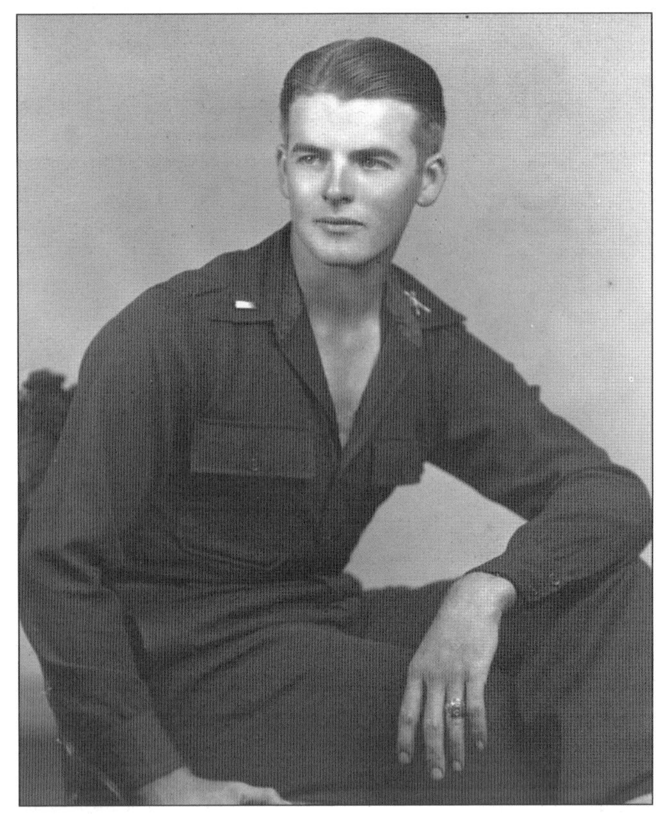

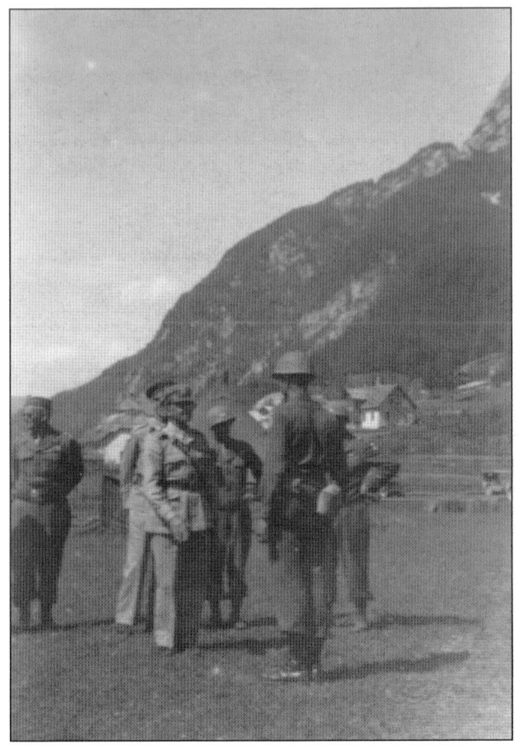

ONE FIELD MARSHALL AND TWO GENERALS. (*c.* 1945) Field Marshall Alexander, two star General Hays, and one star General Duff visit Cave Del Perdil, Italy, to address the troops and express their appreciation. On February 18, 1945, the 86th battalion of the 10th Mountain Division scaled a 1500-foot vertical assent in the darkness to surprise the Germans, who never considered the feat possible. Later the 85th and 87th Regiments attacked and were counterattacked until they secured the peak and opened the way to the Po Valley. (Courtesy Adna Wilde.)

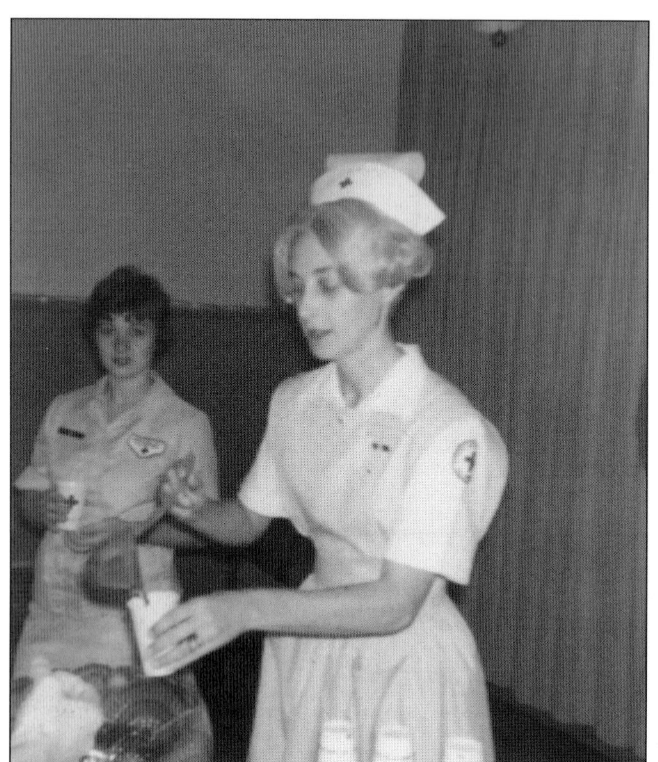

A Red Cross Volunteer Gives Aid. (*c.* 1950–1952) The Red Cross was an integral part of soldiers' lives while they were away from home. While the paid workers of the Red Cross were at the front line, many volunteers spent literally thousands of hours tending to the soldiers' needs. They provided liaison with the soldiers' families and dealt with everything from financial problems to health problems at home. The volunteers read and wrote letters for the soldiers and also purchased their personal needs from the Post Exchange. (Courtesy Adna Wilde.)

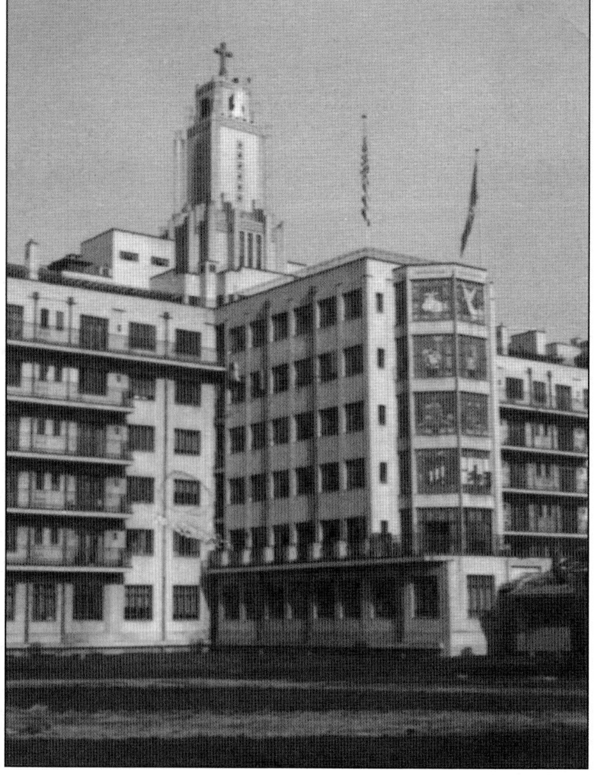

The Tokyo Headquarters Include the Red Cross Locater Service. (date unknown) The Red Cross Headquarters in Tokyo directed the activities of the field and hospital staffs in Okinawa, Japan, and the Philippines as well as Korea. So important was the Red Cross that an American serviceman said on seeing Miss Margaret Sutton, a Red Cross worker, "This is the first time I have seen an American girl in ten months—I would just like to shake your hand." (Courtesy Adna Wilde.)

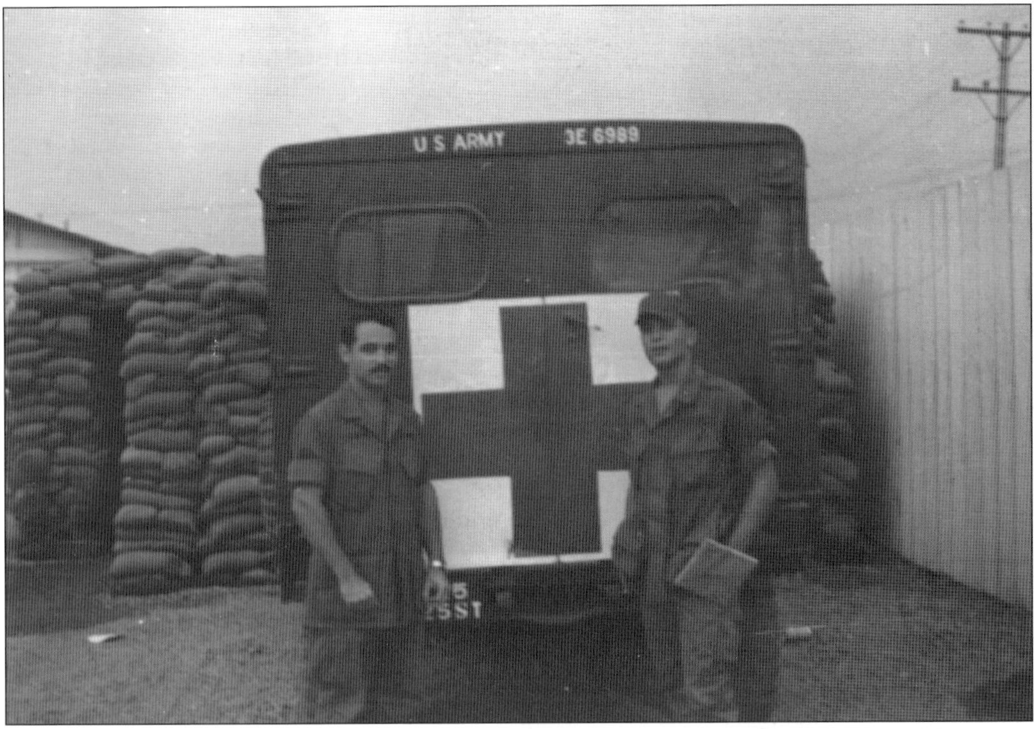

SOME JOBS WERE BETTER THAN OTHERS. (*c.* 1967) Wearing jungle fatigues, Bill Luke and Specialist 4th Class Lamb are standing just in front of their bunker next to the Medivac Hospital in Tan Son Nhut Air Base. On his return to the States, Bill Luke spent almost two years at Fort Carson, Colorado Springs, as part of "Project Transition:" a program designed to help Vietnam veterans adjust to civilian life. The Luke families are natives of Colorado Springs and several members still live in the area. (Courtesy Bill Luke.)

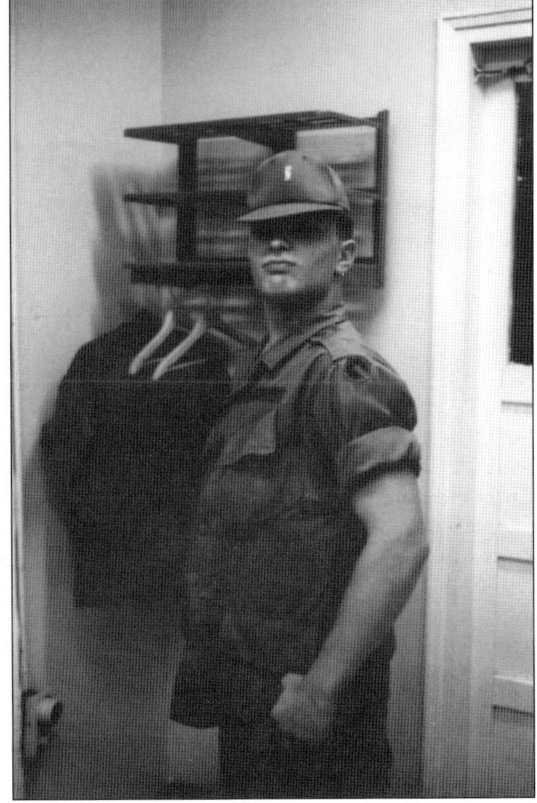

JUST HAVING SOME FUN. (*c.* 1967) Bill Luke takes advantage of using Lieutenant LeBaron's hat as he poses for a photograph taken by Private First Class Solosy. "Life was often difficult in Vietnam and any time we could poke fun at each other, we did. But if Lieutenant LaBaron had caught me with his hat, I could have been busted to a Private." (Courtesy Bill Luke.)

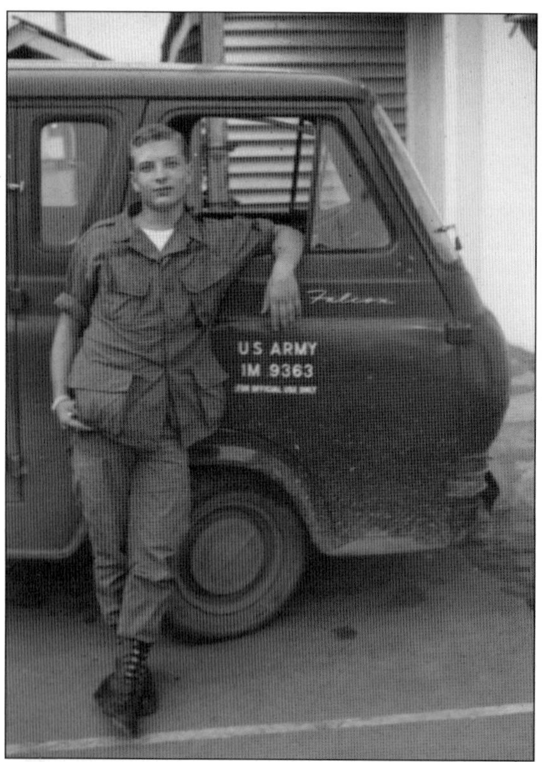

VOTED THE BEST DRIVER. (*c.* 1967) Lance Smith, a civilian, took this photograph of Bill Luke. Bill was involved in a sniper incident driving a similar van near the Phuto race in Saigon. "The AK's hit approximately 12 to 25 inches behind my head on the driver's side. It didn't seem a big deal at the time since it happened quite often but mostly to others." (Courtesy Bill Luke.)

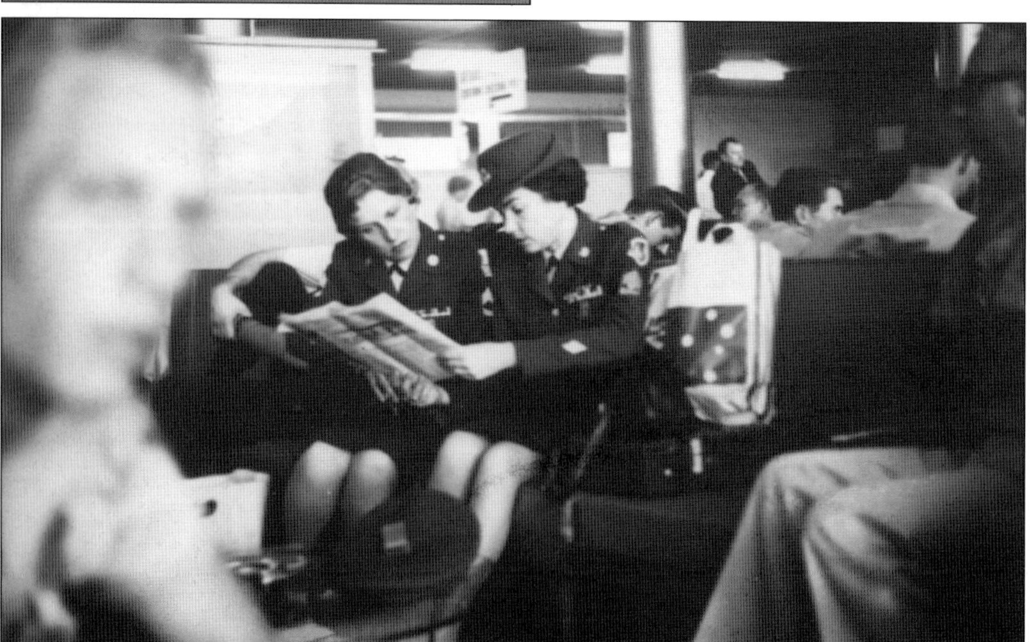

THE WOMEN WHO SERVED. (*c.* 1968) Two unknown women await their plane at the Tan Son Nhut airbase. The photograph was taken in late January 1968, just before the Tet Offensive. The women's insignia show they were sergeants in the army serving in Vietnam. Bill Luke took the photographs because these women were the first American women he had seen in months and besides, "they were good looking." (Courtesy Bill Luke.)